to The Jones family,

WALLED-IN

A West Berlin Girl's Journey to Freedom

So nice meeting you

D. Elke Ette

WALLED-IN

A West Berlin Girl's Journey to Freedom

J. ELKE ERTLE

Mentobe Press

Walled-In: A West Berlin Girl's Journey to Freedom
By J. Elke Ertle.

Library of Congress Case 1-833430741

Media Inquiries:
Mentobe Press
P.O. Box 60625
San Diego, CA 92166

Published by Mentobe Press

First Printing May 2013

ISBN: 978-0-9884061-1-7

Cover and Interior Design: GKS Creative, gkscreative.com

Editors: Jared Kuritz and Mary Altbaum

Printed in the United States of America

This is a memoir. In some cases, people's names and identifying details have been changed in consideration of privacy, but all other accounts and events are true to the best of the author's recollection.

Website: www.walled-in-berlin.com

Mentobe Press

Dedication

I want to dedicate this book to the more than 60,000 pilots, airmen, mechanics, air traffic controllers, loaders, and weathermen—40,000 of them Germans—who worked on the Berlin Airlift within Germany and the half a million more who were involved in some fashion around the world. On close to 280,000 flights they airlifted almost 2.5 tons of food and supplies into West Berlin. Thanks to the courage and tenacity of these men and women I lived to write this book.

Table of Contents

Acknowledgments

To all the publishing professionals from whom I have learned so much, my heartfelt thanks for their expert help and guidance.

My very special thanks go to

- Barbara Richter who encouraged me to share my story. Without her insistence and unwavering support, I would not have attempted it.
- Scotty and Marilyn Kelly who opened my eyes to new possibilities.
- Sonja Brzostowicz for making my America-dream possible and for turning my first year into one of the best times of my life.
- Donna Boyle, and Roger Legare, for their valuable suggestions.
- The men and women in my San Diego Writers' Workshop whose probing questions made me dig deeper.
- Gwyn Kennedy Snider of GKS Creative for designing the cover and interior exactly the way I had visualized them.
- Jared Kuritz of Strategies for his expert and judicious counsel.
- Mary Altbaum for her skillful edits.
- My husband, Burch, for helping me discover the person that always lived inside of me, and, above all, for taking my mother in stride.
- And finally, to all of those who helped in some other way to bring about this book, my sincere gratitude.

A Brief History
of Postwar Berlin

In May 1945, Germany unconditionally surrendered after years of Allied bombing and war on two fronts. Berlin, the capital, fell to the Russians after two weeks of vicious street fighting. In the aftermath, Great Britain, France, the United States, and the Soviet Union concurred, in the Potsdam Agreement, to slice the country into four occupation zones. The wartime Allies were to rule Germany through a control council, called the Allied Kommandatura. Because each power also wanted control of Berlin, located in the middle of Soviet territory, the city was divided as well. Each Ally was to govern its zone and sector unilaterally and also jointly through the Kommandatura. All decisions were to be reached unanimously.

The first to conquer Berlin were Soviet forces. US and British armies did not reach the city until July and the French not until August. During the intervening four months, the Russians created a soviet-patterned municipal administration and issued ration cards in all four sectors. Although the Soviet sector housed only 37% of the population and occupied 55% of the area, the three Western Allies, who shared the remainder of the city, voted to keep the Soviet orders in effect to avoid the risk of damaging East-West relations.

By the end of the war, scarcely a building was standing in the city center. Forty percent of all structures in the city had been destroyed, and the population had been reduced to roughly one-half of its prewar level. To help pay for reparations, railroad tracks were transported east. Most factories that had survived the war were disassembled and shipped both east and west. Power, sewage, and public transportation systems no longer functioned.

Daily, thousands of refugees, expelled from the former German territories ceded to Poland and the Soviet Union, flooded the city. Berlin became unable to support itself, and the Allies had trouble sustaining the roughly 1.5 million Berliners under their care. There was not enough food, coal, or electricity to go around. Initially, civilian rations ranged from nine hundred calories per day for nonworking adults to eighteen hundred calories per day for manual laborers, with almost all of the calories coming from bread. Then caloric allocations had to be reduced even further. Many Berliners augmented their rations by trading their possessions for food on the black market where, despite the shortages, almost anything could be had for a price. Still, during the first winter, many Berliners died of starvation, cold, or illnesses associated with malnutrition.

To prevent Germany from waging future wars, the four Allies had agreed before war's end that it must never be allowed to rise to power again. Thus, occupation policies were designed to keep the country's economy depressed. However, when Germany began to drag down the entire continent, the Western Allies rethought their strategy and decided to rebuild the country, thereby ensuring stability on the European continent. The Soviets opposed this line of thinking. As Western policies toward Germany changed, the former Allies grew apart.

In 1947, US President Truman's new secretary of state, General George C. Marshall, introduced the Marshall Plan, a comprehensive system of recovery aid for Europe. Viewing it with suspicion, the Soviets declined participation. In the Western zones of Germany, the plan produced some economic progress, but purchasing power remained dangerously low. On June 20, 1948, without Soviet concurrence, the Western Allies withdrew the worthless reichsmark in both West Germany and West Berlin and introduced the new deutsche mark. Existing cash could be exchanged at a rate of 1:20 and savings at a rate of 1:10. People lost most of their money.

The Russians denounced this unilateral move as a breach of the Potsdam Agreement and refused to recognize the new legal tender of the West. Three days later, they introduced their version of a currency with the same name in Soviet territory. Germany, including Berlin, now had two currencies. This dispute may have been the most crucial factor leading to the development of the Cold War between East and West.

Irked, the Soviets closed all rail links between the Western zones of Germany and the Western sectors of Berlin and stopped the supply of food and electricity to West Berlin. Just after midnight on June 24, 1948, the Berlin Blockade began. Impending blackout, cold, and starvation loomed for Berliners. There was only enough food to fend off starvation for thirty-five days and enough coal to continue the lifeline power supply for forty-five days. Electricity was available for only 2.5 hours each day. West Berlin's future was in peril.

In an unprecedented logistical feat, the three Western Allies began flying all foodstuffs, coal, and building materials—anything West Berlin needed to survive—from West Germany to West Berlin. While the United States and Great Britain provided the planes, France participated in an administrative capacity. Cargo flights to West Berlin were scheduled around the clock and required complex flight patterning. After the system was perfected, planes landed in closely timed intervals of about three minutes. The total number of miles flown was close to the distance between the earth and the sun.

Coal was distributed only to utilities, bread factories, and hospitals. Private homes and businesses did not receive heating fuel. Instead, during the winter of 1948/1949, decimation of one-half of all park and street trees for firewood was authorized. Eleven months later, when the Soviets realized that, against all odds, the Western Allies' attempt to supply West Berlin from the air had proved successful, they lifted the blockade.

By 1952, the standard of living of ordinary East Germans, compared with 1947, had actually declined. Around half a million employees throughout East Germany and East Berlin went on strike for higher wages and a higher living standard. As the gap continued to widen, increasing numbers of East Germans exited westward. Each year, approximately 150,000 to 300,000 refugees fled to West Berlin. This massive exodus caused problems, both for the East and the West. The East experienced severe shortages of professionals and skilled workers. West Berlin was slowly dying because businesses relocated to West Germany to escape political uncertainties, and the continuing stream of refugees intensified the already existing housing shortage. Unemployment doubled.

To offset these developments, the West German government offered generous subsidies, extensive tax benefits, compulsory relocation of administrative government offices to West Berlin, and incentives to move to and work in the ailing city. Still, West Berlin slowly depopulated. Older people tended to stay because of family ties. But young people, eager for advancement, left the city in droves. Nevertheless, conditions in West Berlin continued to improve.

In the ensuing years, the West Berlin economy had finally improved, and by 1960 there was virtually no unemployment. The West began to look extremely attractive to East Berliners. By August of the following year, one third of the entire population had fled East Germany. Their economy was in danger of complete collapse. On August 13, 1961, East German leaders issued orders to erect provisional coils of barbed wire along all East German borders. By the time dawn broke, construction brigades were already at work. Next, they added cement barriers. Waterways were fitted with iron barriers. At the risk of loss of life, organized escapes by tunneling under, flying over, driving through, or swimming across to West Berlin became regular occurrences. Death statistics along the wall climbed every month.

Eventually, the provisional wall would be replaced by twelve-foot high, reinforced concrete panels and topped by smooth round pipe to prevent scaling. It would extend for ninety-six miles, with spotlights, alarms, guard dogs, armed guards, watchtowers, bunkers, and trenches along the way. Along the border with West Berlin, an additional hundred-yard "*Todesstreifen*—death strip" was created, and anyone who dared to set foot on it was shot on sight. The area contained antivehicle trenches, beds of nails, and smoothly raked sand to allow the tracing of footsteps of fleeing East Germans.

Prior to the arrival of US President John F. Kennedy, on June 26, 1963, the leaders of the Western protective powers had avoided the city. When Kennedy spoke the unforgettable words "Ich bin ein Berliner—I am a Berliner" in front of Schöneberger Rathaus, West Berliners saw in him a guarantor of freedom.

In June 1987, during the height of the Cold War, US President Ronald Reagan challenged Soviet leader Mikhail Gorbachev to "Tear down this Wall." Two years later, on November 9, 1989, after a twenty-eight-year existence, the Berlin Wall tumbled. Not one shot was fired. It was brought down by the people, not by world leaders or by diplomacy.

Allied Occupation Sectors of Berlin—1945 to 1991

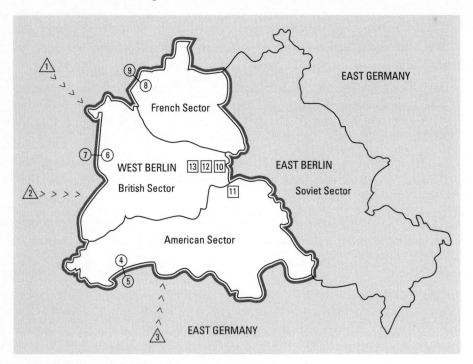

Allied air corridor to Northern Germany/Europe

Allied air corridor to Western Germany/Europe

Allied air corridor to Southern Germany/Europe

④ Ground transit checkpoint Dreilinden (Allied Checkpoint Bravo)

⑤ Ground transit checkpoint Drewitz

⑥ Ground transit checkpoint Heerstraße

⑦ Ground transit checkpoint Staaken

⑧ Ground transit checkpoint Heiligensee

⑨ Ground transit checkpoint Stolpe

10 Brandenburger Tor

11 Checkpoint Charlie

12 Knesebeckstraße

13 Lietzensee

▰▰	Berlin Wall
△	Allied Air Corridors
○	East/West Ground Transit Checkpoints
☐	Points of Interest

Allied Occupation Zones of Germany—1945 to 1991

△1 Northern Allied air corridor
△2 Western Allied air corridor
△3 Southern Allied air corridor

Ground transit checkpoint for travellors from Dreilinden/Drewitz:
④ Ground transit checkpoint Marienborn
⑤ Ground transit checkpoint Helmstedt (Allied Checkpoint Alpha)
⑥ Ground transit checkpoint Horst
⑦ Ground transit checkpoint Lauenburg
⑧ Ground transit checkpoint Wartha
⑨ Ground transit checkpoint Herleshausen
⑩ Ground transit checkpoint Hirschberg
⑪ Ground transit checkpoint Rudolphstein

▬▬ The Wall
△ Allied Air Corridors
◯ East/West Ground Transit Checkpoints

*Our lives begin to end
the day we become silent about things that matter.*

Martin Luther King, Jr.

ONE

THE BIG DAY

I LIE MOTIONLESS under my soft, warm comforter. My head nestles into the thick, square eiderdown pillow and my back and shoulders melt into the mattress like butter on toast. Tapsi, my four-year-old dachshund, lies curled up between my feet. Cradling the covers with my legs, I take a deep, long breath. I feel content from head to toe. Today is a big day. Today is my twenty-first birthday. Today, unfettered life will begin.

The hypnotic tick-tock, tick-tock of the alarm clock on the small laminated table cuts through the silence. I sit up, forcing Tapsi to adjust her position. Inky darkness. Shivering in the sudden cold I strain to read the time: 5:45 a.m. Through the small bedroom window, I gaze outside. No stars. Droplets hit the windowpane. A typical November day in Berlin. I glance at the clock a second time. Only a few more minutes before I'll have to get ready for work.

Briefly, I relive the pleasant sensation of having luxuriated in soapsuds for a full forty minutes the evening before. My skin still tingles. I loofahed each limb with a vengeance so that my arms and legs would feel as fresh as the new chapter of my life that is about to begin. I even slept on nylon brush rollers, held in place by pesky pink plastic picks. No price was too high for the beauty I intended to flaunt today.

Today—my twenty-first birthday! The words still sound like a ceremony to me.

Retreating deeper under the warm comforter, I pull Tapsi into my arms and gently press her hot little body to my chest. Her soft heartbeats

1

echo the ticking of the clock and tone down my excitement. Here at the gateway to adulthood I recall exactly at what point I began to pull away from my parents. It happened soon after I befriended Scotty, Marilyn, and Sharon Kelly, an American military family stationed in Germany. They introduced me to a different world, one that welcomed teen involvement in family decisions. Until then, my life had been mapped out by a series of unassailable rules and restrictions. When I began resisting my parents' authority, I triggered a conflict that paralleled in intensity the Cold War between East and West. While the infamous Berlin Wall restricted physical liberties, the walls my parents put up curtailed not only my physical, but also my emotional freedom. They proved to be ten times harder to topple than the stone Wall.

And so, for the past few years, I have been waiting impatiently to achieve adulthood so that I may break out of my quasi-jail and choose my friends and pursuits without having to ask permission. That time has come. Today is the first day. Eyes closed, my head snuggles into the down pillow as I dream of boundless freedoms ahead.

Suddenly, the six bare bulbs of my Sputnik ceiling fixture light up in a blaze. Startled, I squint toward the bedroom door where I see two shadowy silhouettes: my mother and my father. My slender, six-foot-something father's scrawny legs poke from his calf-length tan nightshirt. My petite mother, a foot shorter than he, is clad in a yellow batiste nightgown. She leans heavily on his arm as they lumber toward my bed. They probably have come to congratulate me on achieving adulthood. My mind spins with excitement and expectations of anticipated well wishes. After all, everything is going to change today!

Instead, my mother utters six unexpected words that turn my world upside down. Their echo still hangs in the air when my father flicks off the light, and my parents close the door behind them. Alone again in the darkness, it feels like a psychic earthquake has hit my universe. Unable to absorb the implications of my mother's startling statement, I crawl even deeper under the covers. Tucked away safely, I cradle Tapsi's little frame and allow the past twenty-one years to pass in front of me as if they were a single image.

TWO

THE PERFECT
LITTLE GIRL

After the War

WHEN MY MOTHER STEPPED into my aunt and uncle's pub, *Zum Kühlen Grund*, holding me, a newborn, in her arms, she consoled herself by saying, "I've lost almost everything in this war. This little bundle is mine. I won't let anyone take her away from me."

Ruins. Desolation. Despair. More than 2.5 billion cubic feet of rubble, the city's 4.4 million inhabitants of 1943 reduced to 2.3 million, two-thirds of them women—that was Berlin in 1945, the year I was born. Germany had capitulated in May, and the four Allies—Great Britain, France, the United States and the Soviet Union—had divided the country geographically according to the Potsdam Agreement of June 1945. Germany was now split into four occupation zones with Berlin in the middle of the Soviet zone. Since each power had wanted the capital to be within its jurisdiction, the four of them had compromised by dividing the city's 371 square miles into four occupation sectors.

Each of the powers was to govern its zone and sector individually but also jointly in matters that affected the country or the city as a whole. Decisions in shared responsibilities would have to be reached unanimously. For all of Germany, that supreme administrative authority was called the Allied Control Council. Its members were Marshal Georgy Zhukov representing the Soviet Union, Army General Dwight Eisenhower for the United States, Field Marshall Bernard Montgomery speaking for Great Britain, and Jean de Lattre de Tassigny for France.

For Berlin, an administrative body was established that mirrored the Allied Control Council on a smaller scale. It was made up of Berlin's four Allied commandants and was called the Kommandatura, a term created by fusing Russian and German.

Ruins everywhere. More than one-half of the buildings in our district, Charlottenburg, were destroyed. Near the center of the city, word had it that only 604 of the 11,075 residential buildings were still standing. In some blocks, there was nothing left but piles of debris. The city looked like a moonscape with forlorn souls staggering through the wreckage, still looking for someone or something. The majority of Berliners had lost most of their belongings to bombing attacks during the war or to Russian lootings after the war. Food was rationed; allocations were meager. Bullet holes pockmarked walls and roofs. Sewers dumped directly into the city's waterways. Medicine was in short supply; electricity was available for only 2.5 hours each day with turn-on time uncertain. The water could not be consumed without boiling, but heating fuel was next to impossible to find. Due to their weakened state, ten thousand Berliners starved or froze to death or succumbed to typhoid, diphtheria, or other diseases.

To these conditions my mother returned home from the hospital in November 1945, as she recalled often. She had just left the Paulinenhaus, one of the few hospitals still in operation in our part of the city. Forty-three out of forty-four hospitals had been seriously damaged or destroyed in the British sector where we lived. Dysentery was killing sixty-five out of every one hundred babies born in the city.

Three months before I was born, my mother had received word that my father, declared missing in action since his deployment to France, was a prisoner of war in a British camp somewhere along the Rhine River in Germany. The husband she had believed to be dead was alive; but whether he was still whole, she did not know.

Because my parents' apartment in the central part of Charlottenburg had been leveled during a British air raid two years earlier, my mother and I now shared a small two-room apartment above the pub with her sister Michen; her niece Rita and her nephew Manfred, ages ten and eight; her stepmother Helene; and her oldest sister, Anni. The flat had a small kitchen but no bathroom. A toilet was located downstairs and served the seven of us plus the building's other eight tenants. In the winter, when the pipes froze, the water had to be turned off. Then, each tenant brought his own pail with water for flushing.

With the exception of my Aunt Michen and cousins, the rest of us were *ausgebombt*—bombed out of our residences. My aunt and uncle's apartment, like most quarters still standing, had been damaged during the war. Air raids had blown out the window glass, and flying shrapnel had ripped a hole into the roof. Most of my parents' belongings had gone up in flames in the bombing of their tenement building two years earlier. My mother counted precious little as her possessions. "*Wir hatten ja nichts*—we didn't have anything," was how she summed up the postwar years. When she, a married woman without children, was conscripted into the war effort, she gave her remaining few personal things to Tante Michen for safekeeping. But when my mother returned to Berlin in August, the Russians had beaten her to the city and taken what was left. All of the women living in the flat at the time the Soviets conquered the city—my two aunts, my grandmother, and my cousin—hid on the rooftop and watched them loot the building. The Russkies took whatever they could get their hands on. Hundreds of thousands of Berlin women were raped during the two months between the arrival of the Russian troops on May 2, 1945 and that of the Americans on July 3, 1945.

My Aryan Name

"YOU CAN'T NAME THE GIRL UTA," the registrar informed my mother and Tante Michen in a straightforward manner, leafing through a hefty hardcover tome.

"But that's the name I picked," my mother replied, annoyed. "It goes with our surname—Umbach. What's wrong with Uta?"

"Uta isn't listed here. Apparently, it's not an Aryan name."

"An Aryan name? Why does it have to be an Aryan name? The war is over. The Nazis are gone."

"I know. But the list hasn't been replaced yet," the registrar said, pointing to the heavy volume. "It takes time. Until that happens, you can't name the girl Uta. There's nothing I can do."

Exasperated, my mother looked at my aunt. "What shall we do?" she muttered in frustration.

"How about 'Jutta'?" The registrar piped up, thumbing through the tome. "That's available. That's in the book. Jutta Umbach. How about that?"

After a moment of silence my mother capitulated. "All right, I guess Uta will have to be a Jutta."

"And put down 'Elke' as her middle name," my aunt added. "Elke is my choice. I'm the baby's godmother."

My mother and my aunt retold that story many times. I have always been bowled over by the notion that I, born after the war, owe my name to Hitler. The register of allowable names must have been abolished soon after I was baptized because Sonja, Lorena, Heike, and Yvonne, the names of my classmates, were not on the list either. They were born only a few months after me.

I have no recollection of this event or of the first eighteen months of my life that was spent in my aunt's apartment. But I heard the stories of those years so often that they became as familiar to me as if I recalled them from firsthand experience.

In a gorgeous cloud of white ruffles that my mother had hand stitched from the silk of a downed airman's parachute I was baptized Jutta Elke Umbach.

Making Ends Meet

"ONLY WOMEN AND CHILDREN made up our household during the first six months of your life, because the men had not yet returned from the war," my mother said to me when I got older. In the first few months after the end of the war, the four adults, my mother, her two sisters, and her stepmother tackled all essential tasks. They covered the ceiling with sheets when the dormer windows leaked; they hauled mattresses before the glassless window openings to keep the elements at bay; and they collected the meager supply of firewood that warmed the flat, even though the wood-burning tiled stove was way too small to do an adequate job under the best of circumstances.

Cold, running water was available, but electricity was provided only during a random 2.5-hour period during any given day or night. "That's when we cooked, cleaned, and washed. Sometimes, we got up in the middle of the night. Our rations were meager. On a daily basis, each of us was allowed:

300 grams (10.5 oz.) doughy bread,
400 grams (14 oz.) mushy potatoes,
20 grams (0.7 oz.) meat,
7 grams (0.25 oz.) fat,
30 grams (1 oz.) miscellaneous food items
        (rolled oats, barley, or semolina), and
15 grams (3 teaspoons) sugar."

My mother used to recite the list like a rosary.
"On top of that, our ration cards entitled us to a monthly allocation of:

100 grams (3.5 oz.) *Ersatzkaffee*—coffee substitute,
40 grams (less than 3 tablespoons) salt,
20 grams (less than 1.5 tablespoons) tea, and
25 grams (1.5 tablespoons) coffee beans.

Food allotments were subject to availability, of course. When the rations in our sector dropped to a mere 400 calories per person the month after you were born, we made *Hamsterfahrten*—hamster trips for food," my mother said. It meant that the women strapped packs to their backs, climbed on board the train, and visited the nearby countryside. If lucky, they succeeded in bartering a few possessions for food and returned with their pouches full, much like a hamster.

"During that first spring and summer, I minced the leaves of the basswood tree in front of your aunt and uncle's pub into my breast milk, so we could feed you kids something nutritious," my mother recalled. "The leaves tasted like spinach. First, I made a bottle for you, and then I thickened my leftover milk with flour and added it to a watery soup for Rita and Manfred."

In April 1946, my father escaped from captivity and, without major injuries, returned to Berlin. Four months later in August, Onkel Kalle, in whose apartment we all lived, also returned from the war. He had been declared missing in action following combat in Russia. His wife, Tante Michen, had received no word for many months and assumed that he was killed, or captured and sent to a Siberian forced labor camp. Then one day, my uncle walked through the front door. He had been released along with a trainload of other prisoners. His unexpected appearance caused unbelievable joy, but also some awkwardness. In his absence, Tante Michen had tried to manage alone, with the occasional help of a new friend, Onkel Fritz.

Now we were nine people in two small rooms, and day-to-day life became even more problematic. Our small rations had to be augmented by purchases on the black market where, despite shortages, almost anything could be bought for a price. But since bank savings had been confiscated in the first few months after the war, there was little cash. Black market deals depended heavily on barter as long as one still had, or could acquire, something to exchange. Because the occupation currency had become nearly worthless, cigarettes became the unofficial currency; even cigarette butts had value.

Although a black market had existed in Berlin during the war, it did not blossom until Soviet troops entered the city. The reason was that the Russian government prohibited their soldiers from converting the occupation marks they were paid into take-home rubles. Consequently, soldiers spent all of their compensation on the spot. But first, they turned their military pay into something of value: mainly cigarettes, fountain pens, and watches.

And as soon as the American troops arrived in Berlin, the black market became a major economy. Unlike their Soviet counterparts, US servicemen were allowed to convert their pay into American dollars at the official rate of ten to one. They were allowed to send that money home but could do far better by first participating in the black market. For example, they might purchase a carton of American cigarettes for fifty cents at the PX and resell it on the black market for 1,500 occupation marks and convert those into 150 dollars. Servicemen caught on quickly, and soon half of all business transactions in the city now took place on the black market. Cigarettes were the currency.

My father decided that he needed to return to work as soon as possible so that he could earn either hard cash or objects worth trading. But he needed a camera to reenter the photography business. His *Leica*, if it had not been stolen already, remained hidden in the rain gutter of a farmhouse in Thuringia.

"After we got married and before your father had to report back to his military unit, he gave me his camera for safekeeping," my mother explained. "Later, I, too, was conscripted and took it with me to Thuringia. Toward the end of the war, just before the Russians reached our area, I hid it with the help of a local girl I had befriended. We concealed it in the rain gutter of her parents' home. But there were rumors that the Russians would demand that all valuables be turned in. It would have made it extremely dangerous for her family to hide a camera. People were shot for lesser crimes than that. Therefore, my girlfriend and I agreed that we would not tell her parents. There had been no opportunity to retrieve it before or after we fled from the advancing Russians."

By the summer of 1946, my father was desperate for work, and my parents decided to travel to Thuringia to look for his *Leica*. Overjoyed, they found it still tucked in its hiding place. I don't think the owners of the farmhouse were ever told that they had harbored an illegal object.

Still, it remained difficult for my father to reestablish his business. He needed a darkroom, an impossible quest in our already crammed situation. Pressure mounted for our family to find separate lodgings.

Mutti

COMPLEX AND FULL OF CONTRADICTIONS, my mother, Mutti, displayed reserve as a rule, often to the point of timidity. But when enraged, she could demonstrate incredible nerve. Although I seldom saw those facets of her, I cobbled together much of her past not only from stories she shared, but also from fragments my father and aunts contributed.

She was the youngest of four sisters. Her father, Paul, spent sixty-five of the sixty-eight years that spanned his working career in the employ of Fürstenbrunn, a Berlin mineral water bottling company. Fifty years earlier, the firm had acquired the rights to a natural spring that had been discovered as far back as the 1600s when a German *Kurfürst*, a prince-elector, was said to have stumbled upon it during a hunting expedition. "Against strict order from our parents, we often snuck into the attic as children and played 'house' with the life-sized *Kurfürst* mannequins," my mother recalled.

In the early days of my grandfather's employment, Fürstenbrunn water was still delivered by horse-drawn carriage. Paul worked his way up from bottle filler in 1907 to stable master and coachman, and eventually to driver of the chief's private motorcar.

He met the love of his life at a company summer fest. Wladislawa Kempska, my grandmother, had left her native Poland together with a brother and sister for better job opportunities in neighboring Germany. The sisters moved to Berlin where Wladislawa soon found employment at the bottling plant. There she met Paul. Following a brief courtship, they married in 1909 and moved into a cottage on Fürstenbrunn grounds where my grandfather could be close to the horses in his care. Throughout his life, Opa talked about "Pfiff" and "Pfaff" and "Max" and "Moritz," his favorite four-legged companions.

In 1910, the couple's first little girl, Anni, arrived. A year later came Helene and then Maria. Once the little ones were born, my grandmother quit working at the plant. The young family kept dogs, cats, rabbits, and chickens and grew their own vegetables. By all accounts, Wladislawa was beautiful, energetic, and talented. "There wasn't anything our mother couldn't do. She sang, danced, cooked, and sewed all day," the sisters agreed.

In 1915, when the youngest daughter, Maria, was three years old, my grandmother was pregnant again, this time with my mother, Gertrud, Trudi for short. As the baby of the family, Trudi basked in love and attention. She was her mother's favorite. But when she was five, her eight-year-old sister Maria, or Michen as everyone called her, contracted polio, a viral disease for which there was no vaccine. Although my aunt eventually recovered, the infection permanently stunted her growth. She never reached five feet in height. During the most crucial time in Michen's life, Paul and Wladislawa heaped all of their attention onto their sick little daughter.

Seven years later, my grandmother died unexpectedly. Suddenly a single parent of four girls between the ages of twelve and seventeen, my grandfather felt the strain of raising his daughters alone. The three older girls were already in apprenticeships or worked full time, but my mother was still of school age. Since she had an hour-long walk to and from school along a deserted stretch of country road, Paul entrusted her care during the week to his sister, Anna, and her husband, Fritz, a postal carrier. His sister and her family lived within minutes of Trudi's school and had one son, Fritz Jr., who attended the same institution. A strong-willed, no-nonsense woman, my mother's aunt was a shopkeeper with a keen sense for business. She owned and operated a stationery and toy store.

"I felt completely abandoned," my mother said later. "Here I was, the only one of the four of us girls who had to live away from home during the week." After completing her education at age fourteen, she returned home for good. But by then her sisters, now seventeen, eighteen, and nineteen worked full time. Their interests and activities had changed, turning home into a different place for my mother.

Following graduation, Trudi also entered an apprenticeship program. Pay was minimal. Since her dream had been to become a hair stylist, she begged her father to allow her to apprentice in a stylish salon. It was customary for parents to compensate the business owner in return for training their progeny. The shop's reputation governed the cost. In her case, the figure exceeded my grandfather's modest resources, and he urged his daughter to consider a secretarial apprenticeship instead.

My mother reluctantly agreed and joined a small household appliance firm. Her initial duties were limited to filing and retrieving records. "I hated that job," she said. Following probation, she quit. Shocked, the business owner asked her what prompted her decision. "I wanted to hole-punch documents once in a while," she complained. The astonished man assured her that she could hole-punch in the future, but Trudi stuck to her plan and left the company.

Next, she started an apprenticeship with a fashionable shoe boutique, but the store declared bankruptcy soon thereafter. Eager for employment in a field that provided personal satisfaction, she asked her father to allow her to apprentice with a dressmaker. They located a skilled tailoress, willing to take on my mother for the customary three-year training program. Being detail-oriented, Trudi passed her exams with excellent grades, but lost all interest in the profession when she discovered that the monetary rewards associated with tailoring fell far short of those achievable in other lines of work. "Why should I settle for less than I could make selling shoes or dresses?" she told her father.

After thinking it over, my mother applied for a position as a sales clerk in an upscale boutique, a job akin to today's personal shopper. But because she had not apprenticed as a sales clerk, the shop insisted on a second apprenticeship. Instead of the standard three years, the firm agreed to a two-year stint. "I worked my way up to the head of the department and purchased, priced, and sold all of Matthiesen's skirts and blouses. And best of all, I was able to buy the most gorgeous, one-of-a-kind garments for myself—at a fraction of the retail price," she added.

Trudi was seventeen and had just finished her dressmaking apprenticeship when my grandfather remarried. His new wife, my mother's stepmother, did not have any children of her own. In each of the following years, one of my mother's sisters got married and moved away.

Having only one daughter left at home, Paul thoroughly spoiled his youngest girl. He was a man of impeccable taste and sometimes surprised her with the purchase of an entire outfit, complete with shoes, hat, and purse. But he also insisted that my mother hand him her entire pay envelope. It was a family tradition. My mother said, "I turned over my wages on the first of the month, and by the fifth, I had every penny back and then some. I owned underwear in every color of the rainbow."

"Working six days per week with an hour and a half commute by steam train each way left little time for leisure," my mother recalled. Still, being an attractive brunette with blue eyes, a stunning figure, and three older sisters, she made the acquaintance of many young suitors. She settled on Egon, a good-looking, well-educated pharmacist with flare. Although the couple contemplated marriage, they decided to wait until they could start their own household. Moving in with Egon's mother held no appeal for them. "*Jung und alt passen nicht zusammen*—Young and old don't fit together," they said.

When the war broke out in 1939, Egon was drafted. He was killed the following year. Trudi was twenty-five when he died. They had been going steady for six years. As more and more young men were sent off to war, age-appropriate matches became increasingly difficult. All of Trudi's sisters were already married. "Why am I always the unlucky one?" my mother began asking herself.

One day in 1942, three years into World War II, she met Karl at a café. He was on military leave. At first, he did not impress her favorably. He just wasn't Egon. Although Karl was tall and slender, he was not particularly athletic. His education did not match hers. He was a self-taught photographer. But there was a certain optimism and vitality about him that appealed to her. In short order, Karl won my mother's heart. However, when he asked my grandfather a year later for his daughter's hand in marriage, Paul cautioned his daughter, "Think carefully. Karl is ONLY a self-employed photographer. Will he be able to support a family?" My mother recoiled at that remark but proceeded with the wedding plans. After the nuptial, my father returned to his Army post, and my mother moved into his studio apartment.

A year later, my mother was conscripted into a German Air Force unit, stationed in the province of Thuringia, about one hundred fifty miles south of Berlin, not far from the Czech border. Her job was to help calculate the unit's provisions. She shared a room with four women in a first-class hotel that had been requisitioned by the military. My mother said she never openly defied orders but resisted in her own way. She often told a story about the time when the entire unit of young ladies was sent into the woods to collect mushrooms for dinner. She deliberately picked the poisonous ones. "I had to give two years of my life to the military. The least they could do in return was to feed me," she said. When her ploy did not get her out of mushroom gathering, she pretended to faint. From then on, she no longer had to participate in collecting her own dinner. Throughout her time in the military, my mother kept mostly to herself and did not form lasting friendships, she said.

When first the American, then Russian units moved into Thuringia during the final days of the war, she fled to Berlin with nothing more than a pack on her back. During those first two years of marriage, she had seen Karl for no more than a few days at a time.

I was already six months old when my father returned from the war. Once he was back in her life, my mother began to withdraw from family and friends. I had become her most prized possession. She often declared, "You are the only thing that belongs to me alone." As I grew up, she devoted her life to every detail of my physical well-being and worked hard at turning me into a small replica of herself.

It was difficult to please my mother. She was a perfectionist and expected the same from others. When she sewed, the inside of the garment looked as beautiful as the outside. She toiled endlessly at housework. If our home was not spic-and-span, all other activities were postponed. Her values were rigid. Those who did not share them were dropped from her circle. By the time I was old enough to register the world around me, she had already terminated her relationship with my grandfather because of his earlier intimation that my father was ONLY a photographer.

My mother spent long hours, hand sewing cute little outfits for me—dresses full of frills and flounces—and welcomed the approving looks and comments from family, friends, and strangers. Even before I reached school age, she curled my geometrically straight hair with curling tongs into *Schillerlocken*—ringlets. It was an onerous task that often led to tears; the tongs had to be heated on the kitchen stove and sometimes singed my hair and scalp. The final step involved tying a huge taffeta bow into my crown where it hovered like a propeller.

One summer afternoon when I was four or five, my mother, father, and I went for coffee and cake to the Strandbaude, an outdoor restaurant along the shore of the Groß-Glienicker See in the district of Kladow. Behind his cupped hand, the proprietor whispered that he had something special to offer: whipped cream. Such luxury had not been seen since the beginning of the war. Overjoyed, my father ordered a portion for my mother and me to share. When our *Kuchen*—cake—arrived, it was topped with a small dollop of whipped cream. "Look what Pappi got for us! This is sooooo good," my mother prompted me as she heaped some of the white stuff onto the tip of her spoon. Her whole face aglow, she steered the cream toward my lips.

I was not an adventurous eater. I sniffed everything before deciding whether or not is was suitable for consumption. That white stuff held no appeal for me. I sealed my lips and shook my head.

"Come on! Try it! You'll like it, I promise," my mother said.

My lips remained squeezed shut, and I stiffened my back with added resolve.

"Come on. Don't be silly. Try it! It's gooood!"

The dollop began to flatten visibly. Not wanting to let the delicacy go to waste, my mother took a couple of disheartened licks.

"See! Mutti likes it," my father encouraged me. Other restaurant guests started to glance at us with interest. After all, whipped cream was quite a sensation. Several futile attempts later, my mother's disappointment got the best of her. With a flick of her wrist, she slapped the entire spoonful smack into my face. As the cream spattered across my little visage, I let out a bloodcurdling shriek, causing every guest in the establishment to crane his neck in our direction. That was exactly what my mother had wanted to avoid.

My father laughed about it for years and never tired of telling the story. But my mother could never see the humor in it. "If I had eaten that cream without sharing it, the rest of the patrons would have said, 'look at that woman. She's eating all that whipped cream by herself without giving any to her little girl. What kind of a mother is she?'"

On rare occasions, my mother could also display unbelievable moxie. One day, as she often retold with satisfaction, my parents, along with my aunt and uncle, visited a neighborhood bar. I must have been about six and probably sound asleep at home. Dressed in a beautiful strapless aqua-colored evening gown, my mother drew admiring glances from a number of male guests. One man, in particular, did not seem to be able to avert his eyes. No words were exchanged between my mother and her apparent fan, but when her party left at the end of the evening, she was the last of the foursome to step into the street. Her silent admirer exited a few paces behind her.

All of a sudden, my mother stopped, turned on her heels, and looked the man straight in the eye. Then she pulled down the bodice of her dress, fully exposing her bare breasts. "There you go. That's what you wanted to see, wasn't it?" she glared.

Pappi

"WHO DO YOU LIKE BETTER, your mother or your father," a neighbor asked.

"Pappi!" I replied without hesitation. I was four years old. I had been taught to always tell the truth.

From the beginning, my father was my clear favorite. Generous and good-natured, he looked after my interests, I was certain of that. When I was little, he often returned from a week or two on photo shoots in West Germany with his coat pockets full of sugar packets. Coffee, served in dainty porcelain cups on saucers, always came with a pack of dual cubes. These were wrapped in thin, white paper, imprinted with the city's emblem or the restaurant's logo. When my father spread out his loot on our living room table, one packet at a time, I squealed with delight, "*Danke schön*, Pappi, *danke*." I had no real use for sugar, but his gifts seemed special. After all, he had collected them just for me.

When the three of us played cards on long winter evenings, Pappi always let me win. We played for pfennigs, and I got to keep the winnings. When, after many nights of card playing, I had saved up the impressive sum of a couple of marks, I would ask my mother, "Mutti, can we go to the bank?" At her hand, I entrusted my savings to the clerk who, in turn, added it to an account my father had established for me. I always pictured the clerk putting my pfennigs into a box with my name on it. I never asked how much money was in the account, and it never occurred to me that the money could also be taken out. I just knew that money belonged in the bank.

My father lived completely in the present. A two-pack-a-day smoker for many years, he quit one evening and never touched another cigarette. Not one comment from him on the subject—ever. He quit! End of discussion.

When I was a young teen, I heard my mother mention that he had been married once before. The comment took me by surprise. I had never heard him talk about a previous wife or seen photographs. When I asked my father, he waved it off, "That was eons ago. Long forgotten."

Tall and slender, fine, straight hair, and sun-sensitive pale skin that peeled in sheets at the slightest exposure, he looked like a brother of the

British-American journalist, Alistair Cooke. The many fine lines that crossed his face created the impression of a happy outdoorsman. They looked like furrows that had taken up residence where a smile had vacated.

My father, Karl (although my mother called him Peter to avoid a mix-up with Tante Michen's husband, also named Karl), was six years older than my mother and born in Kassel, in the province of Hessen. His father, Otto, had been a blacksmith and his mother, Marie, a cook. I met my grandparents only twice, once when I was still a toddler, and again at age four or five. I remember my grandfather as a slender, hollow-cheeked man who was hard of hearing and answered, "Yes, yes my little one," to everything I said.

My grandmother wore her braided white hair tucked into a bun at the nape of her neck. Her smile was warm, her figure pleasantly rotund, and she hugged like a teddy bear. Both grandparents always wore black; Oma even covered her hair with a black scarf when she left the house.

Tante Erna was my father's sister. Her husband was killed in World War II, forcing her to raise their only child, Ottokar, by herself. She did not smile often and her stern demeanor frightened me. My cousin, Ottokar, was fifteen years older than I and definitely an adult in my eyes. I have only one vivid memory of him. I was four or five when he changed his clothes in the bedroom where I pretended to be asleep, and I saw him strip. I had never seen a naked man before and knew instinctively that there was something important about this picture that I should file away for the future.

Many details of my father's life remained sketchy to me. So much was left unsaid. In our few conversations about his childhood, he mentioned that World War I had broken out the year before he started first grade. An uncle of his, Onkel Heinrich, owned a farm in Großenenglis, a small community south of Kassel. Since children were essential to farmwork, particularly during planting and harvesting seasons, they would be excused from school during those times. My father helped on a regular basis and spent even more time on the farm once the men had gone off to war. Although he graduated from middle school, he said, "When you add up the total number of hours we actually spent in school, I don't think it amounted to more than a grade school education."

When World War I ended in 1918, my father was nine, and harsh demands for reparations drove the country into hyperinflation. Germany's currency lost value at breathtaking speed. The year 1923, the last and worst of the hyperinflationary period, was etched into his memory. He was a boy of fourteen who had just graduated from middle school, ready to enter an apprenticeship. Prices escalated rapidly and often doubled within hours.

One day late that year, his mother sent him to the train station. "Go, get two tickets to Großenenglis," she said and handed him a suitcase full of money. On the platform, a long line of people stood already queued up in front of the ticket window. Just before it was my father's turn, the window closed for price revisions. When it reopened, the contents of the suitcase no longer covered the purchase price. "I had to go home and tell Mother that I didn't have enough money for the tickets," he said. He did not remember the price of the train trip, but said, "A loaf of bread cost somewhere around two hundred billion marks. An American dollar was worth more than one trillion marks. People said it was cheaper to burn the paper money than to use it for buying fuel."

Following graduation, my father embarked on a three-year apprenticeship with an upholsterer. He came to hate these years with a passion. From his brief descriptions, I always pictured an employer/employee relationship analogous to that between Dickens' Ebenezer Scrooge and Bob Cratchit. As soon as his three years were up, my father acquired a camera somewhere. He was seventeen. "I figured out how to use it and went to work as a freelance photographer," he said. In Germany, few people owned quality cameras until the 1970s, making photography a lucrative business. Because he never studied the mechanics of it, he shied away from studio work. Instead, he concentrated on shooting weddings, birthdays, special events, and vacation mementos.

My father never forgot his days as an apprentice, though. Throughout his life, he detested manual labor. Even more than that, he detested taking orders. Consequently, he chose to earn a living with independent work and to pay someone for even the simplest manual tasks on the home front, like hanging a picture.

By the time World War II broke out, Karl was well established in his photography business. The German Army assigned him to the

Propaganda Department to photo-shoot frontline action. I know very little about his life in the military, except that I heard him mention France, Finland, Karelia, Estonia, and the Arctic Circle, and he often talked about the cities of Paris, Orel, Minsk, and Murmansk. Since his dislike of orders was deeply ingrained, he was demoted as often as he was promoted.

When my father began dating my mother in 1942, countless bombing attacks on Berlin had already significantly reduced the supply of civilian housing. "The Nazis ordered me to surrender my studio apartment or take in a tenant," he said. Rather than open his home to a stranger, my mother and he decided to marry. The year was 1943.

Near the end of the war, my father was captured in France by American ground units. He never talked to me about the details of his capture. When I questioned my mother years later, she said, "I received a letter from your father's commander, informing me that your Pappi was missing in action. All of your father's belongings were returned by post."

I know from my father that he was shot in the thigh and that the bullet remained imbedded in his buttocks for one reason only: It was part of his future draft avoidance plan. "If there's going to be another war, I'm going to check into the first hospital and have that slug dug out," he used to say. The projectile remained lodged in his thigh for the rest of his life.

Shortly after the end of the war, the American military transferred its German prisoners, captured in France, to British forces. They, in turn, relocated the captives to a former shoe factory on the banks of the British-occupied Rhine River valley of Germany where the prisoners were employed to clear mines and to harvest crops.

Three months before my birth, my father was able to get word to my mother that he was still alive and living in Germany. In April 1946, when I was six months old, my mother left me with her sister and paid him a brief visit at the camp. Husband and wife were allowed to speak to each other for only one hour. Afterwards, my mother took a train to Kassel to share the good news with her in-laws. While there, she received a telegram from my father. He had escaped to Berlin. "The Brits never tried to come after me," he said later.

Throughout my childhood and teens, my father worked almost every day, including weekends and holidays, unless severe weather kept him at home. Photography was his work, his hobby, and his social outlet. I was his favorite subject, and my development was documented in hundreds of photos.

He was dependable, a hard worker, and punctual to a fault. Despite his long hours, he never missed a meal at home. Karl believed in division of labor. He earned the living; my mother kept the house. He considered child rearing to be women's work, a view shared by many. I enjoyed and looked forward to the evenings when my father was home. With his easy laugh and practical approach, he calmed the anxieties that clutched my mother.

My father lived through two world wars, three systems of government, and two major currency devaluations. Karl was a preteen in 1919 when the Weimar Republic was created, Germany's ill-fated first experiment with democracy. He was a teenager during the hyperinflationary period of the 1920s which ended in a drastic currency devaluation and replacement of the mark in 1923 with the provisional rentenmark which turned into the permanent reichsmark. "It took one trillion marks to get one rentenmark," he remembered. As an adult in 1933, Karl watched the Weimar Republic collapse and the Nazis rise to power. He was drafted into the Army in 1939 and lived through six years of hostilities and the unconditional surrender of the Third Reich. Three years later, during my lifetime, he witnessed another devaluation when the reichsmark was replaced by the deutsche mark. My father also lived through the Berlin Blockade in 1948/1949; the creation of the German Federal Republic in 1949, Germany's second democracy; the Cold War; and the construction of the Berlin Wall in 1961. These events left permanent thumbprints on his outlook. Twice, he saw promises remain unfulfilled and savings evaporate. For the rest of his life, my father never believed a word a politician or a government spoke. His motto was, "It's best to stay as far away as possible from those guys. Never, never trust any of them."

Knesebeckstraße

IN LATE 1946, I CELEBRATED my first birthday. The following winter was particularly brutal with snow, ice, and subzero temperatures at

levels that Germany had rarely seen before. Due to the large-scale de-
struction in the final years of the war, Berliners now lived in extremely
crowded conditions with little protection against the elements. Firewood
and coal had become largely unavailable. Over 60,000 people suffered
from pneumonia, influenza, or the effects of frostbite. Many froze to
death. In response, the three Western occupation forces raised food rations in their sectors. But the Russians did not follow suit, and the people in Soviet territory continued to subsist on rock-bottom allotments.
Since his return from captivity, my father had pestered Berlin's provisional government for allocation of an apartment of our own. "We need
the additional space to install a darkroom for my photography business,"
he pleaded. To no avail. Nothing seemed to be had when, at last, he
got word through black market sources that there might be a potential
vacancy. All parties to the rental agreement expected a payoff. The flat
would go to the highest bidder. I have no idea how Pappi finagled the
transaction, but he managed.

In April 1947, we moved to Knesebeckstraße. Since we lived there
until I was thirteen, I remember it well. First constructed in the late
1800s, our apartment was located just two miles west of the heavily
damaged heart of the city. Rows of six-story Victorian tenements lined
both sides of the street in the once upscale neighborhood of Charlottenburg. Each apartment building consisted of four structures, arranged in
a square around a central courtyard. Retail shops occupied the street-side
ground floor; residences made up the remainder. Prior to World War II,
the ornate front buildings had served the posh middle class. Workers and
servants had resided in the back. To ease the post-war housing shortage,
the once roomy apartments had been divided into several smaller units,
creating unusual floor plans.

Our flat was located on the fourth floor in one of the *Seitenflügel*—
side wing buildings. Each flat was also assigned a small cellar, and we all
shared a *Hängeboden,* a large communal drying loft. A sea of white sheets
and underwear often filled this space.

We approached our wing through giant oak double doors that led from
the street into the tiled vestibule of the front building. The gilded mirrors
on the left of the foyer had seen better days. A striking curved wooden
staircase on the right ascended to the front units. Smaller, less pompous

double doors at the opposite end of the hall led into a shadowy courtyard which was dominated by a large chestnut tree next to a tall carpet beating structure. To get to our apartment, we entered the wing building from the courtyard and climbed four musty flights of stairs to our own set of double front doors which were lined with thick sheets of steel to deter potential burglars. There were no elevators in any of the buildings.

When we first moved in, we were assigned the larger of the apartment's two rooms and shared the kitchen and bath with a lady tenant who already occupied the smaller room. Our living space was about three hundred square feet in size and located at one end of a very long hallway. In this room our family slept, dined, lived, and worked. A built-in floor-to-ceiling wood-burning tile stove took up the corner opposite the exterior wall. My baby bed stood near the window. Little by little, my father acquired two brown couches which also served as my parents' beds at night, a round table, two upholstered chairs, and an ebony buffet. He purchased some of the furniture from the previous tenant and acquired the rest on the black market. There was little privacy.

Later in the year, when the lady tenant moved to the back building, Pappi turned her small room into an office and darkroom, and for the next thirteen years, the larger room remained our combination living room/dining room/bedroom. Kitchen and bath were located at the other end of the long corridor, the double front doors smack in the middle of it.

The kitchen was my favorite place in the apartment. A wood-burning stove in the corner opposite the window spread warmth and *Gemütlichkeit*; a small built-in cabinet underneath the window formed a comfortable seat for reading and watching my mother cook. There was also a small walk-in larder to one side. Over time, Pappi acquired a table, chairs, and a small utility cabinet. Though the kitchen was the warmest place in the apartment, a pail of water left on a winter evening would be frozen solid by morning.

In the adjacent bathroom a toilet, sink, freestanding bathtub, and an old-fashioned boiler lined up against one wall. The tiny bull's-eye-shaped window was almost hidden behind the heater so that little daylight entered the room. Prior to taking a bath, the boiler had to be tended, and an allotment of fuel yielded only enough hot water to fill the tub once. In the early years, that meant that all three of us bathed in the same water. During the once-a-week bath ritual, my father stepped into the tub first and took a near scalding bath. Then it was my mother's turn. When it was time for me to get scrubbed down, the water was barely tepid and definitely sudsy. On all other days of the week, the use of the tub was limited to "watering" the photographs which my parents had developed in the darkroom the night before. Because my father had to run back and forth between his office and the bathroom, carrying trays of acid, he soon relocated the darkroom to the end of the hallway adjacent to the bath. Each night, my parents sat there and developed the day's orders. Until my teens, I was banned from this area at night. In case of emergency, I had to use a potty.

I have only a few fond memories of Knesebeckstraße. Although I often felt lonely there because I had no one to play with, on Thursdays the flat came to life. That was when Frau Mandel, our cleaning lady, arrived to spend most of the day cleaning, waxing, washing, and ironing. She was a tall, big-boned woman who lived in East Berlin. Her features were rough and her hair fried by too many permanents, but her heart was as big and as warm as a teddy bear. I would not let her out of my eyes. "Can I go with you to the *Hängeboden*?" I'd ask. She never refused. There, under the building's roof, she boiled our wash in a huge pot and stirred it with a thick, wooden stick. The steam that escaped from the tub in thick clouds settled in pearls on Frau Mandel's brows. When the wash had boiled long enough, she wrung it out and hung it on clotheslines that stretched from beam to beam.

Other times she rolled up our old, faded Persian carpet, threw it over her shoulder, and descended the four flights with a rattan carpet beater in hand. "Can I help you?" I'd ask eagerly and traipse along. Downstairs, she threw the rug over the structure beneath the chestnut tree and beat the living hell out of it. With each whop, big puffs of dust rose into the air. Standing to one side, I would jump with joy. That was fun. I would have loved to give it a whop myself, but I had to be careful not to get dirty. Otherwise, my mother would have put a quick end to my entertainment.

Since all windows faced north, the bare stucco walls felt cold to the touch, summer or winter. Not even the geraniums in the window box outside the kitchen wanted to thrive. I also remember the uneasiness with which I approached our poorly lit stairway whenever I had to enter the building by myself. One late afternoon, many years later—I must have been almost thirteen—a young man, maybe seventeen years old, followed me from the street, through the vestibule and courtyard, and into our wing building. Initially, I quickened my steps to outpace him. But he kept pace. I began to run, but he caught up with me in the stairway. "Wait, I want to talk to you," he called out.

Panting, I stopped on the first landing and turned around. "What?" My heart raced. *What does he want?*

Slowly, the man came closer until only one or two steps separated us. I clutched the bag of bread my mother had asked me to pick up at the grocer and glanced at him. His smile looked somehow menacing. But despite feeling vulnerable in the secluded stairway, I remained glued to the landing, trying to look casual. Without diverting his eyes from me, he slowly spread open his beige trench coat and said, "Do you know what this is?"

My heartbeat quickened. I did not dare to look down. Instead, my eyes swept past his head as I shrugged, "Yeah?"

"Wanna go to the park with me?" he asked.

Heart pounding, I said, "I've to run up and take this bread to my mother first," holding up the bag. "Otherwise, she'll come looking for me. But I'll be right back," I added, hoping he would buy my little lie.

"Okay, if you promise to be right back down."

"It'll only take a minute," I said, turned, and ran up the remaining three flights as if in pursuit by a wild animal. Looking back to see if the man had followed me, I leaned on our apartment's doorbell.

"Is there a fire somewhere?" My mother asked as she opened the door. "Do you have to lean on the bell like that?"

"Sorry," I said, "I think it got stuck. Here's the bread." Then I squeezed past her and into our apartment. Once safe, I wondered if I should tell my mother. Would she ever let me leave the house by myself again if she knew, I wondered? Better not tell her, I decided. But from that day on, I felt uneasy whenever I was alone in the stairway and was relieved when we moved to the Lietzensee soon thereafter. Fortunately, I never saw the young man again.

Berlin Blockade

BUT I AM GETTING AHEAD OF MYSELF. Since the end of the war, ideological differences between Soviet and Western objectives regarding Berlin had grown, and sixteen months after our move to Knesebeckstraβe, the Soviets stormed out of the Allied Control Council. It was in March of 1948 when the four-power Kommandatura effectively, although not formally, ended.

Our currency, the reichsmark, was worthless. The cigarette economy still dominated the market. When the streets buzzed with rumors of an impending devaluation, my parents, like everyone else, rushed to the black market to buy as many of the remaining few goods as possible. By doing so, they hoped to convert their little cash into viable currency, but the cost of commodities had already climbed to unattainable levels. A single cigarette cost upwards of three thousand reichsmarks, my father said.

Then, in June of 1948, when I was two and a half, the rumors became reality. The three Western Allies introduced a new currency in their occupation zones of West Germany and a short time thereafter in West Berlin: the deutsche mark. Up to six hundred reichsmarks of existing cash could be exchanged at a rate of 1:1. The exchange rate for additional funds was 1:15. With this move, West Berlin became economically, though not politically, part of West Germany. The Soviets objected vehemently, but the Kommandatura no longer met, and the Allies no longer cooperated with one another.

Three days later, while people still wrestled with the ramifications of the situation, the Russians countered by introducing their own new legal tender within their zone and sector. It was also called deutsche mark. Germany and Berlin now had two currencies. In either case, the monetary reform had greatly reduced the little savings the populace had accumulated since war's end. It was the second devaluation loss my parents had experienced within a twenty-four-year period.

From the start, the Soviets refused to recognize the new Western currency, and shortly thereafter, the West no longer accepted the new East marks for rent or food. East-West tension mounted. Soviet-controlled Radio Berlin broadcasted that the Americans, British, and French occupation forces were getting ready to leave the city and advised West Berliners to turn to the Soviets. Russia promised to provide food and fuel to all sectors for Eastern currency and ration cards. Few West Berliners took the bait. "We tried to second-guess what was going to happen next," my aunt said later, "but we didn't know what to do. And so we waited."

US military governor, General Lucius D. Clay, made the next move. He halted all shipments of dismantled German industries to Russia. Since the Soviets had captured the city in May 1945, they had removed thousands of factories and over a million pieces of industrial equipment and shipped them to Russia. Even Berlin's 7,000 heads of cattle were rounded up and driven east. In response to Clay's action, the Soviets became uncooperative in administrative affairs. By now, they were convinced that they had made a huge mistake by allowing the Western powers to co-occupy Berlin and wanted them to withdraw their new currency and to surrender West Berlin. To hasten those outcomes, Russia declared "technical difficulties" the following day and blocked all ground and water access to West Berlin. Then they announced that their sector would no longer supply food or electricity to West Berlin. Thus, on June 24, 1948, the Berlin Blockade went into effect.

West Berlin's breadbasket and utility plants were located in the East and all of its coal needs had been met by shipments from West Germany. But since the Western powers had failed to negotiate contractual ground and water rights to and from West Berlin, they lacked the power to intercede. There was only enough food in the city to last for thirty-five days and enough coal to continue a lifeline power supply for forty-five days. A blockade foreshadowed nothing short of impending starvation for West Berliners. My parents, along with everyone else, were terrified. However, leaving the city for West Germany never became a serious option for my family, because my mother was unwilling to sever her Berlin roots.

If life during the post-war years had been difficult, during a blockade it promised to be far worse. My parents set out to gather dandelions and other edible plants, and hoarded what they could. For the remainder of their lives, they rarely spoke about what they felt during that time—what it was like to live day by day, what it was like to wonder whether the end was near, whether life under Communism beckoned, or whether a satisfactory solution could be reached.

Three years earlier, in November 1945, as part of the partition agreement, the four Allies had contractually agreed upon three twenty-mile-wide air corridors which converged over Berlin from Frankfurt, Hamburg, and Hannover. Now, General Clay decided to supply the Western sectors of Berlin from the air because the Western Allies had come to believe that West Berlin must be held to prevent Communism from spreading in Europe.

The first Berlin-bound cargo plane lifted off on June 26, 1948. It was the start of the *Luftbrücke*—The Berlin Airlift. For eleven months, cargo planes flew around the clock. Initially, a plane landed every eight minutes. The first aircraft was dispatched at an altitude of five hundred feet. The next plane flew five hundred feet higher. This pattern was repeated five times before it started all over again. If a landing had to be aborted, the pilot had to return to the beginning of the lineup. Once landed, all cargo had to be unloaded with utmost speed. Toward the end of the blockade, planes landed in closely timed intervals of about three minutes. While the United States and Great Britain provided the aircraft, France participated in an administrative capacity. Pilots from England, the United States, Canada, Australia, New Zealand, Japan, and South Africa flew the missions.

Coal flown in from West Germany was distributed to utilities, bread factories, and hospitals only. Private homes and businesses did not receive any heating materials. To keep from freezing to death the following winter, the population was authorized to cut down one-half the city's park and street trees.

Due to limited availability of electricity and a resulting work-hours reduction, unemployment soared. By the middle of July 1948, half of Berlin's workforce had been laid off and three-quarters of West Berlin's factories were headed for closure. In addition, refugees from the East flooded to the Western sectors. The currency reform and the earlier confiscation of bank accounts by the Soviets had reduced the amount of money in circulation. There was almost no cash in the city. Soviet agents seized this opportunity to spread propaganda that, if West Berliners did not evict the Western Allies, they would soon be subjected to the same conditions that prevailed when the Russians first conquered the city: rapes, lootings, and murders. During the first couple of weeks following war's end, women from all walks of life—grandmothers, prepubescent girls, nuns, pregnant women, and nursing mothers—had been subjected to rampant rapes. Few women had remained untouched. Now, rumors intimated that those days might return, and even that the Western Allies themselves might be sent to concentration camps. The prospects were frightening for Berlin's women. One to two hundred thousand of them had already given birth to Russian babies as a result of the rapes, and close to two million woman throughout the country had had abortions. Panic spread among the populace.

Finally, in the middle of May 1949, after the Soviets realized that the Western Allies' attempt of supplying West Berlin from the air had proven successful and that the Western counter-blockade of industrial exports to the Soviet Union had stifled reconstruction efforts in Russia, they lifted the blockade.

It became clear that, rather than having deterred the Western Allies from holding onto Berlin, the blockade had strengthened their determination to transform West Germany into an autonomous state. Nowhere did this East-West struggle become more obvious than in Berlin.

During the preceding year, one additional airport in West Berlin (Tegel) had been built. Two existing airports (Tempelhof and Gatow) had been modified to accommodate larger planes. Two-thirds of the cargo flights had carried coal, one quarter of them had transported food, and raw materials had made up the rest of the trips. Almost 2.5 million tons of food and supplies had been airlifted to Berlin on close to 280,000 flights. The total distance flown equaled two hundred trips to the moon.

Although the airlift operations officially ended on May 12, 1949, they continued, in fact, until the end of September so that supplies of food, fuel, and industrial materials could be stockpiled in case of a second Soviet blockade. Seventy-nine men had lost their lives to the airlift. More than 60,000 people had contributed their labor. 40,000 of them were German citizens who helped build the runways, unload the planes, and maintain aircraft.

The function of the airlift had been not only to sustain the lives of the just over two million West Berliners, but also to allow the Western

Allies time to negotiate a reinstatement of their access rights. Until agreement over the fate of Berlin could be reached, West Berlin would have to remain a jointly governed territory, located in the middle of East Germany.

I was three-and-a-half years old when the blockade ended and oblivious to the anguish and triumphs of the previous year. There is only one thing I clearly recall: A huge burlap sack of *Kartoffelflocken*—instant potato flakes—propped against our hallway wall, adjacent to my father's curtained-off darkroom. My mother said the flakes were used to make soup. My cousin, Rita, recalled that her family ate potato "steaks" supplied by the United States. "They were dehydrated and looked like French Fries," she remembered. "Maybe they were called potato 'sticks' rather than 'steaks.' At any rate, they were awful," she said. "We also got something from America, called 'grits.' It was supposed to taste like creamy wheat, but it wasn't even close."

Some airlift pilots had dropped small handkerchief parachutes filled with chewing gum or chocolates. These *Rosinenbomber*—raisin bombers—as the children called them, became legendary. Because I was still too young, I did not learn of them until much later, but Rita told me that the planes did not release goodies over our area anyway. "They did not drop them until they were in an airport approach pattern."

Before and during the blockade, my father purchased film and film processing equipment on the black market which operated more or less openly during the airlift. He built a thriving business photographing Allied soldiers in exchange for food, cash, or clothing. His business was doing so well that he employed first one, then two, full-time employees. My mother spent long nights in the darkroom, helping him develop, dry, and trim photos. Because the night work took its toll on her during the day when she needed to shop, cook, clean, and take care of me, my father hired Halla, a young woman who lived in the front building, to be my daytime nanny and caretaker. Such luxury was ordinarily reserved for wealthy families.

The years surrounding the blockade were, in fact, my family's most prosperous years because by the time I turned five in 1950, the nanny years were long forgotten. Education, status, and wealth had begun to reclaim their time-honored places as prerequisites for a substantial income. But even then, life remained somewhat skewed. My father had acquired a polar bear costume, the bear being in Berlin's coat of arms. He often photographed tourists hugging the Berlin Bear in front of famous landmarks. Herr Grabowski, the man who spent six to seven hours each day in the costume, had been a flight controller prior to the war. Although he spoke seven languages, he was unable to find suitable employment because the German airline industry was grounded. Not until the new Lufthansa re-formed in the midfifties, did he have the opportunity to resume the line of work he was trained to do and to receive compensation commensurate with his skills.

Following West Berlin's first free elections in 1949, the military government ended, and an occupation statute went into effect. The Federal Republic of Germany (West Germany) was created in May of that year and included special provisions for West Berlin. Bonn became the new West German capital. Five months later, in October 1949, the German Democratic Republic (East Germany) was founded with East Berlin as its capital.

Arthur

SHORTLY AFTER THE BERLIN BLOCKADE ENDED, I made a special friend. According to my mother, it happened late one midsummer afternoon when I was not yet four years old. She took me by the hand, and together we made the over-an-hour-long walk from home to the *Messehallen am Funkturm*, the trade-fair grounds, surrounding the well-known radio tower. Built as one large steel framework similar to the Eiffel tower in Paris, it is almost five hundred feet tall and could be seen from far away. My father often chose this spot to photograph tourists who fancied a memento with Berlin's famous landmark. "Pappi will soon be finished. Then we can all walk home together," she said.

As we drew near, my father was in the middle of snapping pictures of a British soldier in his late twenties or early thirties. Living in the British sector of Berlin, uniformed Allied soldiers were a familiar sight. Although I was eager to run straight into my father's arms, my mother held me back until she sensed that the transaction was completed. Then, we continued our approach.

My father waved and broke into a broad grin when he spotted us. I let go of my mother's hand, ran to him, and threw my arms around him. "Pappi, Pappi!" He lifted me high above his head while the soldier slowly put his billfold in his pants pocket. On solid ground again, I eagerly stretched up my little hand to the man in uniform, curtsied, and beamed, "*Guten Tag*—good day."

Taking my small hand in both of his, the soldier squatted until his eyes were level with mine and said, "I'm Arthur. What's your name?" Giggling, I squirmed in his gentle grip. Slowly, he repeated, "What's your name? Nah–may?" He asked with a thick British accent, untrained in our language.

I looked to my mother for help. "*Der Onkel will wissen wie Du heißt*—The uncle wants to know your name," my mother clarified with some alarm. Behind her cheery façade she wondered why the solder was so friendly. What did he want from her daughter?

Unaware of my mother's uneasiness, I took note only of his friendly smile.

"Jutta," I answered in my high-pitched little voice.

"U–tah," he repeated and pulled a small bar of chocolate from his breast pocket. "Cadbury," he said as he handed it to me. "I'm Arthur."

Without hesitation, I reached for the chocolate, then stopped halfway and turned to my mother. Her recurrent admonishment, "Never accept anything from strangers," probably resounding in my young head. But when my mother, despite her apprehension nodded, my eyes lit up, and I eagerly reached for the chocolate.

"Cat–berry," I beamed. *"Danke."*

Arthur laughed, bid good-bye, and went about his business.

Barely a week went by before Arthur reappeared at the radio tower. As soon as he spotted my father, he waved, walked up to him, and pressed a small blue teddy bear into my father's hands. "U-tah," he said, "U-tah."

My father was moved. Unable to speak more than a few words of English, he thanked the soldier profusely in German and touched his arm in gratitude. "Asa," he finally murmured, unable to pronounce the English "r" or "th" in Arthur's name. "Tank you."

When my father returned home that evening, he handed me the toy and told me it was a gift from the kind uncle in uniform. Delighted, I danced up and down the hall with my teddy. I worshipped that toy. It would remain my bed companion until almost threadbare.

"Onkel Asa" became a much welcome and appreciated sight to our family. He adored me and indicated with words and gestures that he hoped to have a little girl, just like me, some day. Over the next few months, he frequently stopped by our apartment or surprised us in the street with small toys for me, cigarettes for my father, or staples for the whole family. Sometimes, he filled my baby carriage with potted flowers for my mother. Arthur's generosity was evident throughout our home: canned corned beef, a small slab of bacon hanging from the ceiling in our air-cooled larder, and, of course, Cadbury.

Then one day, Arthur hinted in words difficult to understand, but underscored by his gestures, that he would like to adopt me. He tried to explain that he could offer me a better life in England than my parents could in war-torn Berlin. My parents were shocked. At first, they assumed they had misunderstood. Then they were horrified. They asked themselves whether Arthur was exceedingly presumptuous or whether he had a valid point. Did he know something they didn't? Was something going to happen to Berlin? Would their daughter be better off in a world far away? Were they being selfish? But as soon as my parents had recovered from their initial shock, my father made it clear that I was not available for adoption. I was their daughter and would remain with them, for better or for worse.

Soon thereafter, Arthur's tour of duty in Berlin ended. He waved farewell for the last time. Unable to grasp the finality of our friendship, my chubby little hand waved to and fro. "*Auf Wiedersehen*—until we see each other again—Onkel Asa." It was the last time we saw or heard from the nice man in uniform.

The Rules

SILENCE. EXCEPT FOR SINGLE IMAGES, silence is my earliest memory. I must have been about five. There was something ominous about the quiet that covered our apartment like a veil. "Not so loud."

"Pssst." "The neighbors!" It was one of the many rules that regulated my existence. My parents always spoke in hushed tones and admonished me when I forgot.

Since television was not yet generally available, radio was our sole entertainment. But it was only turned on when my parents listened to the morning and evening news or to a few select programs on RIAS (Radio in the American Sector, the Voice of the Free World). *Günter Neumann und seine Insulaner*—Günter Neumann and his Islanders— was one of the broadcasts they enjoyed. I cannot remember whether it was aired weekly or monthly, but the poignant political spoof had made its debut in December during the middle of the Berlin Blockade. Radio actors poked fun at Berlin's status of being a capitalist island in a communist sea.

Despite my youth, I, too, began to listen to the program. From age five to about ten, I paid close attention to the skits and songs in which the artists pitted capitalism against communism and mocked fanatical adherence to ideology. Through the sometimes compassionate, sometimes biting wit of Neumann's group, I learned on an elementary level what the impasse between East and West was all about. Without realizing it, I received my first inoculation against communism.

The program always opened with the same catchy tune:

Der Insulaner verliert die Ruhe nicht,
(The islander doesn't lose his cool)

Der Insulaner liebt keen Jetue nicht,
(The islander doesn't care for any fuss)

Der Insulaner hofft unbeirrt,
(The islander hopes unperturbed)

Dass seine Insel wieder'n schönes Festland wird
(That his island will once again become a beautiful mainland)

In one of my favorite recurring segments of the show, a party functionary "reschooled" a group of workers to embrace Walter Ulbricht's (head of East Germany) Stalinist Communism. Each time, the lovable but misguided comrade threw his heart and soul into the task of converting the men and women in his class. He spoke in the heartwarming, dyed-in-the-wool *Berliner Schnauze.* This working-class dialect combines earthy humor with friendly disrespect. The "r" is typically silent, and the "g" sounds like a "ch" or a "j." The resulting "Berlinese" comes across as the vernacular of the uneducated and sounds much like the German equivalent of cockney English. While the bumbling functionary sang praises to the East German Socialist Unity Party and denounced the "Fascist warmongers" of the west, his students, without fail, got him into hot water with probing questions.

The program always opened with the familiar, "*Und damit, liebe Jenossen und Jenossinnen, komme ick zu unser heutijet Themata, nämlich…*—And with that, dear comrades, I'm getting to today's theme, which is . . ." And it always ended with the poor man shouting in frustration, "*Die Sitzung ist geschlossen!*—The meeting is closed!" when his students had, once again, assailed him with questions that defied party-line logic.

Frequently, the show poked fun at the inferiority of East German consumer products when compared to similar Western goods. One time, the comrades argued whether Western Black & White whiskey or their state-owned Scotch was superior. After a hilarious taste test, they came to the conclusion that their state-owned product was definitely better because it got them drunk faster and, in a pinch, could double as a stain remover.

Another time, the group focused on the persistent shortages of consumer goods in the state-owned East German *Handelsorganization*—commerce organization. When the HO placed a sign in the window one day that raincoats had arrived for sale, hundreds of people lined up at the door. Unfortunately, only five raincoats had come in. And when a customer inquired in June about the arrival time of bathing suits, he was told, "in early December at the earliest."

Throughout the fifties, people joked about East Germany copying Western ideas and then insisting that their innovations were unique. I remember a skit performed after East Germany introduced the concept of buying on credit, a practice that had already been introduced in West Germany. The new purchase model was, of course, discussed among the comrades. The amiable functionary fully supported the scheme and encouraged his comrades to think of other useful schemes that might be copied from the West. "How about free elections?" a comrade piped up.

When it became widespread knowledge that East Germans were leaving their country in droves, the functionary espoused party-line rhetoric when he admitted that maybe 500 misguided souls had fled to the West since the end of the war. He then added that that number also included close to 50,000 criminal elements. And, he said, according to the latest reports in *Neues Deutschland*, the official party newspaper, no less than 500,000 had returned to the German Democratic Republic as soon as they had realized that life in the West was rather substandard when compared to that in the East.

Elections on both sides represented never-ending fodder for Neumann's group. One time, communist propaganda claimed that the results of the latest Western elections had been rigged. One of the comrades voiced his disbelief because if the vote was truly rigged, he argued, "the 'riggers' must have done a poor job because polls showed that only 50% of their people supported the government. If it had been a bogus election, wouldn't results have shown 99.5% support for their government, like ours do?" In those days, my entire understanding of politics was limited to Günter Neumann's radio broadcasts.

But my all-time favorite program was "Onkel Tobias" on Sunday mornings. Ear close to the fabric-covered speaker, I would crouch in front of the radio. Each week, the same group of five preteens visited Onkel Tobias and Tante Erika. The children asked questions, and the two adults gave helpful answers. The young people looked for suggestions on how to respond to the death of their best friend's beloved pet or how to increase their chances of being picked for the soccer team. Amid song and laughter, there was a moral to every story. But mostly, I relished the notion that there were adults out there who took children seriously.

As a rule, our household was a quiet one, compelling me to tiptoe about the flat. We moved through the day in an orderly fashion. We got up at 7:30 in the morning. Meals were taken at set times: breakfast at eight o'clock, lunch at noon, coffee at three, dinner at six. I had to be in bed by eight. The end of the world would not have put off my bedtime even by a few minutes.

Windows and doors remained closed unless it was time for the morning *auslüften* ritual—the airing out. Summer or winter, every morning after breakfast, my mother, like most housewives, opened the windows wide and draped our feather quilts and pillows over the sills to puff up with fresh air. Fresh air. It was considered a miracle drug. No matter how blustery the outdoors, we took a turn in the neighborhood to take in fresh air. However, turning on a fan, opening a car window, or windows and doors on opposite sides of a room, gave rise to *Zugluft*—a draft— and that was a known killer. "Close that door immediately, the window is open," my mother would yell in exasperation. It took less than an hour to complete the airing-out process. Then, the windows would be shut again; the courtyard clatter would fade, and silence would return.

Obedience, discipline, and loyalty were imparted at birth with the first slap on the buttocks, I believe. They were concepts that I, and probably many other children at that time, had internalized even before we knew the words. The most important principle was obedience. I learned quickly that children did not have rights. It was our job to gratify grown-ups. To demonstrate deference was helpful. Curtseying with downcast eyes and not talking unless spoken to were proper displays of submission. It was expected that we carry out commands without question. "No" was a final answer. In my family, once a verdict was pronounced, right or wrong, my parents never went back on their word. There was also no point in playing one parent against the other. Mutti and Pappi stood united on every issue.

Daily, my mother made plain which behaviors were unacceptable: "Slow down. Don't run. Not so fast. Hands on the table. Don't touch anything. Play quietly. Don't interrupt." It was called discipline. Independent thought and back talk were nipped without delay. I was taught to live within the rules. The rules were predictable and provided constancy. Compliance brought rewards. Broken rules carried undesirable consequences. Boundaries were clear, and I knew what was allowed. Resistance brought withdrawal of affection and stony silence. And silence meant isolation.

During meals, my mother watched and made sure that I finished everything on my plate, including the mutton fat. At times, I would sit for hours, skillfully pressing the greasy fat against my upper palate and into the jowls until my plate was empty. Then I waited patiently for an opportunity to visit the bathroom to spit it out. For that, I had to wait until the end of my afternoon nap, because an hour-long nap after lunch was also mandatory.

Sometimes I sat at the table with a mug of hot milk. If I did not finish fast enough, a membrane formed on its surface. In trying to remove it, I would end up with countless disgusting little pieces. They made me sick to my stomach, but I had to remain seated until the last drop of milk was gone. By then, it had long gone cold.

Discipline was a socially sanctioned tool for building character and enforcing obedience. Even if used to excess, there was no public intervention. When I started school, teachers were still allowed to smack us across the fingers with a ruler. And what occurred in the home was up to the family. One day, when I was in grammar school, my classmate, Michael Erben, found himself at the receiving end of discipline. Herr Müller, our music teacher, was jumping back and forth on top of the three rows of our student desks, as usual. Each flattop table served as a desk to two students. Jumping from one desk to the other allowed him to swiftly attend to developing problems. Violin tucked under his chin, Herr Müller made sure we followed his instructions to the letter. He was a small, pinched man, given to sudden outbursts of anger. That particular day, he was in the middle of teaching us a new song and insisted that we tap out the beat to the text in our music books.

"*Tupfen, tupfen*—tab, tab," Herr Müller yelled as he ran across the rows of desks. We tapped as instructed. But Michael, in the back of the class, had forgotten his music book at home and tapped in his math book instead. Since all school-issued books were wrapped in blue packing paper, the substitution was hardly noticeable.

Michael might have gotten away with his ploy, except that he was neither musically gifted, nor interested, and tapped offbeat. When our teacher tried to correct him, he discovered the ruse. The boy's audacity caused Herr Müller to turn the color of a red apple and to leap to the ground, violin flying. Then he grabbed Michael by the neck, hauled him to the front of the class, and banged his head repeatedly against the blackboard. Michael ended up with a concussion. There was no uproar. There were no sanctions. Nearly all of us experienced at some time what would be considered abuse today.

My parents never punished me physically. They withdrew some of my privileges instead, usually the ones I valued most. I became convinced that my mother observed me carefully to find out what mattered most to me so that she could rob me of that joy. It did not take long before I learned the ropes and which ones to skip. I learned to hold my disappointments and sources of pleasure inside and not to express my desires candidly. To ask for something only turned into a lecture on greed and ingratitude. Silence or a mournful look proved to be the better tactics. I would go through eloquent pantomimes: I'd gaze longingly at this or that object of desire, and then sigh profoundly while raising my eyes timidly at my mother or father.

And of course, there was the loyalty tenet. Children were bound by duty and gratitude to their elders. Even complete strangers expected both. Violation of those moral standards only brought on agonizing guilt attacks. After a few painful lessons, I had learned my role. An eager student, I had child's etiquette down pat. It became my deepest desire to please. I spoke with a baby voice; I played quietly; I did not soil my hands or clothes; I did not ask questions; and I did not touch what I was not supposed to.

But life was not at all bad as long as I obeyed the rules. Despite indisputable decrees and restrictions, I was a happy child because I had figured out the system and lived comfortably within its confines. I grew up thinking all families functioned like ours. By the time I was five years old, my mother had virtually succeeded in turning me into her perfect little girl.

The Sibling

DAYS ROLLED INTO ONE ANOTHER in seamless succession. I had become accustomed to playing quietly by myself. Family and strangers had drummed into me that I was lucky to have a mother and father at home, a warm bed at night, and enough food to keep from starving. Many children did not. I was indeed grateful, but I also often felt a strange sensation deep inside. I woke up, feeling an emptiness that made me want to weep.

Then one day, when my mother took me on an afternoon stroll through the neighborhood, I saw children shoot marbles into a small hole under a large basswood tree alongside the curb. Suddenly it struck me: What I was missing was a playmate. I longed for someone to play with, someone my own age, a brother or a sister. As we walked, I pulled a small wooden duck on wheels behind me with one hand and held onto my mother with the other. Every few yards, when we crossed the narrow gap between the large, square granite plates that made up the sidewalk, the duck fell over. Then I let go of my mother, righted the duck, and returned to her hand. It made for slow progress, but my mother smiled with pride at oncoming strangers. "Mutti, can we get a little brother or a sister?" I asked all of a sudden.

My mother struggled for an answer. The last thing my parents needed was another mouth to feed. These were hard times. Although Mutti and Pappi tried to restore normalcy to our existence, our way of life was, in fact, far from routine. My mother still gathered nettles and linden leaves for substitute spinach. She boiled potato peels to make thin soup. She hand sewed little dresses for me from old curtains and worn-out clothing by opening seams and turning the fabric inside out. My father applied for a permit to dig up the roots of a dead street tree to supply us with soggy firewood. But the truth was unsuitable for young ears. Rather than confessing to the real reason for limiting our family to one child, my mother attempted to dissuade me from wanting a playmate.

"So, you'd like a little brother or sister?" she began.

"Ja," I said squirming at her hand. I had just violated an unwritten rule: Never ask for anything. Wait until it is offered.

But my mother did not seem to mind. "Do you want a little baby girl or a baby boy?" she asked.

"I'd like a brother," I replied without hesitation. "I'd like a big brother, like Manfred." Manfred was my cousin and eight years older.

"The stork only brings babies," my mother replied. "He doesn't bring older children."

I thought for a minute. I had seen pictures of the stork delivering babies in diapers, but I could not recall having seen him bring older children. "A little brother is okay, too." I conceded.

"Have you thought about what it would be like to have a little baby brother?" my mother probed.

"Then I'll have someone to play with all day long."

"That, too. But you'll also have to share everything with your little brother," my mother said and paused, allowing time for me to process the information. "The banana you ate earlier," she began again. "Instead of eating the whole thing, you'll have to share it with your baby brother."

I looked at her. I had not thought of that.

"You'll have to share your toys, too."

My world was beginning to wobble a little.

"And you can't play all day, like you do now because you'll have to push your little brother in his buggy in the afternoon. He has to get out into the fresh air, too," my mother continued.

I had turned quiet. The duck had fallen over, and I was dragging it sideways. A playmate had sounded so good. But having to give up half of the toys and half of the food? And not being able to play in the afternoons anymore?

At home later that afternoon, I marched to the front door and put the chain across.

"Why are you bolting the door?" my mother asked.

"I don't want the stork to come in."

Bath Day

I EAGERLY AWAITED FRIDAYS. Fridays were bath days. The weekly ritual ranked a close second to a visit from my favorite aunt, Tante Michen. At the top of my list was the opportunity to frolic in the water without reprimand. But I also looked forward to the ambiance that filled the long, narrow room on Friday evenings. Heat and humidity turned it into a make-believe storybook land.

Curved claw feet supported the cast-iron bathtub at the far end of the room, next to the tall green boiler with the small firebox at its base.

To prepare for a bath, my mother stuffed the box with wood and paper, ignited it, and when the flames leapt high, she added two charcoal briquettes. Within the hour, the heater was sizzling hot and ready to dispense enough water to fill the tub, once.

One of those Fridays, my mother lifted me into the sudsy water so that I could play with my rubber toy prior to being scrubbed down. Having just finished her own bath, she left the bathroom to get dressed.

I loved water. Splashing about prudently, the way I had been taught to avoid getting the walls and floor wet, I wondered whether Margit, my doll, might need a bath, too. She was a present from Onkel Asa. Made from papier-mâché, Margit had blond braids and wore a blue-checkered skirt and blouse. As I played in the bathwater, she watched from her perch on the small table next to the tub. Mutti had stitched a whole wardrobe for Margit, and I spent countless hours each day dressing and undressing her, teaching her table manners, helping her with her homework, and at my mother's side, pushing her through the streets of Berlin in a rickety doll carriage. I was in training to be a mom, and I wanted to be a good one.

"Look at you. Look at your hands! Margit, goodness, how did they get so dirty? Didn't I tell you not to touch anything? And your face! You were a bad girl, Margit. You'll have to go to bed early tonight," I scolded, imitating my mother. "But first, you need to get scrubbed."

I reached for the doll, removed her clothes, and submersed her. With the big washcloth I began lathering her hands, face, and limbs when, all of a sudden, her eyes dropped into her head. Two big black holes stared back at me. Dumbfounded, I gawked at the doll. I lifted her out of the water and reached for her face. But when I touched her blond bangs, her hair slid off her scalp. Unable to comprehend the doll's sudden transformation, I screamed for my mother. "Mutti, Mutti, Margit is dying."

My mother came running down the hall as fast as she could, but papier-mâché-Margit's flaxen braids floated already on top of the water. I flung the doll as far as I could.

"Margit can't take a bath like you," my mother tried to explain. "She's a doll."

I was inconsolable. The bath had lost its charm. The doll had lost her appeal. I cried and cried until I finally fell asleep.

To my mother's amazement, I made no mention of Margit the next morning. And not the day after that. Instead, I played quietly with Teddy or traipsed, well behaved at my mother's hand, to the zoo, pulling my wooden toy behind me on a string. Margit was a nonsubject.

A couple of weeks later, when my mother and I were on our way to the zoo again, a neighbor asked, "Is your dolly sick today, Jutta?" My mother winced, fearing the reopening of a fresh wound. But I only replied, "I don't play with dolls anymore." Unable to interpret my change in attitude and not wanting to stir up trouble, my mother left it at that.

Overnight, my interest in dolls had evaporated. Now cars, trucks, and trains fascinated me, having watched how much fun my cousin, Manfred, had with them. It seemed to me that boys were allowed to scuttle all over with their windup toys. Indoors, their cars zoomed across the floor into table legs and baseboards, and no one got scolded. Boys made all sorts of noise playing "fire engine" and "conductor" without being asked to quiet down. Outdoors, they ran, climbed, and fought, and got covered with mud without repercussions. For some reason, boys were allowed to have fun while girls were not. I wanted to be a boy, too. And to become one of them I wanted to wear lederhosen—leather britches, wear my hair short, and get dirty like a boy. My father was delighted; my mother was dismayed.

The disaster with the doll caused me to want to become a boy, and that desire became the first serious hurdle to my mother's wish of raising the perfect little girl.

Frau Kardos

IN 1951, EAST AND WEST BERLIN CONTINUED to function as one entity in most respects. Although sector borders were posted and there were some restrictions, citizens moved freely from one sector to another. Telephone lines, sewage lines, and transportation were all shared. People from East and West visited Ursula Kardos, for instance. She lived on the fourth floor of a bombed-out building in the Courbièrestraße in the British sector near the KaDeWe, Berlin's famous department store. "Die Kardos," as she was generally referred to, had become Germany's most prominent clairvoyant after correctly predicting the burning of the

Reichstag—Germany's parliament building—in 1933, as well as the failed assassination attempt on Hitler in his headquarters in 1944. Politicians, actors, and industrialists, rich and poor, influential and inconsequential, were among her regular clients. She did not need cards, a crystal ball, or tea leaves. She did not read palms or astrology charts. She said she "saw" events play out before her like a silent movie and thought herself the narrator.

My mother was among the many who looked to Frau Kardos for help. People came to get advice on important decisions, to locate loved ones, or to determine the basis of health problems. But my mother had a different reason. As she admitted later, her main concern was the unusual developmental direction I had taken.

"She wants to be a boy," my mother confided to Tante Michen. "Do you think that's normal? Peter just laughs, but I think it's kind of unnatural. Aren't girls supposed to act like girls? Aren't they supposed to be interested in dolls?"

"It's probably just a phase," my aunt suggested.

But my mother remained adamant. "I'm going to see Die Kardos. I'm curious what she has to say about Jutta's future."

Frau Kardos lived within walking distance of our flat. She never advertised her services and charged according to ability to pay. The poor did not have to pay anything. My mother recalled having walked up the four flights of stairs on the appointed date for her fifteen- to thirty-minute session. Not entirely comfortable with the thought that a clairvoyant can actually see into the future, my mother did not want to influence the prediction with words or body language. Instead, she decided to take along a photograph of me. Stone-faced, she slid the picture in front of Ursula Kardos.

The clairvoyant studied it. "This is your daughter?"

"Yes."

"Is there anything in particular you want to know?"

"What can you tell me about her future?"

With her alert, light-colored eyes the fortune-teller scrutinized the photograph a second time. Shifting her gaze toward my mother, she said, "This isn't a current photo, is it?"

How did she know? "That's true," my mother replied, determined not to give anything away, "it's a couple of years old."

After examining the photograph for what my mother thought was an eternity, the clairvoyant revealed what she "saw." Her prediction must have been startling, depressing, or embarrassing because my mother never disclosed to a soul what was said in that session, except maybe to my father. The most I could ever get out of her, and then only many years later was, "She said you're strong willed."

Volkswagen

LATER THAT YEAR, IN 1951, my father purchased our first car, a used Volkswagen Beetle. The car was put up for sale by the British occupation forces after reaching the end of its useful military life. Prior to the sale, the Brits had sprayed the once khaki-colored car a dark blue.

At the end of the war, it had been the US Army who had first occupied KdF-Stadt where the bombed-out Volkswagen factory was located. Later, they turned it over to the British Army who renamed the city Wolfsburg, after a nearby castle. The Brits placed Major Ivan Hirst in charge of operations, and he succeeded in interesting his superiors in putting the car to service as an inexpensive light transport vehicle. He got approval to produce 20,000 Beetles. Under his direction, the plant turned out 2,000 Beetles in 1945 and 10,000 the following year.

Ours was one of these cast-off Beetles that my father acquired secondhand five or six years later—no chrome, no radio, and no carpet. A central bar divided the oval rear window. Two flag-like yellow batons waved up and down when turning a switch and served as turn signals. The manual transmission was unsynchronized. Still, to own a car was a big deal.

By the time my father purchased our Volkswagen, the British Army had already turned over the factory to the German government because the British military did not intend to remain in the car business. But first, they had offered it, free of charge, to British and French car manufactures as well as to the Ford Motor Company. Their offer was turned down by all three of these industry giants. They all agreed that the cars, designed by Porsche's chief designer, were "too ugly and noisy" and building them would be "a completely uneconomic enterprise."

The following winter, my mother took driving lessons so that she, too, could operate our Beetle. She did so for one reason only: She wanted me to attend Catholic school, which was located at a considerable distance from our home, and she planned to chauffeur me there. Since the use of babysitters was practically unheard of, I accompanied my mother to all of her classroom instructions and driving lessons. In her theoretical lessons, I followed with interest the various traffic scenarios the teacher simulated by using miniature cars, pedestrians, and bicyclists. During practical lessons I rode in the backseat. I became as familiar with the rules as my mother did.

Contrary to the original plan, I ended up in a nearby public school. Nonetheless, my mother continued with her training and obtained her driver's license. In the middle of that winter Mutti, permit in hand, took my father and me for her maiden drive. She wore her black Persian lamb coat, black felt hat, and leather gloves. I think the plan must have been to chauffeur us to a neighborhood *Konditorei* for afternoon coffee and cake.

I sat in the back, my father in the passenger seat, and my mother behind the wheel. In order to shift from one gear to the next, the first Volkswagens had to be double-declutched. This involved a daunting procedure of releasing the throttle, pressing the clutch, and shifting the gear into neutral. Then the clutch had to be released and the throttle depressed again until the revolutions between engine and gear were roughly equal before the clutch could be pressed again. Only then was it possible to shift into the next gear.

We were stopped at a red light on this maiden voyage. When the light turned green, my mother tried to shift into first gear. I am not sure how far she progressed into the double-declutching process, but our Beetle took a modest jump, and then the engine died. My father chuckled, not expecting to see a woman master this task anyway, and briefly recapped the proper sequence of actions.

"That's not how Herr Bungs told me to do it," my mother snapped back. Herr Bungs was her driving instructor.

"Never mind what Herr Bungs said, I've been driving for years, and I ought to know how to shift into first gear," my father said.

My mother made a second attempt. Another jump. Another engine death.

"You have to step on the gas before you release the clutch," I piped up from the back. I had heard Herr Bungs say it many times during my mother's driving lessons.

"Leave me alone, all of you," my mother said, pitch rising. I could tell by her voice that further helpful suggestions would not be appreciated.

The driver behind us honked his horn. My mother gave it a third try. The atmosphere in the car grew tenser. We hopped forward. The engine died again. The light turned red. By now, my father was practically in my mother's lap. The car in back was honking. There was some commotion in the front seats of our car. Then, my mother opened the door, got out, straightened her coat, and told my father to scoot over. Head held high, she walked around the back of the car, got into the passenger seat and said, "I'll never drive again." And she didn't.

Marbles

LATE ONE MORNING during the following summer, I watched the neighborhood kids play with marbles under the basswood tree in front of our apartment building. Although the sidewalks were paved with cobblestones and granite plates, a ring of black soil surrounded each tree.

"Can I play, too, Mutti, pleeese?" I pleaded. I knew that my mother was not keen on the idea. The trees were close to the busy street. And since she kept office hours in our flat to help with my father's business, she did not have time to watch me play outside.

"Please, Mutti, please," I begged again.

It was a beautiful June day, and despite her misgivings, my mother relented. Even on this warm and sunny day our apartment was dark and damp. She did not begrudge me a little sunshine. "For half an hour, but only if you promise to stay on the sidewalk. Be careful. Don't talk to strangers and don't step into the street. As an afterthought she added, "And don't get your dress dirty."

I was willing to promise anything and followed my mother up the stairs to our apartment to grab the small blue marble bag Tante Michen had given me for Easter. It contained fifty clay marbles, all coated with a shiny finish. Rushing down the four flights at breakneck speed, I dashed through the courtyard and vestibule, marble bag hanging from a drawstring around my wrist.

Emerging from the double oak doors that led into the street, I slowed my pace and hesitated before moving closer toward the group of five children, merrily engaged in the game. This was the first time my mother had allowed me to play with the neighborhood kids, and I felt apprehensive. Uncertain of the proper approach and unfamiliar with the rules, I hung back.

But I quickly grasped the object of the game. Close to the tree trunk, within the ring of soil, I saw a fist-sized hole in the ground, a few centimeters deep. On the first go-around, each child took a turn throwing three marbles toward it, hoping to sink them on the first try. The player with the most marbles in the hole started the second round. If none of the children was able to sink one, the player with the marble closest to the hole started the second round and tried to flick in as many as possible. If he missed, it was the next player's turn. The child who sank the last marble was declared the winner and took all.

By the time I had worked out the rules, my half hour of unsupervised playtime was up, and my mother came to take me back to our flat. Reluctantly, I followed. I had not even had a chance to join in the game yet. But I did not dare to complain because one-half hour of playtime was all that was agreed upon. In our house, agreements ruled out arguments. Without delay, I began campaigning for another opportunity to play with the other children.

The following day was another beautiful summer day. To my surprise, my mother yielded again and allowed me to play. Again, I ran downstairs with my bag of marbles and stopped short several paces from the action.

"You want to play?" a boy, by the name of Detlef asked.

"Yes," I nodded eagerly.

Detlef, the clear leader of the group, told me to step into the semicircle of children while he called out the selection rhyme.

"*Ene, mene, muh, und raus bis Du*—ene, mene, moo, and out are you." Chanting the syllables, Detlef pointed clockwise to each child. The last child had to step out of the circle. He then repeated the rhyme until only one girl, Gabi, was left. She began the first round.

My heart thumped with excitement. I could feel it in my throat. If I won, I stood to double or triple my marble holdings. I had discovered that ten marbles were worth one glass *Bucker*—cat's-eye. While clay marbles were about one-quarter inch in size, the glass ones were one-half inch and valued like pure gold. I did not own any cat's-eyes yet.

The game began. I lost. Three marbles down. I joined the next game. This time, Detlef shouted out a different selection rhyme:

Warte, warte noch ein Weilchen—Wait, wait just a little while,
Bald kommt Haarmann auch zu dir—Soon Haarmann will come to you, too.
Mit dem kleinen Hackebeilchen—With his little cleaver,
Und macht Leberwurst aus dir—He'll make Liverwurst from you.

The rhyme harked back to a song that had gained in popularity after Fritz Haarmann, a notorious serial killer from the northern German town of Hannover, had murdered more than two dozen boys and young men in the 1920s. I did not understand the meaning of the words, but the rhyme was fun. I was learning all kinds of new things.

All too soon, my mother appeared to take me home. By now, I was hooked on the game. Back at our flat, I counted my marble holdings. I sorted them by color and imagined amassing buckets of the tiny spheres.

Soon, I got to play again. My game improved. I even won a few times. Now, I even owned some cat's-eyes.

One afternoon a few weeks later, when my mother allowed me to join the neighborhood kids again, they played for the coveted cat's-eyes. By now, I was adept at the game and carried an assortment of clay and glass marbles. When it was my turn to toss my *Bucker*, the string of my sack broke. The bag hit the cobblestones, opened up, and my prized possessions scattered in all directions. I hunkered down to recover my wealth, but most of it had already rolled out of my reach.

All the kids tried to grab my wayward riches before they could hit the gutter. When all strays had been recovered, I held open my sack, expecting to recapture my fortune. But the children just cackled. "Finders keepers, losers weepers!" they hooted.

Having grown up among adults and never having attended kinder-garten or preschool, I was ill prepared for peer interaction. All my prized *Buckers*, even the pretty purple one, were gone. I was heartbroken. How could my new pals do this to me? It was wrong. Who was going to make it right?

I ran to my mother for help, but she only said, "Now, now, stop fretting. You don't know what trouble is. By the time you're married and have children of your own, you'll have forgotten all about this."

How could I have made her understand that I had just experienced the equivalent of the currency devaluation of 1948?

THREE

THE VENEER CRACKS

Elementary School

IN MARCH 1952, STALIN SENT A MEMORANDUM to each of the three Western occupation powers stating his desire to end the division of Germany and to plan for its reunification and neutralization. It called for free elections following unification and acceptance of the German frontiers as laid down in the 1945 Potsdam Agreement. Adamant about free elections prior to, not after, unification, the West rejected his offer. Furthermore, Germany still hoped for modification of postwar agreements in which it had ceded one-third of its prewar territory to Poland, Russia, and Czechoslovakia.

Having failed to achieve the desired results, Stalin gave Walter Ulbricht, head of state of East Germany, a "thumbs up" on assuming a larger role in shaping the future of the German Democratic Republic. Without delay, Ulbricht went to work by turning the zone boundary into an international one.

In *Aktion Ungeziefer*—Operation Vermin—he gave orders to clear a five-kilometer-wide strip of no-man's-land along the 866-mile-long border between East and West Germany. Thousands of people, living near the boundary on the Eastern side, were removed from their homes. Towns and villages were split in two. Some villages were leveled altogether. Ulbricht's men laid down barbed wire and ripped open local boundary roads to put an end to easy border access. The ninety-six-mile border surrounding West Berlin was also significantly altered, although not fully closed.

Meanwhile, due to the Marshall Plan, West Germany's economy was slowly improving. In East Germany, on the other hand, the standard of living had actually declined since 1947. As the disparity between East and West widened, Ulbricht accelerated his staged plan for *Aufbau des Sozialismus*—construction of socialism. He pressured farmers into joining collectives, accelerated industrial nationalization, escalated arrests of potential opponents to the regime, increased military recruitment, and expanded censorship. These repressive measures created a visible crack in the shiny veneer of the socialist paradise Ulbricht tried to put on display. The number of people willing to leave everything behind to go west increased dramatically. Rather than attempting to cross the now fortified border into West Germany and risking jail, they traveled to East Berlin from where they could simply walk or take a train across the boundary line to the West.

I was seven and did not concern myself with the plight of the East German people. My concerns were much more immediate. I was about to start school.

When my mother and I visited the Catholic school she wanted me to attend, I got frightened by the nuns' flying white robes and linen wimples. Although baptized a Catholic, like my mother, I had rarely been taken to church and had never seen a nun before. I lobbied my father, a Protestant, to let me go to public elementary school. He was happy to indulge me, and close to Easter, my mother took me by the hand and walked me the six long blocks to the *Uhlandschule*, an old brick schoolhouse in our neighborhood. It was early afternoon. Because many schools had been damaged or destroyed during the war, instructions were given in shifts. My class was scheduled for afternoon lessons.

After passing through gigantic iron gates, we crossed a large school yard, walked up a series of wide steps, and entered a long corridor through a set of oversized doors. At the end of it, we stepped into a huge auditorium where other children and their parents were already seated. After a number of speeches, each followed by applause, parents escorted their offspring to various classrooms. Boys much older than I dashed past us in the hallway, and with a loud clang, someone's lunch tin hit the stone floor, spattering its hot content in all directions. My mother's grip tightened as she guided me around the unsightly, smelly mess without comment.

My back pressed against the inside of the classroom door, I surveyed my surroundings. A series of casement windows lined the opposite wall. Three rows of double desks with built-in benches and inkwells filled the center of the room, and a bulky wood desk occupied the front. Behind it loomed a large blackboard. Even though it had only been minutes since we left the auditorium, a cacophony of screams and laughter already filled the classroom. Children ran up and down the aisles. Two boys were slugging it out in the back. A redhead with bushy pigtails performed a one-footed balancing act on top of one of the desks. The ruckus frightened me into immobility.

A trust-inspiring woman in her forties took me by the hand. I turned to look back, but my mother was already gone. "You LIKE school, don't you," the woman said with an encouraging smile. I gave her a faint nod. She led me to a double desk in the back and helped me unhook my tin cup from the leather satchel strapped to my back. The school bag contained my slate, chalk, and a sponge. The tin cup was meant for hot school lunches. The woman pointed to a small ledge beneath the desk, helped me slide my satchel onto the shelf, and asked me to sit down. Then she walked to the front of the room.

"*Guten Morgen, Kinder, ich bin Fräulein Elias, Eure Lehrerin*—Good morning, children, I am Miss Elias, your teacher," she said.

There was commotion in every part of the room. The din was deafening. Of the thirty or so boys and girls in my class, hardly anyone seemed to pay attention to the teacher. And what was even more amazing, no one got punished. Glued to my seat, I watched in wonder. Eventually, the class settled down, and after a while, Fräulein Elias said the first day of school was over. Everyone snatched their satchels and rushed through the doors to reunite with their families.

This was the best part of the adventure. To sweeten the initial school experience, our parents waited for us with giant shiny cones in their arms. They were called *Schultüten*, made from foil-coated construction paper, and almost as tall as we were. The traditional cones were filled with fruit, nuts, candy, chalk, and sponges, their crepe-paper necks tied with huge bows. Screaming with delight, we ran to our relatives and reached for these big, sweet surprises. My mother and Tante Michen stood in the crowd, holding an immense fuchsia-colored cone for me.

In the meantime, my father was hard at work at the gate, photographing students and their parents next to a cardboard Easter Bunny with a slate draped around its neck. The crayon letters read, "*Mein Erster Schultag*—My First Day of School." When he was done with the paying customers, he took my picture. The scariness of the afternoon's experience was already forgotten. Full of anticipation, I looked forward to the next classroom day.

When my mother and I arrived at the school gate the following afternoon, a spunky brunette rushed toward us, thick braids dancing on her back as she ran. "You and me sat next to each other yesterday," she beamed. "Let's sit together again." I did not recognize the girl from the day before, but followed her dutifully into the classroom where she pulled me into a seat in the second row. "My mother and father are opera singers," she informed me.

Felicitas, or Fee as she liked to be called, and I would spend the next six years sharing a desk. We competed for first place in every subject and formed a lifelong friendship.

Before long, I loved going to school. Fräulein Elias was generous with her praise. My grades were excellent, and I felt important and smart for the first time. But school posed unexpected challenges as well. I did not know how to behave around kids my age. They seemed to know so much more than I did.

Even before we finished learning the alphabet, I overheard the boys talk about the origin of babies, a question my mother always answered with, "We'll talk about that when you get older." Now I was shocked. Then Christiane, a redhead considerably taller and more developed than I, told a circle of us that she had peeped through the keyhole into her parents' bedroom shortly before her baby sister was born. Spellbound, we listened to her eyewitness account. Her description did not quite match the boys' version which posed new questions. But I did not ask. I did not want to appear ignorant.

Not much later, the school lunch program was terminated and parents were asked to provide sack lunches. But not all families were able to oblige. As a result, some of my classmates ended up going without a midday meal, but I assumed they had forgotten their lunch at home. Since I had been taught that forgetfulness was punishable, I shook my head when Renate asked for a piece of my sandwich, "No, you have to remember to bring your own." And when Barbara asked for a bite of my apple, I recalled my mother's stern caution that bacteria spread via saliva and protested, "No, your mouth is full of germs."

Without brothers, sisters, or cousins my age, the concept of sharing eluded me. I put my soul into my homework, got excellent grades and believed respect and popularity to hinge upon outperforming my class-mates. I flung myself furiously into the one thing I knew I was good at: book learning. The successful chase of high grades boosted my self-re-spect. When Gabi tried to copy my math work from across the aisle during an exam, I protected my answers by shielding them behind my cupped hand.

I knew how to please grown-ups, but in the presence of peers, I re-mained socially awkward. Still, I dreamt of becoming the most popular girl in class. But it was not working for me. I felt more like an outsider. What am I doing wrong, I wondered? Finally, I asked my mother. She dismissed the question with a sigh, "It's not important to be liked. Your grades are what counts. You'll find that out when you get older. Don't pay any attention to the other kids. Do what the teacher says. And if anybody gives you a bad time, tell me, and I'll have a word with their mother."

Several months later, after she stopped walking me to and from school, I became more vulnerable. Now the boys were strapping their leather satchels to their chests like shields and, howling like fire engines, rammed those of us who could not get out of their way fast enough. I wanted to tell my mother but sprinted like an antelope instead, fearing for my life. I never said a word at home, because I came to recognize that parental interference could make me an even bigger target. Instead of telling my mother, I got protection. I talked my classmate Jürgen, who lived in the next block, into walking me home. We even held hands.

Unlike home, school was not at all quiet, predictable, or orderly. That was one of its attractions. In the classroom, I drank in the turmoil until my bucket of information was filled to the rim. And with my moth-er's encouragement, I spilled its entire content as soon as I arrived home.

But just as Walter Ulbricht saw in West Berlin an annoying escape hatch for refugees, my parents regarded school as a bad influence. Just as the East German regime loathed RIAS, the American radio station, for beaming propaganda into the Soviet zone, my parents suspected that my classmates filled my head with "subversive" information. To reduce my vulnerability, Mutti and Pappi insulated me from my classmates by limiting my interaction with them. And just like the East German people resisted their government's interference, I tried to guard against my parents' influence. Too much talk could result in restrictions, I learned. If my mother suspected objectionable traits in a classmate, she vetoed our friendship. I began withholding small, potentially damaging pieces of information and tilted my bucket only so far. This change brought about an almost imperceptible crack in the veneer of my hitherto perfect compliance with my parents' wishes.

Purple Shorts

IN THE YEARS FOLLOWING THE WAR, thousands of East Germans had left for the West. The massive exodus caused problems for both, East and West. The East experienced severe shortages of professionals and skilled workers. West Berlin's unemployment doubled. Money and work were scarce, and most families, including mine, carefully curtailed expenses. That included some items I considered essential in second grade.

Physical education was scheduled three times a week in elementary school. During the winter, we concentrated on indoor gymnastics; in the summer, we played outdoor team sports. One of the first ball games we were taught was *Völkerball*, literally people ball, or better known as dodge ball. In the game, two teams play against one another, using a volleyball. The object was to eliminate opposing team members by throwing the ball and hitting them with it or by catching an opponent's ball before it touches ground. Unable to procure a volleyball, we used a weighted leather medicine ball which was difficult for beginners to handle. And a beginner I was.

Growing up, I had had little occasion to play ball of any kind and consequently could barely throw or catch. Having been born prematurely, I remained small and scrawny throughout childhood and was the smallest girl in class. Some of my classmates were almost twice my size, and several of them were pretty good ball players. Whenever the opposing team took possession of the ball, my heart dropped into my shorts pockets. I darted hither and thither across the playing field, hoping to avoid physical harm. But I considered injury the lesser of two evils. The bigger calamity, in my mind, was my attire.

Gym clothes consisted of whatever our parents handed to us. Most kids wore taut black cotton tricot tank tops and briefs that looked remarkably like undergarments. Still, black tricots were considered haute couture among seven-year-olds. My dilemma was that my mother would not squander scarce resources on a store-bought tricot outfit when she could sew up a pair of shorts from a piece of leftover fabric. A quick hunt through her scrap box resulted in a purple piece of satin she considered suitable. In short order, she fashioned a pair of bloomers with three rows of one-fourth inch elastic around the waist. The mass of elastic was intended to insure that the shorts would stay put on my shapeless body during the game's countless contortions.

Thus, instead of in a stylish form-fitted tricot outfit, I was clad in a white T-shirt and a pair of baggy purple knickers. And herein lay the true crux of my trouble. With three rows of elastic, my satin shorts reached almost to my armpits. With every movement, they twinkled in shades of heliotrope, violet, plum, maroon, magenta, and mulberry, making me feel like a comic-strip character. Whenever the two captains selected their team members, they began by choosing the top performers. The worst players were divvied up last. I was usually among the very last players to be picked. I did not know whether their choice was based on my lack of ability or my appearance, or both.

My hideous purple bloomers did nothing to increase my popularity. Already self-conscious about my athletic ineptness, my outfit-caused humiliation was almost more than I could bear. I wanted to blend in, not blaze a fashion trail; I wanted to look sporty, not ridiculous. Although I would have preferred not to have to ask my parents for new gym clothes because such requests tended to lead to lectures on the state of family finances, I considered the problem far too critical not to plead my case. "Don't be ridiculous," my mother replied. "It's only a pair of gym shorts. You're not going to a beauty pageant."

Stuck with the status quo, I enrolled in a free after-school gymnastics class in hopes of becoming a better athlete. Perhaps if I got stronger, I would be less frightened and play better, I reasoned. The plan worked. In time I became a passable gymnast. Soon, I was allowed to coach younger children, and eventually I turned into a tough little volleyball player. Sports of all kinds became my favorite pastime. And eventually, my parents even consented to black tricots.

East German Uprising

TO COUNTERACT THE ONGOING economic crisis, the East German government authorized higher taxes, higher prices for consumer goods, and a ten percent increase in production norms to go into effect toward the end of June 1953. The plan unleashed widespread discontent among workers.

In the meantime, The central committee resolved to turn the Stalinallee, a wide, tree-lined boulevard in East Berlin, into a glittering showpiece of the "workers' paradise" by replacing the bombed-out World War II ruins that lined both sides of the long avenue with a massive residential high-rise development. When, on June 16, the project's construction workers were told to increase their output in accordance with the new quotas or to expect pay cuts, they balked and called a general strike for the next day. As protesters marched toward the House of Ministries in the city center on June 17, other workers joined along the way, and soon, demonstrators numbered in the thousands. The unrest spread to other cities, towns, and villages throughout East Germany, and people began demanding additional changes. They called for price decreases for consumer goods, an increased standard of living, and ultimately for free elections, and the resignation of the East German government.

When demonstrators stormed the government seat in East Berlin and set fire to state-owned shops, Red Army troops quelled the uprising by sending in tanks and firing into the crowd. Throughout East Germany, close to half a million employees went on strike, and military force was used in many parts of the country. Dozens died. Thousands were imprisoned.

While Red Army tanks rolled across East Berlin's Potsdamer Platz and demonstrators sought cover from machine-gun fire, my parents sat close to the radio, absorbed in the commentator's words. Although I could not fathom what the East German uprising had to do with us, Mutti's and Pappi's white knuckles suggested that we, too, were in some sort of danger.

Year after year since the founding of East Germany in 1949, approximately 150,000 to 300,000 refugees had fled to West Berlin. Following the events of June 17, 1953, the East German population's desire to go west intensified.

First Travel Abroad

UNLIKE THE PEOPLE IN EAST GERMANY, people living in the West were free to travel to any destination of their choice. My parents and I took advantage of that liberty, and in the summer of 1953, we took our first voyage abroad. I was seven. Since German summers could be unpredictable, Herr and Frau Döbler, business associates of my father's, had successfully planted the seed of a vacation in the sun. And so, for the first time, the five of us took a trip to the Adriatic coast. We motored in our Volkswagen Beetle to Munich in the south of Germany, and then boarded a train to Riccione in Italy.

Due to border delays and poor road conditions, the 650-mile trip to Munich took one-and-a-half days. Of the three transit routes through the Eastern zone, my father chose Dreilinden/Helmstedt because it involved the shortest distance on East German roads. In the outskirts of the American sector, we crossed checkpoint Dreilinden (also called Checkpoint Bravo). After scrutinizing our identification cards and inquiring about our destination, military police waved us on. A few hundred yards farther down the road, we had to stop at the Eastern checkpoint, Drewitz. Because of frequent spontaneous border closures, rigorous vehicle inspections, and potential interrogations, delays could be expected. But we were lucky and passed without incident. Next, we traveled on the one-hundred-mile stretch of East German autobahn to the Marien-born/Helmstedt checkpoints. While there were no speed limits on West German highways, East Germany enforced a maximum of 100 kilometers per hour (60 miles per hour) and imposed hefty fines on violators. To maintain the imposed limit presented no problem for us, however. Our Volkswagen's top speed was 62 miles per hour. Circumventing the countless potholes in the poorly maintained roads slowed us even further. Upon leaving the Eastern zone, procedures were repeated in reverse. First, we crossed the Eastern checkpoint Marienborn, then Helmstedt (Checkpoint Alpha) in the American zone.

Once in West Germany, we traveled on the autobahn as much as possible, although many stretches still required detours through small towns due to poor road conditions on the highway. Unless passing another vehicle, right lane use of the autobahn was mandatory. That meant that Mercedes and Porsches routinely used the left lane, while all other traffic, especially Beetles, stayed stuck in the right.

If motoring slowed by construction and poor road conditions made passing difficult, having to share the road with military convoys made it next to impossible. The last three hundred miles of our journey to Munich led through the American zone which extended south from the Frankfurt/Main area all the way to Stuttgart and Munich. Several US Army and Air Force units were repositioning for maneuvers that summer, and we were trapped between convoy vehicles for extended periods. My father's sporadic attempts at venturing into the passing lane brought on barrages of honks and flashing lights from quickly approaching faster cars. The slow progress increased our travel time between Helmstedt and Munich to one full day.

Meanwhile, I sat in the backseat, perched on beach towels and blankets, squeezed between my mother and Frau Döbler. None of the car windows were cracked open. *Zugluft,* the killer! While the adults studied road maps and discussed overnight options, I was bored. For a while I amused myself by watching our car's *Winker,* the orange turn signals in back of each door, which looked like one-sided arrows and operated like human arms. Flicking a switch, my father made them move up and down whenever he wanted to change directions. Although the signal arms "winked" at slow speeds, at autobahn speed, air resistance prevented them from functioning properly. Then, they remained permanently suspended in midair, requiring him to use hand signals.

It was crowded in our Beetle with four adults, a little girl, and everyone's luggage. I could barely peek out the front or side windows. After some time, I discovered that, kneeling on the seat facing back, I could peer through the small rear window. For a while, I watched the slow khaki-colored trucks behind us, their operators hunched over their steering wheels. Timidly, I waved to a driver. He waved back. My heart jumped with joy. Someone noticed me!

Soon, I made a game of it. Whenever we were trapped between military vehicles, I gave the driver a big smile and waved tentatively, hoping for a response. If there was none, I intensified my efforts. After a while, I began to detect a pattern. Black drivers were much more likely to wave back than white GIs. Many broke into cheerful smiles and animated waves, white teeth contrasting against their black faces. I had never seen black people before. Now, I was thrilled every time I saw a black driver behind the steering wheel because I anticipated a friendly response, and I was rarely disappointed.

During that first Beetle trip abroad, I developed a deep fondness for black Americans. In later years, it would extend to all Americans.

Because my father felt uncomfortable navigating the roads in a foreign country without speaking the language, we garaged our VW in Munich and continued by train to Italy. Although I don't recall the train ride, I remember Riccione. We checked into the Hotel Savioli, right on the beach. The sea was pleasantly warm, the waves gentle. The sand was white and plentiful, and the sun shone all day. Every morning and afternoon, my mother covered me with a thick coat of Nivea, a water-in-oil emulsion skin cream. Afterwards, I busied myself with bucket and shovel at the water's edge.

One day, the four adults took a bus trip to Venice and left me in the care of the hotel staff. I felt proud to be considered trustworthy enough to remain behind by myself. In my parents' absence, I tried to carry on with our routine and took meals at our regular table instead of eating in the *Paradiso del Bambini*, the children's paradise, where most of the other hotel guests' children dined. When the waiter came to my table with the first course, a soup, I waved him off. I had seen my father do it. Instead, I ate small portions of the remaining courses, and when he brought a bowl of fresh peaches, I pulled up my skirt, formed a small basket, and piled in as many peaches as it would hold.

"Promise me. You won't go near the water," my mother had said. Therefore, I only went as far as sitting in one of our rented beach chairs. When evening came, I went to bed at the designated time. I was proud of myself that I had been so responsible and self-sufficient all day.

Summer in Austria

OUR UPCOMING SIX-WEEK SUMMER BREAK at school loomed like a large, empty expanse on the horizon. I was ten and dreaded school vacations. Cut off from friends for most of the summer, I would have to entertain myself day after day. Because of my father's photography business, Mutti would be unavailable until late in the afternoons. By then, it would be close to dinnertime and too late to do anything fun.

I considered being an only child a curse. Except for spending weekends in our *Schrebergarten*, a small, leased garden plot in the outskirts of the city, there was nothing to do. On Saturdays and Sundays, I tended my own small flower garden in the back corner of the lot or played with Marianne, whose parents leased the plot next door. But that covered only the weekends. The rest of the time, I was stuck at home. I was bored.

Lately, tears had welled up in the early mornings. Sometimes it would be noon before I was able to stifle them. I didn't know why I was crying; I just felt sad. I never mentioned my melancholy to my parents because complaints of any kind tended to prompt lectures about unappreciative children. "You don't know how good you have it, young lady. We work our fingers to the bone so you won't want for anything. Other children would gladly trade places with you."

Words like these made me feel guilty. Therefore, I kept my misery to myself.

One day, shortly before the start of summer vacation, my father asked if I would like to spend six weeks in the mountains of Austria. "Mutti and I can't go. We have to stay here and earn money so that all of us can eat. But other kids are going. How would you like to join them?"

I was thunderstruck. I'd never been to the mountains; we always vacationed at the seaside. And I'd never been away from home without my parents. The choice was mine? Usually, I did not get to make decisions. This is an opportunity for me to demonstrate my maturity, I thought, and tried to simultaneously display exuberance and grown-up restraint. The result was that I shifted tentatively from one foot to the other with a stupid grin on my face.

"For the entire summer? What other kids are going?" I inquired, still at a loss for words.

Bit by bit, my father explained that he had seen a classified ad in the newspaper. Each summer, a woman, who operated a small orphanage, took her charges, about twenty kids altogether, to an *Alpenhütte*—an alpine chalet—in the mountains of East Tyrol. To help finance the trip, she liked to include ten paying children.

"How would you like to go with them?" my father asked again.

I was still speechless. On one hand, I was more than ready for playmates and adventure and welcomed the opportunity to demonstrate that I was old enough to cut away from my mother's apron strings. On the other hand, I was unpracticed in the art of socialization and a little afraid. Would I fit in? I certainly did not want to be the odd kid out.

"How old are the other kids? " I asked with curiosity.

"It says here, the orphans' ages range between four and ten. Only children under age twelve will be accepted," my father read aloud from the paper.

I was not keen on younger children because I thought they didn't have anything to teach me. But I welcomed opportunities to associate with older kids, thinking they would be my ticket to adulthood. To grow up as quickly as possible was my quest because, from all I could tell, only adults were taken seriously.

Knowing that my father had a penchant for sound risk-taking and frowned upon scaredy cats, I threw all caution to the wind and answered with as much confidence as I could muster,

"I'd love to go." Then I took a deep breath. It felt good. I even believed my own lie.

Next, my father checked the legitimacy of the orphanage and that of its owner, Frau Fuhrmann. When satisfied, he signed the necessary releases. A few days later, my parents chatted across the fence with our garden-plot neighbors and mentioned my upcoming adventure. Immediately, Herr and Frau Tornow signed up their daughter, Marianne, as well. Jani, as she liked to be called, was two years my senior. I was thrilled.

With a list of items required for the trip, my mother and I went shopping. She bought me a pair of sturdy hiking boots and a bright yellow plastic drinking bottle with a red-and-green stopper. Then she labeled all of my clothes, toiletries, and incidentals.

Before I knew it, Jani and I boarded the charter bus to Prägraten in the Austrian mountains. Frau Fuhrmann, her young assistant, Anneliese, and about thirty kids filled the coach to the last seat. I was delighted that Jani was coming along. Her familiar face made the adventure much less frightening. Still, when we pulled away from the curb and I saw my parents become smaller and smaller on the sidewalk, I had to hold back tears.

We drove all night, slept on the bus, and arrived in Prägraten midday. The village was nestled in a scenic valley at an elevation of 4,300 feet. High mountains reached up toward the sun on both sides.

The bus stopped in front of a small inn, the *Gasthaus Hatzer*. Everyone got out, stretched, and looked around in awe while the driver unloaded our luggage. We had barely made a full circle around the bus when Frau Fuhrmann said, "Come on kids, stretch your legs. We have a little hike ahead of us." Only then did we learn that we had not actually arrived at our final destination. To reach the 5,900-foot-high *Alpenhütte*, we had to climb 1,600 feet to the top of a steep, zigzagging trail that started next to the *Gasthaus.* "The luggage will be brought up later," someone yelled.

It was a slow ascent. The little ones had to be carried or assisted. The rest of us had trouble adjusting to the thin mountain air. Used to atmospheric conditions at sea level, most of us were physically unprepared for the vigorous hike. Jani complained, "This is ridiculous." I paid no attention to her and pressed toward the head of the group, huffing and puffing all the way. I hoped to impress Frau Fuhrmann with my stamina. But my efforts went unnoticed.

The mountain hut consisted of four or five bedrooms, a large living room that also doubled as a dining room, and a bare-bones bathroom, devoid of tub or showers. "This is it," Anneliese, Frau Fuhrmann's assistant, said. "This is going to be our home for the next six weeks." As we found out by evening, our quaint little cottage was not wired for electricity. Only the moon provided night light. And there was no kitchen either. All meals were sent up daily by cable lift, just like our luggage.

Dead tired upon arrival, we were fed a small meal in the dining room and then sent straight to bed. Five to eight children were assigned to a room. The group consisted mostly of girls, although some of the youngest children were boys. There were only three twelve-year-olds in the group, my friend Jani being one of them. I was the fourth oldest child and fully expected to share a room with them. But because of my small stature, people routinely mistook me for a seven-year-old. Frau Fuhrmann was no exception, and I was assigned to a room with younger kids. Her directive was a devastating blow to my self-esteem.

"But I'm older than *her*," I protested, pointing to the fifth girl assigned to the room that would house Anneliese, the three twelve-year-olds, and "her," a fully developed nine-year-old. My pleading and crying did not change anything. Neither did my red eyes and stuffy nose at the breakfast table the next morning. Frau Fuhrmann remained unimpressed. Dejected, I drank my cup of ice-cold milk and munched on buttered country bread covered with homemade plum marmalade. When sulking did not result in the desired outcome, I gave up and focused on my new environment.

On this first day in Prägraten, there was no agenda, and we were allowed to explore our surroundings. It felt like I had gone to heaven. Berlin was forgotten. Our *Alpenhütte* was located at the far corner of a beautiful valley. A small glacial brook meandered through the picturesque meadow that stretched from our chalet to the distant high mountains. The field was covered with thick, green grass and dotted with patches of bright yellow, purple, pink, and white wildflowers. A few black-and-white cows grazed at the far end near a leaning barn. Moss-covered boulders popped through the grass here and there. Sun flooded the valley in soft gold. The clear blue sky seemed to jump out of its frame of mountain peaks. A photograph could not have done justice to the beauty before me. It was so different from Berlin or the Adriatic Sea.

Soon after arrival, Jani struck up a close friendship with one of her roommates. I was distraught at first, but found a wonderful friend in Helga, one of Jani's roommates, also two years my senior. In addition, I became good friends with Traudl, one of the Hatzer daughters, whose family owned the *Gasthaus* as well as our chalet.

Every morning, there was milk fresh from the cows, chilled in the icy creek. I was introduced to delicious apple strudel, homemade jams, and cow brains that looked like scrambled eggs. Because I was a picky eater, I had a little trouble getting used to the unfamiliar foods, but I managed.

Frau Fuhrmann kept us busy. We hiked to nearby mountaintops and waterfalls whenever the weather allowed. Other times, we visited the towns of Hinterbichl, Lienz, and Mattrei. We also spent many hours in our own beautiful valley, close to the *Alpenhütte*. Despite being a greenhorn hiker, I quickly became a sure-footed mountain goat and learned to jump from rock to rock, like a local. Traudl, who was my age, taught me to identify, pick, and press wildflowers and assemble them into a small book. She also showed me where to look for and find the coveted *Edelweiß*.

Because we had no tub or showers, we soaped up by the creek and rinsed off in the cold mountain brook. To do this, we stepped into the narrow streambed, lowered ourselves onto its slippery river rocks, and allowed the icy water to briefly run over our naked bodies, from shoulders to toes—holding our breath all the while. Afterwards, we quickly hopped onto the grassy bank and wrapped a towel around our numb limbs before assisting the next girl. Feeling the tingle of blood rushing through our veins again, we felt proud to have survived another character-building experience. *Mutti and Pappi will be so pleased with me, especially Pappi.*

The days passed with lightning speed. By the time vacation was over, I had acquired a great deal of self-confidence and formed lasting friendships. When word reached me that my parents had checked unexpectedly into the *Gasthaus Hatzer*, I ran down the jagged trail to reach the valley as fast as I could. I wanted to thank Mutti and Pappi for allowing me to join Frau Fuhrmann's group of kids and could not wait to share my new experiences.

"Did you have a good time?" were my father's first words.

"That blouse could use a washing," were my mother's. Without missing a beat, we reverted to our familiar family dynamics.

A Matter of Faith

ALTHOUGH BAPTIZED A CATHOLIC, I lacked a religious up-bringing. I knew the difference between God and the Devil, but was unfamiliar with the sacraments, apostolic teachings, confession, conse-cration, and purgatory. I knew how to put my hands together to ask God for help, but could not recite a prayer. The reason was that my Catholic mother had married a Lutheran.

At the time of my parents' nuptials, the Catholic Church was ad-amant that secular partners convert before being allowed to marry in church. Partners were also required to pledge that any children from the union be raised in the Catholic faith. My parents had married in 1943 while my father was on a brief military leave. There was neither time for conversion nor did he wish to change faiths. "I have no objections if you want to raise our children as Catholics," he told my mother, "but I'm not going to convert."

Thus, my parents were married in a civil ceremony, never in the church and, according to Church tenets, remained unwed before the eyes of God. After their nuptials, the parish priest passed over our home whenever he visited the members of the congregation, even though my mother had remained Catholic. Offended, she never took me to church.

I was introduced to Catholicism in *Religionsunterricht*—religious instructions—in elementary school. The north of Germany, including Berlin, was primarily of Lutheran faith, so I was one of only five or six Catholic girls in class. A Catholic vicar and a Protestant pastor came to school two or three times a week to conduct regularly scheduled class-room sessions. Our small Catholic group was led to a separate room. Vicar Bethke was a young, shy man with boyish features and rosy cheeks. His assignment was to teach us catechism, the summary of doctrine from the New Testament to the present. He was to educate our young minds in the Catholic faith by asking probing questions and helping us work out the answers.

Although the church's teaching method had worked well in the first two grades, by the time we reached third grade, our young minds were far less susceptible to indoctrination than education theories presumed.

To us, the purpose of *Religionsunterricht* had turned into an opportunity to mortify the poor vicar with questions that would make him blush. We would not quit pestering him until his rose-colored cheeks turned a deep burgundy. Toward this goal, we worked up collective questions that were guaranteed to make him squirm. Our queries usually centered on the Immaculate Conception.

"Vicar Bethke, what is conception? How does it come about?"

"Vicar Bethke, what do they mean by 'the moment of conception'? When is that?"

"Vicar Bethke, I don't understand how the Blessed Virgin Mary conceived Baby Jesus free from the stain of the original sin. What does that mean?" We took turns peppering questions at the poor man we were sure would embarrass him. Afterwards, we sat in our seats with hands folded and backs erect. Holding our collective breaths, we gazed at the vicar with wide eyes, trying to look innocent. Then we watched him sidestep our questions. He would clear his throat several times, fumble, stare helplessly into space, and finally change the subject. Like cats playing with a mouse, we would return to our devious line of questioning and keep him fidgeting.

At age nine, I started preparation for First Communion by entering a two-year program with Pfarrer Opfermann, our parish priest. Unlike Vicar Bethke, he was relaxed, funny, self-assured, and knew how to make learning fun. During this twenty-four month period, I turned into a pious Catholic.

But following First Communion when I was eleven, my religious fervor began to subside again. I no longer attended church regularly, and stories I had heard made me doubt some of the tenets he had taught. My confidence in the pulpit Gospel lessened immensely when Tante Michen spoke of an incident that involved an acquaintance of hers.

Her friend was a well-to-do married man who found himself in a rocky marriage. As time passed, he met an attractive younger woman and fell in love. Although he had lost all hope for matrimonial bliss with his wife, he saw great potential for happiness with the other woman and decided to get divorced. But because the Catholic Church frowned on such things, he was unable to remarry with the priest's blessing. The church would not bend, but because he made substantial contributions toward the repair and replacement of the war-damaged stained-glass windows, he decided to try his ace. "I'm not making another donation unless you can get me divorced and remarried in church," he told his priest. "How about getting my marriage annulled?" It took a long time, but eventually, he got what he wanted. Tante Michen's story ripped a sizeable hole in my belief in the Catholic faith.

Then my Protestant father added to my confusion when he considered leaving the church altogether. In lieu of tithing, church taxes were imposed and ranged from four to nine percent of gross income. They were collected by the *Finanzamt*, the equivalent of the Internal Revenue Service, and distributed to the appropriate faiths. Since my mother was a homemaker and had no income of her own, our family's church taxes were based on my father's income. In my parents' case, he was obligated to pay taxes to both faiths. "Isn't that amazing?" he thundered, "The Catholic Church is willing to take my money but unwilling to recognize my marriage. I'll fix all of them. I'll leave the church altogether. Then neither the Lutherans nor the Catholics will be able to collect."

My mother pleaded until my father held off on making a final decision. But his logic for wanting to leave the church made sense to me. My faith had been stretched beyond its limits, and I remained a Catholic in name only.

Camp Experiences

THE SIX WEEKS IN AUSTRIA, my first trip away from home, had turned out to be a formative experience. I had become enchanted with the majestic beauty of the mountains and developed an affinity for hiking in their serenity that would last a lifetime. After Prägraten, I could hardly wait for another chance to go to summer camp. My parents saw benefits in summer camp as well. I had returned a happy child, and they had enjoyed a respite from parenting. During each of the next three years, they signed me up for camp, and I got to go on a class trip to boot. Each time, I made new and unexpected discoveries.

The first year, when I was eleven, I spent four weeks in Milano Marittima on Italy's Adriatic coast. The camp was run by *Caritas*, a charitable Catholic relief and service organization. On the train to our destination, I shared a compartment with seven girls, all close to my age. By the time the train had reached the international border that allowed Italian customs agents to check our travel documents, we had become friends already. Passing time, three or four of us pulled down the window and watched the activity on the platform. Pleasantly warm air wafted into the compartment. "Nice! Feels like Italy already," someone giggled.

The platform teemed with activity. Loudspeakers announced incoming and outgoing trains. Porters propelled carts, stacked high with luggage. Well-dressed men in suits rushed to and fro. Children played hide-and-seek. People hugged, kissed, and gestured enthusiastically. Vendors hawked their wares, shouting foreign-sounding words. Caught in the general gaiety, we leaned out the window. Karin yelled the only Italian word she knew, "Italiano!" We all laughed. Vonnie hollered, "Molto bene!" Then the rest of us chimed in, "Italiano—molto bene, Italiano—molto bene," the only three words we could come up with. We spoke Italian and were pleased with ourselves.

A black-haired, olive-skinned man, pushing a cart of candied almonds and lemon sections, passed by the window shouting, "Canditi, canditi, croccante alle mandorle, canditi." We howled just as loud, "Italiano—molto bene, Italiano—molto bene." We had fun.

Suddenly, the man turned, his fiery black eyes skewering us. Halting his cart for just an instant, he spat at us. We shrieked, ducked, and lurched back into the compartment, heads knocking against one another. Aghast, we saw a rivulet of spittle run down the windowpane. Without a word, the vendor glared at us one more time and moved on. We stood speechless, a good couple of feet behind the open window.

One of the camp's nuns, who apparently had witnessed the incident, entered our compartment and closed the window. "Sit down, girls, and don't talk to strangers," she said in a calm tone of voice. Quietly, we returned to our seats, unable to grasp what had just occurred. We had only wanted to participate in the general commotion. The nun took a seat amongst us. Quietly she said, "Because of World War II, Germans are still unwelcome in many parts of the world. Time will heal. It has only been twelve years since the war ended. Forgive the man."

On this trip I learned that one could be spat at just for being German and that one should forgive people who don't understand all of the ramifications of their actions.

When I was twelve I spent three weeks at summer camp in Soderstorf in the Lüneburger Heide of northern Germany. This area is covered with heather and junipers. Its terrain is sandy and flat, and much of the region is part of a natural preserve.

Herr Schultke, a schoolteacher and friend of a business associate of my father, ran the camp. I knew him casually and assumed that our acquaintance would make me one of his favorite children. It didn't. Fortunately, I was far more interested in making friends with the other kids than in being the teacher's pet. I relished the wide-open spaces around Soderstorf, our daily hikes, and the eerie midnight walks during which the white bark of the surrounding birch trees reflected the moonlight. Above all, I loved our weekly scavenger hunts.

Almost all of the boys in camp were fond of the game, but I was the only girl with a keen interest in participation. Even though most of the girls did not care for physical exertion, I could not wait to prove that I had just as much stamina as the boys. I implored Herr Schultke to allow me to join one of the boys' teams, but he would not give in to my pleas. On our first scavenger hunt, he assigned me to a group of girls. We lost so badly that I was embarrassed.

The following week, Herr Schultke relented. Beating out some of the less coordinated lads, I made it onto a boys' squad. Given maps with important landmarks, teams were dispatched at thirty-minute intervals. Within the shortest time possible, each group was to spot telltale ribbons, locate clues, and scout out dead ends. I did my best to outperform everyone on my team. I ran so hard that I could feel my heart thump in my throat. Our group won.

For the last hunt, Jochen, one of the team captains, chose me along with four boys for his team of six. Since I was the only girl elected to a boys' team, I exploded with pride. Although I did not consider the girls fun when it came to team sports, I enjoyed their company at night when we saw movement in every shadow outside the window after having told scary ghost stories.

When I returned home from Soderstorf that year, I was even more convinced that I wanted to be a boy. Boys had much more fun.

In fall of the same year, my entire high-school class went to Storzeln, not far from the Swiss border. The four-week trip was subsidized by the German federal government to allow Berlin children to get out into the countryside. Many of my classmates had never left Berlin. The landscape around Storzeln was dominated by apple trees and sloped gently toward Lake Constance.

Our entire class of thirty girls, including Frau Brunk, our homeroom teacher, spent mornings in the classroom and afternoons on hikes. We slept in large dormitories, washed in community bathrooms, and ate in a common dining room. In Storzeln, I learned two things: I became proficient in a form of sign language, and I learned to love food.

Tante Ruth, one of our camp mothers, strictly enforced the rule of no talk once bedded down for the night. Since we had to retire when it was still light outside, we found it difficult to go to sleep right away. One of the girls knew how to sign, and in no time, each one of us was proficient in lengthy conversations without uttering a word. There were endless experiences to be shared. Years later, I would build on that Storzeln experience. When I wanted to prevent my mother from reading my diary, I developed a secret code of my own.

The second thing I learned was to eat everything without first sniffing it. Still the finicky eater I had been since early childhood, I continued to pick at my food. But in the company of my classmates, I soon began to wolf down whatever was placed before me. When I got off the bus at the end of the trip, my parents were astounded to see I had gained six pounds.

The following year, at age thirteen, I joined Herr Schultke's summer camp again, this time in Oberwarmensteinach in the mountainous Bohemian Forest of southeast Germany. Christina, my best friend and classmate at the time, joined me. But after only one week, she got homesick, visited her father who vacationed nearby, and never returned to camp. Again, I was forced to make new friends. By now, I was getting better at it. At camp, we followed the same routine of hiking, sightseeing, games and leisure time as we had in Soderstorf.

In the heart of the village of Oberwarmensteinach stood a small *Gasthaus*. Two couples and their sons vacationed at the inn. Their boys were maybe a year or two older than my new friend, Siggi, and I. One day, the four of us happened by chance to enjoy a piece of *Schwarzwälder Kirschtorte*—Black Forest cherry cake—at the same local café.

Jürgen, with jet-black hair, made my heart thump when our eyes first met. Siggi and I named his friend Charly Brown after the song that played in the jukebox at the café all day. Its American version was one of the top ten hits for the Coasters that year. We crooned to Hans Blum's German lyrics:

Wer lernt die Vokabeln nicht
(Who doesn't learn their vocabulary)

Wer spielt Skat beim English Unterricht
(Who plays cards during English class)

Charly Brown, Charly Brown, das ist ein Clown, der Charly Brown
(Charlie Brown, Charlie Brown, he is a clown, Charlie Brown)

Und es gibt für i-ihn
(And there is for him)

Keine Medizi-in
(No medicine)

Charly Brown, der hat nur immer Unsinn im Sinn
(Charlie Brown, he only thinks of tomfoolery)

Whenever the schedule read *Freizeit*—free time—we hung around the village with Jürgen and Charly. One day, time got away from us, and we stayed out past our mandatory shoe-polishing period. When we returned to the compound, the gates were already closed. My heart stopped. What now? Jürgen had the answer. "Just climb over the fence!"

We followed his advice. The chain-link fence swayed back and forth as Jürgen helped me scale it. Charly assisted Siggi. Giggling, we made it into the compound and said our good-byes. That's when Jürgen's eyes met mine. His dark pupils shone brightly. I felt a lightning bolt pierce my heart and quickly looked at my shoes. I steadied myself with my hand resting on top of the fence post. When, a moment later, I felt his hand cover mine, I let go and ran. I did not dare to look back until I had put a good ten feet between us. Then I saw Jürgen blow me a kiss. As fast as we could, Siggi and I continued our run back to the camp. We hoped to sneak in through the back door. Too late. Herr Schultke stood squarely planted in the doorway.

"And where have you two been?"

"We, ah, we . . . we had coffee and cake in the village."

"Do you know what time it is?"

"We didn't realize it until a few minutes ago."

"That's no excuse. You're grounded. You're not to leave the camp again without my explicit permission. Understood?"

"Yes." We averted our eyes.

"And if it happens again, I'll have to inform your parents. Are we clear on that?"

Oh God!

Heads hanging, Siggi and I hauled our shoes from the dorm and polished the life out of them. I didn't sleep all night. *Am I in love?* I never saw Jürgen again, but I thought of him often. After that, I no longer wanted to be a boy.

The Fish-First-Say Method

THE YEAR PRIOR TO MY TRIP to Oberwarmensteinach, in 1958, I was twelve and had graduated elementary school. There had been three available high-school paths for us:

Track 1—a three-year curriculum for pupils with below-average grades. Its goal was an apprenticeship in a trade of choice.

Track 2—a four-year curriculum for students with average or higher scores. With emphasis on mathematics or foreign languages, this program aimed at careers in administration.

Track 3—a seven-year curriculum, called *Gymnasium*, preparing its graduates for entry into university. This program included all general collegiate courses, including Latin. The *Gymnasium* was available to top students only.

Upon completion of elementary school, the homeroom teacher handed each student a document, proposing an educational path. I had been recommended for Track 3. But because my parents did not consider higher education necessary, I chose Track 2 with emphasis on languages. My father fully supported my choice. "Girls don't need a college degree. They get married. All they need is something to fall back on," he said. Although kids from our economic class did not ordinarily go to college, my mother questioned whether I shouldn't pursue Track 3 because of my teacher's recommendation, but my father and I overruled her. I preferred to attend the school my friends had chosen, and only one student from my class, a boy whom I never associated with, chose Track 3. Fee and I decided on the *Max-Liebermann-Schule*, a brand-new school with a four-year curriculum. As part of an experimental program, the principal gave parents the choice of placing their offspring in an all-boy, all-girl, or a mixed class.

"Boys are distracting. They'll only hold you back," my mother said and signed me up for the all-girls class. I was not alone. Fee and three girls from my elementary school ended up in the same class.

On the first day in the new school, English was on the lesson plan. Although we already had two years of rudimentary British-English behind us, most of us knew little more than "Peter Pim and Billy Ball—Peter is slim and Billy is tall." Having selected the foreign-language track, we expected an increase in instructional intensity, particularly since we were also scheduled to begin French lessons. But we were in for a surprise.

Shortly after the bell rang, a middle-aged, wiry man, barely five foot five, burst into class.

"My name is Kraschinski. You may call me Count Schinski. I'm your English teacher," he said in rapid-fire speech, throwing several books on the desk. His smile was infectious. Twenty-six pairs of eyes attempted a cursory assessment of the feisty little man. *What will English with him be like?* "I know from years of teaching experience that students coming from elementary school are unprepared to construct even the most basic

English sentence," Herr Kraschinski began. "This has to change immediately if you want to pass my class."

The twenty-six of us stopped inhaling in midbreath. This was a different tone than we were used to from elementary school. It felt more like moving from kindergarten to medical school. We sat at attention.

"A foreign language involves very different muscles," he continued. "If you want to speak good English, you'll have to develop them. Here's a little crutch. It's easy. Pay attention. What is the English word for an animal that lives in the water?" he asked.

Silence. No one moved. We held our collective breath.

"Class participation is mandatory," Herr Count Schinski reminded us. "If you don't participate, I'll note a 'seven' in my book." He waved a little black book through the air. "Three notations require a parent-teacher conference."

That was a new one. Our grade system was based on grades one (very good) to six (failed). Count Schinski had just added another grade.

"So, what do you call an animal that lives in the water?" he repeated.

"Fish?" a tenuous whisper from the front row.

"Good," he praised. "Now tell me what comes before second and third."

"First?" a few more voices could be heard.

"Right again," Herr Kraschinski said. "Now the last question. What do you do when you express something in words?"

"Speak!" Many of us shouted.

"True," he replied, "but that's not the word I'm looking for. Try another one."

After a number of nervous guesses, we hit on the word he had in mind.

"Say," we proposed.

"Excellent," he praised the class. "The three words I was looking for are: Fish, First, Say."

He wrote them on the blackboard. "And that is also the name of the method I have personally developed. It's my

FISH-FIRST-SAY Method."

Dumbfounded, we stared at the teacher. Was he kidding?

"Let's all say the word 'Fish' together," he prompted.

"Fish!" The class called out with a little more enthusiasm.

"Now, pay attention to the shape of your mouth and the position of your tongue as you pronounce 'Fish.' Keep mouth and tongue in the same position and say 'Fish' and immediately afterwards, say 'First.'"

"Fish–First," we said.

"You're not keeping your mouth and tongue in the same position!" Herr Kraschinski admonished.

"Fish–Firsht?" we whispered, wondering if that was the outlandish sound he had in mind.

"Very good," he exclaimed. "Now, keep your mouth and tongue in the same position and try to pronounce all three words."

"Fish–Firsht–Shay," we yelled, grinning at each other. English with Count Schinski was going to be pretty funny.

"From now on, keep your mouth in that very position throughout the English session and you'll do well."

For she nexsht four yearsh, we shpoke English, ushing Herr Kraschinshki's Fish–Firsht–Shay Meshod. We all sounded like we had speech defects, but he kept his word. We passed his class. Did his method help us learn English? Who knows.

The Constitution

ALTHOUGH AS A PEOPLE, Germans have a long history, as a country the history is much shorter, and as a democracy it is shorter still. The German state was created in 1871 when Otto von Bismarck, chancellor under Emperor Wilhelm I, unified a number of small kingdoms into the first German Empire. The first democracy, the Weimar Republic, was not created until 1919 and lasted only fourteen years. When it failed in the midst of an enormous economic crisis, Hitler came to power. In April 1949, the second democracy, the Federal German Republic, was formed, and a new constitution went into effect on September 1, 1950.

The most recent German history had been a thorny subject when I went to school, a subject educators liked to avoid. They had seen "facts" change rapidly during the Nazi years and were not about to stick out their necks for fear of potentially disastrous consequences. Frau Lange, our high-school history teacher, had covered the Egyptians, Babylonians, Persians, Greeks, Romans, and the old Germanic tribes, but we barely got to the outbreak of World War I and certainly did not discuss World War II. Most parents shunned the subject as well, because just a few years earlier, an innocent comment to your child, if repeated by the youngster, could land you in prison.

Although an "A" student, I knew virtually nothing about recent German history. Unlike twenty-first century teens, who are accustomed to locating a wealth of information on the Internet, most postwar German teens were anything but worldly. Even though I had grown up in a large city, I was not even aware of the existence of public libraries.

In early 1960, I was barely fourteen years old. One morning, Frau Lange, our regular history teacher, was sick and Dr. Novak, a young substitute, taught the class. Upon entering the room, he looked around and said, "Let's talk about the *Grundgesetz*—the constitution—today. What do you know about that?"

With blank stares, we looked at the slender man who walked with an almost imperceptible limp. *What about it?*

Trying to approach the subject from a different angle, he prompted, "We'll be celebrating the anniversary of our constitution's tenth birthday later this year. What has the *Grundgesetz* accomplished?"

Clueless, we shifted our eyes away from the teacher and focused on the back of the girl in front of us, our usual avoidance tactic. *I hope he's not going to call on me.* I turned to my neighbor and whispered, "Fee, did we talk about this before? Did I miss . . . ?"

Dr. Novak's gaze bored right through me as he thundered, "You, with the polka dots, would it improve your attention span if you had to turn in a two-page essay, entitled, 'Ten Years *Grundgesetz*?' Have it in my office tomorrow morning, 11:00 a.m. sharp."

I lifted my eyes and glanced cautiously in his direction. Was he talking to me? Our eyes met. I blushed and stuttered something, but he had already moved on.

I was aghast. *Two whole pages? By tomorrow? What can I say about the constitution? I don't know a thing.*

Upon returning home from school, I quizzed my mother, "Mutti, I'm supposed to write an essay, on ten years of the constitution. What shall I write?"

My mother was in the middle of preparing the evening meal and growled, "If you had paid attention in class, you'd know what the constitution is all about. I'm sure your teacher didn't pull the subject out of thin air. You haven't been listening. You'd better take a good look at your books."

I was on my own. The paper was due the next day. Unable to find any information on the subject in my textbook, I grabbed pen and paper and reached for our family encyclopedia, the "*Volks-Brockhaus A-Z.*" I looked up "*Grundgesetz*" and copied the printed passage onto a clean sheet of paper.

> The constitution is the highest law, addressing the form of government and the relationship between the executive power and individual freedom of the citizens and the form of the execution of government and the participation of the citizens therein.

That sounded impressive! *Executive power? Execution of government? Participation of citizens therein?* I had no idea what the paragraph meant, but it sounded intelligent. So far, I had only covered one-half of a page with large block letters. But "Constitution" led me to other subjects. Bold arrows indicated I might also look up ▶ Weimar Constitution, and ▶ Führer principle.

Why not string these entries together? I copied the passage printed under "Weimar Constitution."

> The constitution of the Deutsche Reich, created August 11, 1919 (Weimar Constitution) was an expression of a democratic form of government. The new form of government is the authoritarian state based on the Führer Principle.

I now had just over one page and still needed more. I moved on to "Führer Principle."

The Führer Principle is at the base of the National Socialist State. Decisions are not derived by majority resolutions (democratic principle) but from the resolve of a responsible Führer. Authority to the bottom. Responsibility to the top. Parliamentary rule is a form of government in which decisions of a state are derived from the majority rule of the people's elected representatives and the leaders can only remain in office through the confidence of the majority. It existed first in England but also in Germany 1918-1933. As the mark of a liberal democratic state, parliamentary rule was removed by the National Socialistic Revolution and replaced by the Führer Principle.

Keeping wide margins and writing in big block letters, I managed to fill two pages. With that, my remedial homework was completed, and I turned it in the next day.

A few days passed before my mother remembered my task, but then she asked, "How did you fare with that paper you had to write the other day?" I told her about my research and repeated the key ideas, more than a little pleased with the results I had achieved without anyone's help.

"You turned in what?" my mother shrieked. "Did it ever occur to you to look at the date the encyclopedia was published? It was published in 1935. It was published during the Hitler years. It's Hitler propaganda! Oh my God. You repeated that gibberish and handed it in? The man is going to think your parents are Nazis!" My mother threw up her hands in disbelief.

Now it was my turn to look shocked. "What do you mean the encyclopedia is wrong? I thought that's why we have one. So that we can look up information!"

But the deed was done. Every day for several weeks, my mother asked as soon as I returned from school, "Did your teacher say anything to you?"

"No," was my answer every time.

Shortly thereafter, Frau Lange returned. We never talked about the constitution again. Dr. Novak ignored my essay, and for all I know, he never even read it.

The Record Player

I REMEMBER THE EXACT MOMENT when I first realized that my teen years would be an uphill battle. It was in the spring of 1960, shortly after my fiasco with the essay on the constitution. My father had just brought home our first television set. It was built into a gorgeous cherrywood cabinet. Wraparound doors concealed a black-and-white TV; a radio slid out from the bottom; and the top opened to expose a record player. A record player! My heart sang.

I had turned fourteen only a few months earlier, and Ray Charles, Paul Anka, Connie Francis, Elvis Presley, and the Drifters were the rage. Unfortunately, I knew them only by name. My parents followed the news and a few select programs on the radio, but they flipped the switch on any but 1920s music. I was expected to do the same.

"*Schalte das Gejammer aus*—turn off that moaning and groaning," my father insisted when I tuned to pop music.

"Why can't you listen to something we can all understand?" my mother complained when foreign sounds wafted from the speaker.

"Turn that stuff off right now and get back to your English and French books," my father scolded when I tried to tune to the hit parade on Monday nights. As a result I was ignorant of the latest hits.

My parents' contrarian stance on popular music always reminded me of standing in a paternoster in one of our government buildings. These large passenger lifts consisted of a chain of open compartments that moved in a loop without stopping. There were no doors. Passengers stepped on or off as the open compartments crept by. Whenever I saw a crowd go up, and I was the only one going down, I feared that I was going in the wrong direction. Similarly, I worried now that I was the only person in the world who did not know Elvis' latest hits.

To cover up the hole in my education, I pretended to my classmates that I owned Paul Anka, Ray Charles, and Elvis records, and listened to popular music like everyone else. How long could I keep up the charade?

But now, we, too, owned a record player. Thank God! With this overdue acquisition, *fiel mir ein Stein vom Herzen*—a rock tumbled from my heart. I could quit pretending. Which records should I get first and how should I start a collection with my paltry allowance, I wondered. Returning home from school the next day, I headed straight for the cherrywood cabinet. I just wanted to touch our new player again. This weekend, Fee would help me start my collection. I smiled in anticipation.

Gently easing up the lid partway, I reached into the shallow compartment with my other hand, fingers hunting for the stylus. Nothing. I lifted the lid a little higher and peered into the box.

My jaw almost came unhinged. I found myself staring into a gaping hole, right down to the top of the TV set. And the hole had the shape of a record player!

"Mutti, Mutti, what happened?" I shouted as I ran into the kitchen.

"Oh that," my mother wiped her hands on her apron, getting ready to put lunch on the table. "Pappi and I don't want you to spend your time listening to records. You need to concentrate on your schoolwork. That thing would only distract you. One day you'll be glad that we had it removed."

I gasped in disbelief. The earth was still shaking under my feet when my mother added, "Besides, records cost money."

"Well, what happened to it?" my voice skipped up an entire octave.

"A man came and cut it out. Pappi sold it," my mother answered as if it were the most natural conclusion in the world.

"Sold it? Just like that?"

"Go, wash your hands. Lunch is ready."

Since I was used to obedience, I raised no objections. I meekly followed my mother's instructions. But the crack in the veneer of the once perfect little girl had begun to widen.

1946—
A street in Berlin.

June 1946—
I am baptized in a dress
made from the silk of a
downed airmen's parachute.
Behind me from left to
right: Irene, a colleague of
my mother, my mother, and
Tante Michen.

1947—
Most of the buildings are still heav-
ily damaged or destroyed.

Summer 1948—
My mother on the
Kurfürstendamm. Her
dress is made from the
same parachute as my
baptismal dress.

Winter 1948—
Dressed in my
warm rabbit coat,
I look at my Pappi.

1949—
On a bench in the
Berlin Zoo.

1950—
I want to play
exclusively with
cars and trains.

1950—
Tante Michen and
I on the trade-fair
grounds near the
Funkturm, Berlin's
radio tower.

1951—
My mother takes
my father and me
on a maiden drive
in our Volkswagen.

April 1952—
My first day of school.

1954—
I count my
winnings to be
deposited at the
bank.

1954—
I proudly wear my
lederhosen, leather
britches.

FOUR

PARADIGM SHIFT

A Star is Born

TIME SLID BY. Although a day was always twenty-four hours long, some seemed longer. At fourteen, I was a *Backfish*, a teenager. The term was still favored by the older generation and literally meant "baked fish." It referred to a girl in transition from child to womanhood. Upon reaching adolescence, I had looked forward to a longer parental leash and increased participation in decisions that affected my existence instead of merely obeying orders. But, my life remained fixed in patterns that were established when I was a youngster.

I was still a little girl in my parents' eyes. Every aspect of my life was scrutinized, similar to the police monitoring adherence to the speed limit. But in the case of a patrol car, most of us only slow to the speed limit until the cops are out of sight. In my case, the police remained permanently in my rearview mirror. It was frustrating.

Without siblings and only a small extended family, I felt isolated and bored. The majority of my time was spent on school and homework. My mother tested me every day on what I had learned and carefully supervised all outside activities. Not allowed to explore on my own, I began to feel unsure of myself again. I wondered if my friends had already learned things I did not know yet.

To keep myself occupied with outlets acceptable to my parents, I watched afternoon shows on our new television set. When the station solicited program suggestions from teens, I jumped at the opportunity. It was April. The six winning ideas would be aired live in early summer in an hour-long program, entitled, "*Wie Ihr's Wollt*—As You Like It."

In line with an artistic bent I had begun to develop in high school, I proposed to create a simple and inexpensive wall decoration made from insulated electrical wire. My creation would depict a fisherman, made of wire, cardboard, fabric, raffia, aquarium greens, and a plastic fish.

Proud of my brainchild, I showed my proposal to my mother. "*Wäre das nicht dufte?*—Wouldn't this be grand?"

"*Ja, ja, mach mal*—sure, sure, go ahead," my mother replied, her mind on business matters. She was glad I had found something to do with my time.

After mailing off my proposal, I gave it no further thought. But to my surprise, I received a letter a couple of months later, informing me that my idea had been selected along with five other entries. I was invited to fly to Frankfurt/Main for three days of rehearsal and live transmission, all at station expense. I was elated. "On television! Can you believe it? No one I know has ever been on TV!"

Overnight, I became a celebrity at school. Uneasy, my mother wondered aloud, "You don't want to fly alone to Frankfurt, do you? Alone in a strange hotel? Alone at a television studio? I'll go with you."

Her plan to accompany me met with my emphatic rejection. A teen with her mother in tow? Unthinkable! I wanted to appear independent. We argued. In the end I prevailed because my mother could not think of a discreet way of inserting herself into the reservation process. And she did not want to attract the attention of the network because she could not explain her misgivings. I was relieved.

As the day of my trip neared, I came to realize that I did not know how or what to get ready. I quizzed my parents. My father suggested that I bring a set of precut parts and a completed project. "That way, you can demonstrate the assembly process and also show the audience your final piece," he proposed. It sounded like a good plan, and I prepared accordingly.

The long anticipated Saturday morning in June arrived. I boarded a Pan Am flight bound for Frankfurt/Main, where a twenty-two-year-old young man waited for me at the airport. Talk about being flattered! Karsten was tall, dark, and handsome and had been assigned to be my escort for the three-day period. He was an actor. I had never seen him on television, but that did not matter. *Wait until I tell my friends in Berlin!*

Karsten drove me directly to the studio where rehearsals were already in progress. The other participants, all from various towns in West Germany, had rehearsed for two days already. I learned that I alone had received VIP treatment. Because standard travel from West Berlin was cumbersome, the station had paid for an airline passage while the rest of the group had commuted by train, bus, or car. Upon hearing this piece of information, my self-esteem performed somersaults and I felt like I had grown several inches on the spot.

The program began with six young girls and their teacher from Bad Homburg, demonstrating beach games with hula hoops and balls. My wall decoration was listed as the second program segment, followed by five male students from Munich presenting a marionette show. Afterwards, a group of scouts from Stuttgart talked about their travels to Finland. Then a business administration trainee from Schwetzingen showed off his magic tricks, and the hour closed with a skiffle group from Hamburg.

Upon arriving at the studio, I was ushered toward a partly partitioned corner. I laid out my finished art piece next to the parts in order of assembly. Then I watched with interest as three large, moveable cameras were set up. "When the red light is on, we're filming," one of the cameramen said. A harried man by the name of Max introduced himself as the floor director, took one look at me, and announced in a matter-of-fact tone, "That dress has to go. Find something less busy." Then he turned his attention elsewhere.

I was taken aback. He was talking about my best summer dress, a sleeveless fuchsia-colored creation with big white polka dots and a huge collar. My mother had made it for me the summer before. Short of my nightgown, I had not packed anything beautiful. Mortified, I remained glued to the chair and stared at the turmoil around me. I had no idea what to do next.

A young coordinator, taking pity on me, explained that a solid-color outfit allowed the camera to focus on the art rather than on the dress. Why hadn't Pappi mentioned this? He must have known. After all, he was a photographer. The coordinator's explanation made sense, but it was too late for me to come up with another outfit. When Max was unable to locate a suitable garment in the studio, he instructed me to turn sideways and elevate my arms against a solid background during assembly. After several trial shoots, he deemed this a satisfactory solution.

Heart pounding wildly and vocal cords nearing paralysis, I made my first attempt at rehearsing the ten-minute segment with cameras rolling. Watching the red light on the "hot" camera, I explained the assembly process, holding up each part as I spoke.

"Cut-cut-cut. Turn that thing forty-five degrees to the right so that the camera can get a better angle," the floor director yelled, followed by, "Go back to . . . after cutting two pieces of wire to equal length . . ."

Go back? My heart skipped a beat. It had never occurred to me to memorize my speech. While practicing at home, I had simply talked through the demonstration. To my horror, I learned that all the other participants had scripted and memorized their lines.

"Ten minutes, Fräulein Umbach—no more, no less," Max shouted impatiently. My hands shook. *How can I keep the demonstration to exactly ten minutes? It isn't scripted. It just happens!*

"See the clock behind us?" Max pointed to the back wall. "It'll count down ten-nine-eight, and so on. When it gets to three, you'd better wrap it up. If you're falling short, extend your talk. Capito?"

My heart raced. My head spun. But I nodded and quietly practiced my segment over and over while the crew worked with another group. After a while, I began to relax. With practice, it became a little easier to simultaneously manage my arm elevation, explanations, smiles, and assembly. Finally, I let out a huge sigh of relief. I could do it.

That evening, as Karsten drove me back to my hotel, I experienced a new sensation. I could count on myself. It was a wonderful feeling.

The next morning, because it was Sunday and there were no rehearsals, my escort gave me a tour of Frankfurt. I expected him at 10:00 a.m. but was ready by 8:00 a.m. Throughout the tour, I hung on every word Karsten spoke; yet, I heard nothing he said. I felt like a princess in the company of Prince Charming. *Other women must be green with envy.*

After a morning of sightseeing, Karsten invited me to lunch at the imposing Four Seasons restaurant. Live plants reached from floor to ceiling in a parklike setting. Arbors for quiet conversation were tucked into the greenery. Waiters in black-and-white attire floated among the elegantly dressed patrons at small tables covered with starched linens, silver, and crystal. The room hummed with the clatter of dishes, affluence, and hushed conversation. Not in a million years would I have pictured myself in this breathtaking setting.

Although I tried to act casual, lunch turned into a mild disaster. The maître d' ushered us to a small table for two. I was so nervous that my mouth dried up and my lips stuck to my teeth, causing a minor speech defect; I spilled my drink onto the skirt of the only dress I could wear on the show the following day; and I could not decide whether the glass of water was intended as a finger bowl or as a drink. I don't even remember what we ate. All I recall is that I intently studied the floor for scuff marks and blushed every time I met my escort's glance. I felt like a country bumpkin out on the town.

Throughout my trials and tribulations, Karsten remained the ultimate gentleman. He made polite conversation and pretended not to notice my awkwardness. The pleasant smile, permanently affixed to his face, did not reveal whether he saw in me an attractive blond or a retarded fool.

By evening, back in the safety of my hotel room, I had overcome the day's humiliation. Unable to sleep, I sat on the edge of my bed and watched the leafy branches of the trees outside make shadowy patterns on the sheer curtains. Throughout the night, I basked in the memory of having lunched at the *Four Seasons* with a television star.

Monday came, and with it the live airing of the show. By then I had made friends with several of the other participants and felt much more relaxed. To my surprise, I pulled it together. I controlled my nervousness, gracefully assembled my work of art, and watched the time. My segment lasted exactly ten minutes. I was all smiles, knowing that my parents, Tante Michen, and my classmates would be watching on their sets at home.

The television experience kicked off my passage from childhood into teen. The rubber band had stretched, and the bumpy ride of adolescence had begun.

Letter to the General

FOLLOWING THE TELEVISION EXPERIENCE, I craved further exposure to the world beyond home and parents. For the first time, I had explored unfamiliar terrain without parental direction or supervision, and it had turned into a pleasant experience. To my parents' consternation, the small seed of independence that had germinated in those three days became difficult to eradicate. All of a sudden, they detected unfamiliar willfulness in their daughter. "She'll settle down during the summer break. Just give it a few days," my father predicted.

With summer vacation just around the corner, I dreaded the anticipated monotony of life at home which, at times, had almost swallowed me up. What could I do to make this summer more interesting? Were there still programs like Operation Kinderlift, I wondered. Each year during the late fifties, the Red Cross and the US Air Force in Europe had jointly flown close to two thousand underprivileged West Berlin children to West Germany for summer holidays with host families. Wouldn't it be fun to live with another family for a few weeks? When I learned that Kinderlift had been terminated three years earlier, I racked my brain for other options. How about American military families stationed in Germany? With fondness, I remembered how black GIs had waved to me whenever our Volkswagen Beetle was stuck between convoy trucks on the autobahn when I was seven.

The idea of visiting with an American family fired my imagination. I could practice my English. After all, Mutti and Pappi always urged me to keep my nose in my English and French books. If I put a language spin on it, they might agree to a student exchange. I knew that my mother did not champion adventures, but Pappi might support my quest. He enjoyed travel and uncharted waters. But how should I go about it?

One afternoon, not much later, I heard General Ralph M. Osborne on the news. He was the American commandant of the US Army in Berlin, the highest-ranking American officer who also represented the United States in the Allied Kommandatura, the organ through which the United States, Great Britain, and France still exercised their governmental authority over the Western sectors of Berlin even though the Soviets had walked out. I had an epiphany. *I bet he can locate a host family for me.*

I reached for my baby-blue stationery with the letter "J" inscribed in the upper left-hand corner, a gift from Tante Michen for my fourteenth birthday. Then I took Cassell's New German and English Dictionary from the shelf. Checking each word and phrase for proper spelling, I penned a letter to the General.

Dear General Osborne!

I am 14 years old and I go to a girlsclass in secondary school. I am learning English since four years. I would like to spend my summer holiday with an American family in Germany. If they have a daughter as old as I, I would like that. Can you help me? I know no Americans.

Many greetings
Jutta Umbach

Satisfied with content and penmanship, I carefully sealed the letter and addressed it to:

General Ralph M. Osborne
Commandant of the US Army
Berlin

Into the yellow mailbox at the corner it went. I felt that sense of achievement again that I had experienced after filming the television segment. But I also heard a vexing little voice in the back of my head. It kept whispering: You should have discussed this plan with your parents before you mailed the letter, Jutta! I knew the voice was right. But anticipating Mutti's disapproval, I was reluctant to relinquish my big dream without giving it a try first. Speculating that the chances of a response from the general were remote at best, I confessed to my parents over dinner that evening. As anticipated, Pappi was supportive, even enthusiastic, while Mutti was vehement in her opposition and displeased with my unexpected streak of independence.

"You are too young . . . Who knows what kind of family you'd end up with? It isn't safe. What if you don't understand their language? What if you want to come home before the end of your stay?" my mother worried. But in the end, even Mutti had to admit that it was not worth getting worked up over something that was highly unlikely to happen.

Returning home from school a few weeks later, I heard the soft murmur of two female voices coming through the half-open living room door. One voice I recognized as my mother's; the second sounded unfamiliar. Customers were usually led into the small office, not into the living room, and relatives never visited during office hours. Not dressed for company, but in street clothes, I cautiously approached the living room when I heard my mother call out, "*Komm' rein, Jutta. Eine Dame ist hier, die Dich kennenlernen möchte.*—Come on in, Jutta. There's a lady here who'd like to meet you." My mother's voice sounded more solicitous than usual. Quickly scanning my memory for recent events which might have caused a teacher or parent to call on my mother with a complaint or request for disciplinary action, I inched into the room.

A middle-aged, well-dressed lady greeted me. "*Mein Name ist Mrs. Miller. Ich komme von der US Mission.*—My name is Mrs. Miller. I work with the US State Department." My heart wanted to jump out of my chest. *She must be here because of my letter to the general. Mutti will be upset.* I glanced in her direction. Both women were seated at the table. My mother fidgeted with her glasses, but I could not read her mood. Mrs. Miller proceeded to explain that two potential host families had been found.

Trembling, I shifted from one foot to the other while Mrs. Miller continued. "The Peterson family has three daughters. One is your age, Jutta, one is two years younger, and their third girl is one year older than you. The other family interested in hosting you for the summer, the Kellys, have just one daughter. She is two years older than you." Turning to my mother, Mrs. Miller said, "Don't you agree, Frau Umbach, that the Kellys might be the better fit? Not only is Sharon an only child, like Jutta, but, from what I hear, both girls want to be airline hostesses some day."

I glanced at my mother again and waited for her to object. But after a moment's silence, she quietly nodded and her lips formed a nearly inaudible "yes." She hardly seemed herself. *Will Mutti really let me go?*

Still standing next to the dining room table, I felt as if someone had taken everything I believed to be true, thrown it into a box, and shaken it so hard that the contents had rearranged itself. Questions tumbled in rapid succession from the top of my head like ice cubes from a freezer tray. Am I dreaming? Has General Osborne come through for me? Is Mutti going to let me go? Do I get to stay with an American family this summer? Where do they live? Will I get a sister? I did not dare to speak, fearing a rude awakening.

Seemingly from miles away, Mrs. Miller's voice echoed with the story as it had unfolded. Miraculously, the letter had landed on General Osborne's desk. Unable to assist directly, he had forwarded it to his colleague, four-star General Frederic Harrison Smith, Jr., who served as the commander in chief of the 4th Allied Tactical Air Force in Germany as well as the commander in chief of all of the US Air Forces in Europe. Headquartered in Wiesbaden, he had passed the request to his community relations department which, in turn, had dispatched a message to all Air Force subcommands. Someone had placed an appeal in the *Stars and Stripes*, the military newspaper.

According to Mrs. Miller, my plea for help had caught the eye of MSgt. Clarence Kelly, who had casually mentioned it to his wife, Marilyn, and their daughter, Sharon, over dinner that evening. His unit, under the command of General Smith, was in charge of radar surveillance of the Berlin air corridor. "We monitor all Allied air traffic in the twenty-five-mile-wide airspace to and from Berlin," MSgt. Kelly had mused. "I have always wondered what the people in Berlin are like."

Just four weeks earlier, before he and his family had been transferred from the United States to Ramstein Air Base, he and Marilyn had talked about the wonderful learning opportunities this transfer might present for their daughter. "Sharon would be exposed to a different world. She might even learn to speak a second language."

Now Sharon begged, "Dad, can we host the Berlin girl?"

"It did not take long for the Kellys to agree on extending an invitation to Jutta for a three-week stay this summer," Mrs. Miller said.

When my father arrived at home that evening, my mother told him about Mrs. Miller's visit and the invitation from the Kellys. He was so surprised that he could not speak for several minutes, but he was happy for me. "*Weißt Du was?*" He said. "*Wenn Du Deine Sommerferien in Ramstein verbringst, dann laden wir Sharon ein, ihre Weihnachtsferien mit uns zu verbringen.*—You know what? If you're spending your summer vacations in Ramstein, we'll invite Sharon to spend her Christmas vacations with us." My mother remained speechless; this was more than she could assimilate in one day.

As plans for my German-American exchange progressed, public relations departments in Ramstein and Berlin prepared for a human-interest story. Newspapers marked the departure date in their calendars. Pan American Airways offered their full VIP services, seeing in this story an opportunity to advance talks with the US Air Force regarding improved radar surveillance in the Berlin corridor.

Best Summer I Ever Had

CLOSE TO NOON on a beautiful summer day in mid-August, a plush Pan Am limousine arrived at our home to whisk me to Berlin's Tempelhof airport. Neighbors stopped to watch with curiosity as a uniformed chauffeur opened the car door and helped me slip into the back. He then carefully placed my small suitcase into the large, empty trunk. I was fourteen years old. I felt like the Queen of England on a state visit. Taking full advantage of my sudden prominence, I rolled down the window and waved a regal "good-bye" to my parents.

"Don't forget to wash your neck and behind the ears every morning," I heard my mother shout as the limo swung away from the curb, yanking me back to reality.

Twenty minutes later, we pulled into the airport. Pan Am flight attendants presented me with a bouquet of pink carnations and ushered me on board one of their *Clippers* bound for Frankfurt Rhein/Main. Passengers craned their necks as I took my seat.

During the flight, Captain Everett Wood invited me into the cockpit and let me climb into the copilot's seat where I found myself surrounded by a maze of instruments. "Shall we call for a positional fix from your

American host father's radar unit?" he asked. "They can pinpoint exactly where we are. And we don't want our aircraft to stray outside the air corridor, do we?"

I nodded, then shook my head, not knowing which question to answer first.

"Visibility is excellent. Normally, we wouldn't need to call. But in bad weather and during night flights, it's standard procedure. The work of your host father's unit is very important to our safety."

On huge earphones that cupped both sides of my small head, I listened in on the crackling exchange between the copilot and the radar man on the ground as he conveyed the aircraft's position within the corridor. A bit intimidated I asked Captain Wood, "Are ze Russians watching us on zeir radar screen right now?"

"They probably are," was his answer, "but don't worry, our friends are watching us, too. And they're making sure we're going to stay safe."

There was no doubt in my mind that the Americans were our friends.

Upon arrival at Rhein/Main airport, the stewardess asked me to deplane last. When I stepped through the aircraft's open door, I spotted a small crowd at the foot of the ramp: a uniformed American soldier, a woman, a teen, and a slew of reporters. I hesitated. Dressed in a white blouse and a red-checkered skirt that billowed over my starched petticoat, I smiled apprehensively and descended with uncertain steps toward the gaggle on the tarmac. Cameras flashed. *What do I do now?*

"*Velkom in Ramsteen,*" the thirtyish woman said in accented German as she threw her arms around me in a big bear hug. Her hearty embrace went a long way to help me regain my composure, but her American twang broke the ice. We both giggled as she continued in English. "Utah, this is my husband, Clarence—we call him Scotty—and this is our daughter, Sharon," she said, pointing to the two people standing behind her, their faces brimming.

After we hugged and kissed, everyone tried to talk to me at once. Words followed one another in such rapid succession, that they sounded to me like raindrops hitting the pavement. My host family's pace of speech quickly outstripped my translating abilities. Pan Am personnel came to my rescue and ushered us into their VIP lounge for a glass of juice and interviews with reporters from German dailies and American military newspapers. I tried to answer the scores of questions fired at me but had trouble understanding even the simplest sentences. Of the countless British-English words I had committed to memory, not one seemed within reach or matched what I heard. Neither did I find Herr Kraschinski's "Fish-First-Say" method of pronunciation helpful. I opened my mouth several times, but nothing came out. It felt like someone had closed the door to my memory and misplaced the key. Finally, I got so rattled that I could not even understand German.

Soon, it was time to leave for Ramstein Air Base. Scotty led us to the family's big, beige Pontiac with chocolate-brown fenders. The length of the car immediately caught my attention. I guessed it would take two Volkswagen Beetles to make one Pontiac. When Mr. Kelly turned the wheel with only one hand while smoking with the other, I was impressed. I had seen my father expend more energy parking our small Beetle than Scotty spent maneuvering this majestic sedan.

Upon arrival at the Kelly's apartment, we were greeted by the family dog, a small black dachshund, named Mr. Poops. I was in heaven. I had always dreamed of a dog of my own, but pets were not allowed in our Berlin apartment.

"May I valk him?" I asked almost immediately.

"Anytime. I'll show you where we keep his leash," Sharon said, delighted to pass off her daily responsibility. Mr. Poops and I became instant and inseparable friends.

My three-week whirlwind introduction to life in an American military family had begun. Marilyn showed me through their three-bedroom flat. Although very similar to German apartments, I immediately spotted a clever feature in the bathroom. A vinyl curtain hung from a rod and extended all the way into the bathtub.

"Vat a great idea," I exclaimed in amazement. "In our home, ze entire bathroom gets wet when we shower. We don't have a curtain like zat."

"It keeps the floor dry," Marilyn agreed.

Then it occurred to me why my family did not have a shower curtain. The Kelly's tub was built into an alcove so that the rod could be secured between two walls. Our bathroom formed a rectangle without indentations.

"That's why we make cat washes most of ze time," I tried to make conversation.

"Make cat washes?" Marilyn wrinkled her forehead.

"You know, when you put a little soap and water onto a cloth and wash yourself like a cat?" I mimicked.

Marilyn laughed. "Oh, I see. We call it a sponge bath. You don't have to take a sponge bath here. You can shower anytime you want to."

"Really?" In our house, a daily shower was considered pure luxury. We took ours once a week.

"Absolutely," Marilyn assured me.

Next morning, after breakfast, Sharon and I headed for her last day in summer school. Students occupied individual chairs with attached desktops. Classes were held in a discussion format, and students were free to contribute at any time. In my school, two students shared a desk; Classes were held in a lecture format, and students participated only when called upon by the teacher.

"How come there are no foreign languages on your schedule?" I wondered after perusing Sharon's lesson plan. "Everyone in my class studies English and French."

"I don't know," Sharon shrugged.

An hour later, we all got an unplanned history lesson. During a discussion of nineteenth-century discoveries, one of Sharon's classmates credited Alexander Graham Bell with the invention of the telephone. I waited in vain for the teacher to correct him.

"Johann Phillip Reis invented ze telephone," I finally piped up when it seemed that the error was going unnoticed, "around 1860. That's before Bell." I swallowed hard. Normally, I was too timid to speak out among strangers. But I was so proud that it had been a German who had invented the phone, that I overcame my bashfulness. Then I shared what I remembered from physics class, namely that Reis had successfully transmitted the sentence, *Das Pferd frißt keinen Gurkensalad*—the horse doesn't eat cucumber salad.

Sharon and her friends stared at me in disbelief before they broke into laughter. "The horse doesn't eat cucumber salad? I don't think so. Who is this 'Djohan Rees' anyway?"

"No way," another of Sharon's classmates rejected my assertion. "Bell invented the telephone. That's a fact."

Now it was my turn to look bewildered. I knew from physics class that Reis had invented the phone and that Bell had improved on his contraption. I glanced at the teacher, hoping for backup.

The instructor delighted in the controversy.

"All of you are right to some degree," he said. "Alexander Bell is generally credited with the invention of the telephone, but there were many others before him who made discoveries that helped Bell perfect his apparatus. One of them was Johann Reis. But the Frenchman, Charles Bourseul, and the Englishman, Cromwell Varley, also contributed."

The debate then turned into a lively discussion of history versus politics and the ability to spin the truth one way or another. "History is not always as dry as it appears, is it?" the teacher grinned.

Toward the end of the school day, the class discussed current politics. To my amazement, these American kids knew far more about West German Chancellor Konrad Adenauer and Berlin's Mayor Willy Brandt than I did. In my school, current politics were rarely discussed. When Sharon's classmates asked whether I preferred Willy Brandt to Konrad Adenauer, I had no answer. We studied ancient history: We knew about the Dark Ages, the Teutons, and the Prussians. But we had been taught very little about World War I or World War II. Teachers and parents alike seldom touched upon these subjects. My knowledge of World War II did not go much beyond watching the documentary, "The Diary of Anne Frank." Once each year, our entire school, one class at a time, was marched into the auditorium. Like most young Germans at the time, I knew very little about what was going on outside the narrow frame of my world. Now, I felt completely ignorant.

One evening during the middle of my visit, Sharon took me to a beatnik party at the youth center. Girls in calf-length skirts and bobby socks danced with boys to swing tunes from a jukebox. I watched in frank admiration as both sexes appeared completely at ease with one another. I usually became tongue-tied and uncomfortable in the presence of young men. When one of the boys asked me for a dance— probably because Sharon had made him—I tripped, red-faced and nervous, all over my feet. As long as I could remember, my parents had discouraged my association with the opposite sex by saying, "There's plenty of time for that when you get older. Right now, you need to concentrate on your studies." And I had always complied without protest. Now I wondered if I had given up too easily. Why did Marilyn and Scotty allow us to visit the teen center on a weeknight when my parents forbade outings like this?

"On weeknights I have a 10:00 p.m. curfew. On Saturdays, I can stay out until midnight," Sharon had explained. With the exception of parent-supervised activities, my parents did not allow me to go out in the evening at all, weekdays or weekends. I began to feel pangs of jealousy. What a fabulous unsupervised existence Sharon leads, I thought.

Sometimes, we joined Sharon's friends to see a movie and visit the commissary afterwards for a hamburger, French fries, and a coke. Prior to my Ramstein visit, I had seen the inside of a movie theater less than a dozen times, and then only when my mother had taken me to watch a children's film. Neither did my parents and I consider going out for a bite to eat very often because we lived by a simple rule: Don't spend "good money" on something you can get at home for free.

One night, Sharon invited her girlfriends to her apartment for a slumber party. The six or eight of us talked, laughed, and played games all night, trying to keep each other from falling asleep. I struggled but was the first to doze off. The strain of listening to foreign words all day had tired me out. But it also saddened me to know that a slumber party in my home would be out of the question. My parents would never put up with the giggles throughout the night or the commotion in the bathroom the next morning. I was not even allowed to invite a single girlfriend to stay overnight. Suddenly, I felt cheated. There was a whole life out there I had never known.

"American teens have so much more freedom than German girls," I lamented.

Of course, we wrestled with the typical language-based misunderstandings. One Monday morning Sharon informed me, "We'll drive to the base in Landstuhl next Thursday. Be sure to bring your ID."

I nodded, but when we arrived at the base a few days later, I could not produce the paper.

"Don't you remember, I told you to bring your card today?" Sharon asked.

"I remember. But you said next Thursday, not this Thursday. Isn't next Thursday a week from now?"

And there was the matter of the long fingernail. Sharon and her girl-friends worked hard at convincing me to let the nails of my little fingers grow ad infinitum. Each girl proudly showed me a long, curved claw on each hand.

"Doesn't that get in the way?" I asked.

"The fun is in seeing how long it'll get," they assured me.

Despite their passionate arguments, I was unable to grasp the concept, and the girls finally gave up.

The Kellys also enjoyed many activities as a family. Bowling was one of their favorite pastimes. I had never heard of the sport, but knew its German cousin, *Kegeln*. I quickly caught on, and, within a few days, bowled with the best of them. "Bowling is *prima*," I concluded.

One sunny afternoon, Scotty, an avid member of the Ramstein Aero Club, invited me to join him and his instructor for a flight to nearby Saarbrücken. The flight did not last nearly long enough. To take off, cruise, and land in a four-seater, to feel the breeze, and to see the world from above were experiences I could not describe in words. I had been on a commercial airliner, but to fly in a small plane was altogether different.

"This is how God must feel when he looks down on earth," I told Scotty.

When the Kellys celebrated their wedding anniversary, I helped clean, cook, and decorate for the occasion. "At home, I am not allowed to clean," I admitted to Marilyn, "because my mother thinks I use too much water. My mother lets me dust, but that's no fun." Sharon was amazed that I should be unaccustomed to chores. She would have gladly handed over her duties for good.

"Do you know how to cook?" Marilyn asked.

"I know how to make a cake, but I've never cooked a meal."

I loved American food. Aside from steaks the size of dinner plates, we had many unfamiliar and delicious foods: fresh corn on the cob, baked potatoes, barbeques, packaged sweet rolls, pancakes from a mix, iceberg lettuce, broccoli, and banana splits. Aside from a lack of variety when it came to cheeses and sausages, the meals could not have been better.

"The vegetables look so green after they're cooked. They make the water in my mouth run together," I told Marilyn. "Don't your vegetables at home look green?" she laughed.

"They look khaki," I admitted. My mother cooks them for a long time."

With special permission from the base, I was allowed to join the Kellys at the exchange facilities. Aside from the greatest American invention, the sweatshirt, I could not get excited about American fashions. "The skirts and the shorts are way too long," I complained to Sharon. "Why do you wear those funny-looking Bermudas? Shorts should be short. Isn't that why they're called 'shorts'?"

Bobby sox were ruled out as well. "I've waited for a long time to wear nylons. No way am I going back to wearing kids' socks, Sharon."

But Marilyn guessed what item I secretly coveted. On a hunch, she took me to the lingerie department and asked the sales clerk to lay out several training bras. In truth, I had little need for a brassiere. My father had a point when he teased me, *"Zwei Erbsen auf ein Brett genagelt—* Two peas nailed to a board." But a bra was a status symbol. Teenagers wore bras, children did not. My face turned crimson when the sales clerk returned with a small white brassiere in my size. Overjoyed, I tried it on and refused to take it off again. Four weeks later, when it was grey in color, my mother had to pry it off so that it could be washed.

Much too soon, the three weeks with the Kellys ended. It had been the best summer I had ever had. When I returned to Berlin, my mother was in the hospital. My father said that she had developed pleurisy because my escapades had diminished her immunity. His words made me feel bad. Nonetheless, as I sat by her bedside recounting my many new experiences, I sat tall, shoulders pulled back and chest pressed out. In my tight-fitting ribbed sweater that left no doubt of a brassiere, I wanted to convey that I had made the important transition from childhood into adolescence. When my mother finally asked, "Are you wearing a bra?" I replied with a hint of ridicule, "It was a present from Marilyn."

"I see," Mutti said and turned away. The subject was closed.

Christmas in Berlin

TO RECIPROCATE, MY PARENTS HAD EXTENDED an invitation to Sharon to spend the last three weeks of December in Berlin. Scotty and Marilyn were to join us for the holidays only and would stay in a nearby hotel.

I had lobbied hard for Sharon to arrive prior to December 6, *Nikolaus Tag*—St. Nick's Day—because I did not want her to miss out on this first in a series of fun German Christmas traditions. When I recalled the many activities the Kellys had organized during my Ramstein visit, I worried that Sharon might get bored in Berlin. Not that Berlin didn't have oodles of diversions to offer, the problem was that my parents thought me, at barely fifteen, too young to participate in any of them. What would Sharon, who was seventeen already, think when my parents scratched a visit to the teen club? And how would she feel when there were no beatnik parties, no sleepovers, no bowling, no golf, and no movies? I prayed that Berlin's history and our many Christmas traditions would compensate her for the lack of teen activities.

When Sharon walked down the ramp at Tempelhof airport in December of 1960, my parents and I, surrounded by a slew of German and American reporters, welcomed her to Berlin. I could not wait to throw my arms around my American sister. After a couple of minutes, it became obvious that Sharon still did not speak any German. Despite her parents' urging, she had not taken any language classes. Since my mother did not speak a word of English, and my father knew only the few British words he had picked up as a prisoner of war, the responsibility for dialogue rested with me alone. But I did not mind. In fact, I welcomed the opportunity to show off my language skills, even if they were far from polished.

"I'm so glad you were able to come tonight because tomorrow is a very special day," I said to Sharon on the way home from the airport. "Tonight, before we go to sleep, we must stand one shoe in front of the bedroom door." Sharon looked at me with a quizzical expression.

"One shoe? Why?" Sharon asked.

Bursting with excitement, I explained, "Because during the night, Saint Nick visits each home. He rewards good girls and boys and punishes bad ones." Then I described how on the night of the fifth of December, children all over Germany polish their best pair of shoes and place them in front of the bedroom door. Then they place their Christmas wish lists inside one of the shoes. St. Nick retrieves the papers for delivery to the *Weihnachtsmann*—Santa Claus. But before departing, he fills the shoes of obedient children with chocolates, candies, and nuts and leaves a switch for the bad ones.

"You were a good girl during the year, Sharon, weren't you?" I inquired with a wink, "or will you get a spanking?"

Sharon laughed, "I most certainly do not need a spanking," she laughed.

Then I told her the story of the real St. Nikolaus, a Catholic bishop who lived in an area that is now part of Turkey and gave presents to the poor, especially the children. "Saint Nikolaus died in the fourth year hundred," I informed Sharon.

She wrinkled her forehead, "He died when?"

"In the fourth year hundred, you know, three hundred fifty or so."

Sharon thought a minute. "You mean in the fourth century?"

"Ja, ja that's it. Don't forget to stick your wish list in your shoe."

Sharon grinned sheepishly, "I'm a little too old for that. What will your parents think?"

"No worries, only Saint Nikolaus will see the list," I joked.

Before we retired that night, we agreed to put our shoes and wish lists in front of the bedroom door. Both papers read: *Stiefel*—Boots. When we got up the next morning, we snickered when the lists were gone and our shoes brimmed with goodies. "See, Saint Nikolaus was here after all," I teased.

After breakfast, we took the subway to attend a *Weihnachtsfeier*—Christmas celebration—at my high school. Each desk was decorated with a spray of fresh conifers, a small white candle, a lantern made from gold foil, and a *Pfeffernuß*—a spice cookie. Several of my classmates entertained. Yvonne played Christmas carols on her accordion while the rest of us sang along. Heike danced to a selection from Swan Lake. Someone read a Christmas story, and then Santa came with token gifts for each of us, including Sharon. The presents were part of our holiday *Julklapp*—Secret Santa—tradition.

"Your celebration was very festive," Sharon commented afterwards. "But I didn't see anyone wear red or green."

"It's not customary. If we dress up, it is usually in black, gold, or silver. But I heard that Christmas in America is celebrated with dances and fireworks. Like New Years. Is that true?" I asked Sharon.

"Not fireworks generally, but I think our celebrations are a little less reflective than yours."

"Would you like to see the sights of Berlin?" I asked the next morning. "Many of the landmarks are right here in our district. We can walk to them."

"Sounds like fun," Sharon replied, not realizing that she would walk all over town, putting more miles on her soles in a single day than she had all summer. Travel by foot, bus, and subway was the norm for a Berlin teen.

Leaving our apartment, I informed Sharon. "The city has twenty districts. Eight are in the Russian sector; six in the American, four in the British, and two in the French zone."

"Which sector are we in now?" Sharon asked.

"We are in Charlottenburg, the British sector."

"Where is the Russian sector," Sharon wanted to know.

"Not far from here. My father will drive us there some other day."

We walked the four blocks to the *Funkturm*—Berlin's famous radio tower—where my father was at work taking photos of tourists next to Santa. "During the rest of the year, my father works with a man in a bear costume," I told Sharon. "The bear is in our city's coat of arms."

We continued to the stadium, built for the 1936 summer Olympics, where Jesse Owens, the black American track-and-field athlete, won four gold medals. "Because he was of color, Hitler refused to shake his hand," I told Sharon.

It had been a long walk, and she swore she would never again go along with my walking tour ideas. "Please," she begged. "I'm bushed."

"You have grown roots like a bush?" I asked.

"No, I mean I'm tired and exhausted."

We hopped on the subway and returned home.

On the second Sunday in December, we lit two of the four candles on our *Adventskranz*—Advent wreath. I explained that the tradition of the wreath harked back to pagan times. We lit the first candle on the fourth Sunday before Christmas, then one more each Sunday until all four candles were lit on the last Sunday before Christmas.

During the days that followed, my parents, Sharon, and I visited one department store after another on West Berlin's glitzy boulevard, the Kurfürstendamm, affectionately called the Kudamm, searching for a pair of black boots for Sharon. Santa hoped to make her Christmas wish come true. In vain. The German fashion rage in 1960 was white ankle boots. Like gulls scurrying along the pavement, white boots were ubiquitous. No self-respecting store stocked black ones.

Defeated, we gave up and visited the *Charlottenburger Schloß*—the Charlottenburg castle, built for the first king and queen of Prussia at the end of the seventeenth century.

Next, we visited the zoo. "It is the oldest zoo in Germany. The first animals were donated by King Friedrich Wilhelm IV, the King of Prussia," I lectured.

"The zoo didn't get damaged during the war? Even though it's right in the heart of town?" Sharon asked.

"It did get damaged. By the end of the war, this entire area was destroyed. I read that less than one hundred animals survived."

"Most of our holiday celebration occurs on *Heiligabend*—Christmas Eve," I said one afternoon when Sharon and I returned home from a walk around the neighborhood. "Here in the north of Germany, Santa arrives on Christmas Eve. In the south, the *Christkindl*, the Jesus child, brings the gifts. We open them on Christmas Eve," I explained and went on to say that Martin Luther started the tradition in the sixteenth century because he wanted to shift the celebration away from St. Nick's Day. He wanted Christmas to honor Christ, not a saint. But both traditions continued side by side.

"Does your Santa come down the chimney?" Sharon wanted to know.

"No, we have radiant heat."

Scotty and Marilyn Kelly arrived on December 23. Our fresh fir tree already resting in a bucket of water on the balcony, it was ready to be placed in a stand in the corner of the living room. Sharon and I decorated it with small white electric lights, gold glass balls, straw ornaments, and silver tinsel. Then we placed a large gold star atop of the tree. "We used to put wax candles on the tree," I told her, "but we are afraid of a fire."

Following afternoon coffee and *Stollen*—the traditional holiday yeast bread with raisins, candied citrus, almonds, and cardamom—Scotty, Marilyn, Sharon, and I took a leisurely walk around the nearby lake. When we returned, the Christmas tree was lit and gifts were placed, unwrapped, underneath the tree. It was time for the *Bescherung*—the presentation of the gifts. A couple of white spots immediately caught our eyes. There was a pair of white boots for me and an identical pair with black elastic at ankle height for Sharon. It was the best Santa could do for black boots that year.

At 11:30 p.m. on Christmas Eve, church bells rang, and we walked to the nearby Canisius Church for midnight service.

To the Kelly's surprise, Christmas Eve was followed by not one, but two legal holidays: the first and the second *Weihnachtstage*—Christmas days. "December twenty-fourth is for the gift exchange between immediate family members. December twenty-fifth is for the goose or turkey feast and the gift exchange with the extended family, and the second Christmas Day is celebrated with friends," I explained. In lieu of celebrating with extended family, which my family never did, everyone squeezed into our car to go sightseeing. My father chauffeured and I played tour guide. Our first stop was the famous *Brandenburger Tor*—Brandenburg Gate. In olden times, visitors had entered the city through such gates. "It was built the late seventeen hundreds," I told the Kellys and explained that the chariot on top was driven by Victoria, the Roman goddess of victory. "After Napoleon defeated Germany in the war of 1806, he brought it back to Paris. Eight years later, the Germans defeated him and returned it to Berlin."

The next stop was the postwar Russian War Memorial, an imposing semicircular set of arches topped by a bronze of the Unknown Soldier. "Even though we are in the British sector," I said, "the memorial is guarded by Russian soldiers."

"Are those Russian tanks?" Scotty asked, pointing to two tanks flanking the monument.

"Those were the first two Red Army tanks that entered the city in 1945." I went on to explain that the monument was built by the Russian government to remind us that it was the Red Army that liberated Berlin from the Nazis. "Berliners call it the 'The Tomb to the Unknown Rapist,'" I added, "because of the hundreds of thousands of *Russenbabies*—Russian babies—that were born as a result of rapes and the equally large number of abortions that were performed."

Then we were off to the *Kaiser-Wilhelm-Gedächtniskirche*—the Emporer William Memorial Church—another of Berlin's famous landmarks. I told our little group that the church was built in the 1890s, and that most of it was destroyed in one of the 363 air raids on Berlin during World War II. Only part of the spire and the entrance survived. The British Royal Air Force bombed the church in late November of 1943. Using his hands and feet, my father tried to add that my mother and he had lived in an apartment building only a few blocks to the west, in the Ansbacher Straße, at that time. Their apartment was also destroyed during that fateful November night. "My Dad says, in that one air raid alone, two thousand people were killed and 175,000 people became homeless," I translated.

I had a difficult time keeping a straight face when I articulated the word "people." Every German child knew "people" to be a German slang word for a phallic symbol. But among our small group of six, interested in the fate of the church and the residences surrounding it, no one but me was aware of the colloquial meaning of the word. Only the corners of my mouth twitched.

Toward the end of the day, my father drove us to the Eastern border of West Berlin where large white signs with big black block letters cautioned:

ACHTUNG!
SIE VERLASSEN JETZT
WEST BERLIN
(Attention! You are now leaving West Berlin)

"It doesn't look like a border," Marilyn said. "How do you know it is?"

"Do you see the white line painted on the asphalt? It marks the boundary between East and West Berlin. It's almost thirty miles long and close to one hundred miles if you also count the border between West Berlin and East Germany which surrounds us. Although people can walk or drive from one sector to another, they must show their identification papers," I explained.

On December 27, Scotty, Marilyn, and Sharon returned to Ramstein, leaving our family to usher in the New Year in solitude. Even though my parents, and especially my father, had thoroughly enjoyed hosting the Kelly family, they breathed a sigh of relief. We had our small apartment to ourselves again. My mother, who had felt anxious about meeting the Americans, had come to adore Marilyn's uncomplicated nature, even though neither of the two women spoke the other's language. My father, far less inhibited, communicated almost without help, using gestures along with the few British words he knew.

In the car, on the way back from dropping off the Kelly family at the airport, my shoulders slowly dropped. I suspected that in the days and weeks to follow, the hated, customary silence would return to our home.

New Years Eve

OVER THE COURSE OF THE NEXT FOUR DAYS I turned quiet. By the time New Year's Eve rolled around, I was downright miserable. During both visits with the Kellys that year, my arc of vision had exploded. I had been introduced to new ways of thinking. Marilyn had talked to Sharon and me with ease and openness and had offered advice only when asked. She had been careful not to use her parental authority arbitrarily. Although Sharon also lived within a framework of rules, she was given some control over her life. Now, I, too, wanted to be allowed to question values, challenge opinions, and debate rules. This time, the rubber band had not only yielded a little; it had stretched permanently. Like a morning mist, the desire for change had slipped into my cells.

But as expected, after the Kellys returned to Ramstein, our life returned to my family's version of normal, which meant that each member of the cast performed according to a script:

My father brewed the coffee in the morning, ate breakfast, departed for work, returned at noon—sharp—for his hot midday meal, took a forty-five-minute nap, went back to work, and headed home in time for a cold supper.

My mother woke me, made breakfast, dusted, shopped for lunch and dinner, cooked and served lunch, napped, took care of infrequent business calls and correspondence while cooking and cleaning.

I ate breakfast ahead of the rest of the family, left for school, returned home for a reheated lunch, took a forced one-hour nap, completed school assignments, and joined my parents for supper.

With the commencement of the seven o'clock evening television news, the daily family drama spiraled toward its climax with my father asking me to fetch his slippers along with a beer and a "bump," a grain-based *Schnaps*. Throughout the news, my parents commented on the ineptitude of government officials while I continued to ferry additional beers and bumps between kitchen and living room.

At eight o'clock, unless it was movie night, the set was turned off, and a hush fell over the room. My father lost himself in the daily paper while my mother thumbed through a magazine. Only the rustling of pages and occasional clicks of bottle and glass on the marbleized tabletop broke the silence. Feeling superfluous, I retreated to my room. I gladly would have traded two of our three daily meals for some conversation.

It was a daily dance in which each family member stepped in perfect synch with one another. Everyone's steps were expected and accepted by the others. I had never done what I wanted to do. I had always done what my parents expected me to do. All my life, I had been the perfect little girl—now I was sick of it.

Something fundamental had changed inside of me. Since my initiation the previous summer into my American friends' active lifestyles, I had wanted to duplicate their level of freedom in my Berlin life. I longed for autonomy and silently scrutinized the rationale behind the many familiar family conventions I had previously accepted without protest. Now, it felt as though I was peering through a pair of binoculars after focusing the lens. All of a sudden, I was aware of the dearth of two-way communication, collaboration, acceptance, compromise, and laughter in my family. Their absence stood in stark contrast to the conviviality and support that had filled these walls just days earlier while we had hosted the Kelly family. It was as if darkness had rolled over the landscape with their departure. I missed Sharon—the sister I never had. And I missed Marilyn—the mother I had always wanted.

Moments later, a tidal wave of guilt came crushing down on me. Its weight almost squeezed the air out of my lungs, making me feel dizzy. *Haven't my parents opened their arms, their home, and their pocketbooks to my American friends? What is wrong with me? How can I be so ungrateful? Doesn't my mother cook for my father and me? Doesn't she wash and sew for us? Doesn't she take care of me when I'm ill?* I struggled with a gnawing ambivalence. Why did I find it so difficult to feel and express affection toward my mother? Sometimes, I had to force myself to hug her, even though I cuddled with my father and squeezed Tante Michen at the slightest encouragement. In short order I had willingly thrown my arms around Scotty and Marilyn, complete strangers until this summer.

Then I recalled how, in first grade, we made Mother's Day cards from construction paper in school and wrote inside, "*Mutti, Du bist die Beste*—Mom, you are the best." In the years that followed, teachers encouraged us to compose our own loving Mother's Day messages. That's when card writing became tricky. Something about my mother—maybe the deep parenthesis of displeasure on either side of her mouth—discouraged me from being intimate. Mutti wasn't uncaring; she hugged me, I knew that. Just the other day, while talking to a neighbor, she had put her arm around me, pulling me closer. "That's my daughter," she had said with pride, bragging about some small thing I had done. But somehow this, like most of her embraces, felt more like an "I own you" hug than an "I love you for who you are" cuddle.

With Marilyn I had often walked hand in hand; but I avoided holding hands with my mother. While visiting Berlin's sights during Christmas, Mutti must have noticed because, when we stopped at the Kaiser Wilhelm Memorial Church, she had tried to slip her hand into mine. As usual, I had pulled away. I suppose I withdrew because Mutti was my master, not my pal, like Marilyn.

When I stayed with the Kellys in Ramstein, I had seen Scotty kiss his wife every morning before leaving for work and again upon returning home in the evening. I had never seen my parents kiss. Until I had watched the Kellys, I had assumed that kissing stopped when people got married. Many times, I had witnessed Marilyn rub Scotty's neck and shoulders after he had had a rough day at the office. I had never seen such intimacy between my parents. Do the Kellys have an exceptional relationship, or is theirs an American-style marriage and different from a German one, I wondered.

Not long ago, our high-school teacher, Frau Brunk, had initiated us into the secrets of matrimony. "Girls," she had cautioned, "if you want to get married some day, my advice is to play down your intelligence. The male ego is fragile. Men don't like brainy girls. They're looking for helplessness because they want to feel superior. Men want to be in the position to teach their little woman. They want her to be an extension of themselves."

On the way home from school that day, a lively discussion had ensued among my friends. "Do you think men are really like that?" Frau Brunk was an attractive, shapely blond in her late forties. She had never married, though some famous men, like the Austrian scuba diver and underwater filmmaker, Hans Hass, were among her closest friends. "She's bound to speak from experience," we concluded. Frau Brunk's remarks had put a new spin on romance and marriage. I had imagined a full partnership with my future beloved in which each spouse respected and supported the other and in which both partners formed a team with common objectives. Now, I questioned whether this notion was realistic. Staying single did not seem like such a bad idea anymore.

By the time New Year's Eve arrived, I was utterly disheartened. The last day of the year was always depressing, but this year, the day was in a class by itself. Nineteen-sixty had been full of excitement and new experiences for me. I had been on television; my name had been in the newspapers on three different occasions during the year; and I had acquired a "sister," host parents, and wonderful friends. I asked myself how the coming year could possibly match that.

As usual at year's end, radio and television commentators summed up the positive aspects of the outgoing year and spun doom and gloom for the future. Someone always alluded to the powerful metaphor of the wise, old man handing over the scepter to the wet-behind-the-ears toddler. My resulting sense of hopelessness had never been more compelling than this year.

In addition, in recent months, the news had been chock-full of speculations about the future for West Berlin. Throughout my life, our political situation had been a precarious one. Since the midforties, when I was born, Berlin had been the focus of an escalating Cold War. The Soviets wanted nothing less than for the Allies to surrender the Western sectors of the city. The 1948/1949 airlift had kept us alive by supplying all food, coal, and raw materials by air. Due to the Marshall Plan, tax credits, and subsidies, our economy had improved over time. Now there was virtually no unemployment.

The East, on the other hand, was heavily indebted and suffered serious shortages of raw materials and food. Attracted by higher salaries, resettlement grants and the ready availability of consumer goods offered by the west, many East German doctors, nurses, teachers, skilled workers, and engineers chose to cross the border. Once in the West, they were directed to the *Marienfelde* reception camp. After potential spies had been filtered out, the refugees were flown to West Germany where jobs and accommodations waited.

But despite West Berlin's improved economy, our businesses had relocated en masse to West Germany. They had done so to escape political uncertainties, and people followed the jobs. Just when my life was supposed to blossom, my hometown was slowly dying.

Now, the Cold War was heating up again. Soviet leader Nikita Khrushchev intimated that he was running out of patience with the Western Allies. At a September meeting of the United Nations, he had put his cantankerous temperament on display again when he banged his shoe on the table. He liked to refer to Berlin as "the testicles of the West." Every time he wanted to cause the Western world a little pain, he said, all he had to do was to squeeze West Berlin. Lately, he had been doing a lot of squeezing. What is going to happen, I wondered? *Might we wake up behind the Iron Curtain one morning?*

Even before the clock struck midnight, I wished I could turn it back and relive 1960. While people around the world ushered in the New Year with champagne, apprehension radiated through my body like a series of low-voltage shocks. A mounting weight of hopelessness settled on my shoulders. Barely fifteen years old, I asked myself whether it was possible that the best part of my life and my greatest successes were already behind me.

The Trouble with Boys

ONCE A WEEK A MOVIE WAS SHOWN at city hall, and many of my friends attended these free presentations. I had been barred from joining them in the past, but at the beginning of the New Year, my parents eased the rules. "From now on, you can go to the Monday night movies with your classmates," they announced.

"Great! How about theater and dances?" I asked, blindsided by a generous dose of hope.

"As long as a parent or a teacher is present."

Wonderful. Nineteen sixty-one was off to a great start. Had Marilyn and Scotty's relationship with Sharon made a lasting impression on Mutti and Pappi? Had my parents weighed their own authoritarian approach against Marilyn and Scotty's democratic style of parenting and come up in favor of the latter? I did not ask. My questions would only trigger sermons on the presumptuousness of children who stuck their noses into things they were too young to understand.

Full of optimism, I interpreted my new freedom to be the first step toward independence. Further autonomy would undoubtedly follow once I had demonstrated responsible conduct. The new rules represented a turnabout, a paradigm shift, in our house. My parents had decided to finally treat me like an adult instead of a little kid. Immediately, I began experimenting with new attitudes, behaviors, and fashions in hopes of discovering my true identity. I feared that I had already fallen behind socially by not having participated in many of the pursuits my friends enjoyed on a regular basis. To create the patina of normalcy, I had often pretended that I had something important planned instead of admitting that my parents kept me from joining in activities. I also still felt a bit awkward in the company of boys. Being in an all-girls class had limited my exposure to young men. But under my parents' new guidelines, I would be able to catch up in a hurry. I was sure of that.

Soon, my parents' new rules were put to the first test. In late spring, my class hosted several out-of-town high-school groups, including a coed class from Sweden. For the first time, I was allowed to fully participate in the goings-on. Since none of my classmates spoke our visitors' language and the Swedes did not speak German, we conversed in broken English. The resulting gibberish added to the charm of the experience. During their two-week stay, our visitors participated in many of our class activities. On several occasions, we took them on tours of the city, to the movies, and to the theater. All of our adventures were teacher supervised.

A blond, curly-haired young Swede awakened my romantic interests. When Gunnar Erikson bestowed on me his black-and-white photograph, along with a pink foam-rubber carnation, generously doused with his musky cologne, it nearly caused me an arrhythmia.

One evening, Gunnar and I—the rest of my classmates must have been present as well—enjoyed a movie at the *Marmor Palast*. My mother queried me the following day about the plot. All I could remember were some Romans in chariots. I vaguely recalled that the name of the film might have been *Ben-Hur*. My mother's alarm bells soared to code red. The more she probed, the less talkative I became. Why should I share my feelings? After all, Mutti and Pappi never talked about such things.

To my mother's relief, the Swedes left shortly thereafter. I turned melancholy for a day or two and then moved on. But my mother got sick. "I have a terrible headache," she said and went to bed for several days. Apparently, the fear that I was still too naïve and could easily be taken advantage of by one of these young, hormone-laden brutes had been too much for her delicate health. I knew it could not have been a migraine that incapacitated her, because she quit getting them while I was still in grade school. In my younger years, she had suffered terribly from the neurological disorder. But when general practitioners failed to uncover the cause of her migraines, my mother visited a specialist who determined that exploratory surgery was required to rule out a brain tumor. Horrified, my mother fled the doctor's office and never again experienced a migraine. Now, they were just headaches.

With the approach of summer, Herr Gimmler, our school principal, entrusted four honor students with the *Kartenamt*, the checking in and out of the school's maps and charts. He appointed Helmut and Achim from the boys' class and Doris and me from my girls' class. The four of us felt honored to have been singled out by the principal and took our responsibility seriously. During midmorning breaks, we rushed to the map room and signed out geography, biology, and history paraphernalia. Initially, we discharged our duties with pride and efficiency while taking little notice of each other. But soon, a friendly banter developed. Helmut, a shy, pimple-faced youth, became rather attentive toward me. He helped me roll up heavy maps, brought me a chair, and paid attention to everything I said. I felt flattered by his overtures.

One day, he asked me to join him for a swim in Lake Jungfernheide after school. He must like me, I thought, not entirely with displeasure, and agreed to a harmless rendezvous at the lake. Upon returning home from school that afternoon, I informed my mother of the invitation and my acceptance.

"You can cancel that plan right now," my mother replied. "You're not going. You're staying home. I'm sure you must have some homework to do."

"But, Mutti, I've already accepted. I told him I'd meet him at the lake at three. He'll be waiting."

"I told you. You're not going. End of discussion."

How I hated those words. "Mutti, please. I'll tell him that I won't be able to go in the future," I pleaded. "But let me go today. I've promised."

I was not romantically interested in Helmut, but I recoiled at my mother's arbitrary decision.

"Who is this boy anyway? What makes him so important that you have to meet with him today?"

"He's one of the four of us Herr Gimmler appointed to the *Karte-namt*. And I told him I'd be there. That's why."

"He's probably some *Halbstarker*," My mother said. "He'll figure out soon enough that you're not coming."

My back stiffened. *Halbstarker* was a derogatory term, suggesting immaturity and lack of breeding. It literally meant "half-strong." "We're only going swimming!" I said with a tinge of defiance in my voice. "Why can't I go?"

"Because I said so. Do as you're told. Now, go and do your homework, and quit pestering me."

I was taken aback. "Because I said so" was hardly a valid argument. Marilyn and Scotty would never have responded like that.

Under the guise of going to the library with Tina, and contrary to my mother's directive, I got on the bus to the lake. At least, I would tell Helmut that I would not be able to stay for a swim. Since admitting the truth was too humiliating, I invented an excuse. Then I immediately rode the bus home, still fuming.

I had barely entered our flat, when my mother asked, "Where have you been?"

"At the library with Tina. I told you."

"What book did you get?"

"I didn't get one."

"What book did Tina get?"

"I don't know." Unprepared for my mother's line of interrogation, I felt heat rise from my neck to the top of my scalp. *I'm giving myself away.*

"You didn't go to the library at all, did you?" my mother barked. "You went to the lake against my wishes and met with that boy, didn't you?"

"Yeah," I admitted, caught in the act.

The consequence of my disobedience was four weeks of house arrest for insolence. It was my first experience with prolonged punitive confinement. Four weeks. For lying because I wasn't allowed to display good manners? I seethed internally but feigned indifference. I was not going to let my mother see how much she had hurt me.

In my mind, I kept going over the incident and concluded that I was being punished for something other than my unauthorized trip to the lake. My mother doesn't trust me alone with a young man. She's afraid that Helmut will take indecent liberties with me, I decided. Dialogue with my mother involving subjects of a sexual nature had been awkward since I was a little girl. I remembered the time when I was six and had inquired about the stork for the second time. After concluding that sharing life with a little playmate would be better than a lonely existence, I had asked her, "Mutti, how does the stork know which house to bring the babies to?"

"Because the moms and dads sprinkle sugar on the windowsill."

For days, I sprinkled sugar on the kitchen sill, but the stork never came.

Eventually, my mother took me aside. "The stork doesn't really deliver babies. That's just a fairy tale, like Snow White. You're a big girl now. The truth is, the mom carries the baby under her heart until it's ready to come out."

That was earth-shaking news. I mulled it over. "But how does the mom know when the baby is ready to come out?"

"People tell her."

I was baffled. How did people know? Was I carrying a baby under my heart and didn't know it? Could I be a mom tomorrow? Prodding my mother failed to extract further details.

"You'll understand some day when you get older," was all she said.

Sex was the one phase of my education my mother had not pressed vigorously. Until I started school, pregnancy and childbearing remained mysteries. Elementary school proved eye opening. Reproduction was the number one topic of interest among second graders. During breaks, we secretly circulated drawings of male and female reproductive organs. By age eight, all of the kids in my class were well informed on the physical aspects of reproduction. But I did not share my newfound knowledge at home. I held out for the *Aufklärung*, the revelation. A number of my classmates had already had this elusive one-on-one with their mothers. I waited. When nothing happened, I took matters into my own hands.

One day, when I was twelve, my mother was dusting knickknacks in the living room. The moment was perfect. Fiddling with the radio knobs, I blurted out, "Mutti, do you know what a midwife is?"

My mother froze, looked at me sideways, and said, "Yes?"

I waited for the "revelation," but Mutti remained mum. Apparently, knowing about the midwife's role in childbirth made an *Aufklärung* superfluous.

Now, I figured I was barred from going swimming with Helmut because the one-on-one with my mother had lacked a few details. My dating future could turn out to be problematic, I speculated.

Storm Clouds Gather

IN THE EARLY PART OF 1961, a pall seemed to gather over West Berlin. The Cold War between East and West that had begun after World War II, had picked up speed in the fifties, and now unfurled in the sixties. Like a strand of hair in a braid, West Berlin's destiny was intertwined with the negotiations between the superpowers. Bombarded daily by reports of unsettling events and powerless to act on our own behalf, we prayed that the Western Allies would not sell us out in exchange for a deal with the Soviets. Sometimes, Berliners felt like dependent little children, a feeling all too familiar to me.

Since 1950, first secretary of the East German Socialist Unity Party, Walter Ulbricht, had pushed five-year plans for the formation of *Landwirtschaftliche Produktionsgenossenschaften*—agricultural cooperatives. Now, in 1961, he boasted that ninety percent of all agricultural land had been collectivized. The *Deutschlandsender*, East Germany's chief radio station, praised his reforms. According to their broadcasts, state production goals were not only met, but greatly exceeded.

The Western Radio in the American Sector, RIAS, on the other hand, reported that the East German economy was in serious trouble. It claimed that production lagged far behind demand, and that the East suffered serious shortages of raw materials, industrial products, and food. Only three years earlier, Walter Ulbricht had predicted that East Germany would soon overtake West Germany in the production of goods. Instead, the disparity between East and West became more apparent every day. RIAS commentators upheld the view that Ulbricht had failed to create a healthy economy. They said he had only created the illusion of one when he had ordered an East German currency reform in 1957. At that time, he had limited the amount of funds eligible for exchange to three hundred marks (less than fifty dollars at the time) and required that the entire process be concluded within ten hours.

Western analysts suggested that the real purpose of that intervention had been a reduction of the amount of money in circulation. Less cash in people's pockets meant less buying power. Diminished purchasing power assured that goods remained longer on the shelves. And well-stocked shelves created the impression of a healthy economy. In reality, RIAS said, the only thing Ulbricht had achieved was that most East German citizens had lost their life's savings. All of these past and present issues were talked about in early 1961 again. Interpretations differed sharply.

In the meantime, Walter Ulbricht continued his reforms. Troubling changes were announced daily. Although the East German government did not allow its citizens to move to West Germany, East Germans could go to East Berlin. From there, many crossed to West Berlin and never returned. Now, Ulbricht was closing that door, Western reports stated. East German citizens were now forced to acquire near-impossible-to-obtain permits to cross the border into West Berlin. Violators faced three-year prison sentences.

Powerless to change their government through elections, East Germans chose to leave. Some two and a half million people had fled since 1945, about fifteen percent of the state's entire population. But the numbers were not all that concerned the East German government. What was even worse, most of those who fled were young people. More than three-quarters were under the age of forty-five, and half were younger than twenty-five. East Germany was losing the cream of its educated professionals and skilled workers, Western sources said.

Ulbricht also made transit between West Berlin and West Germany more difficult. Increasingly, Western travelers were searched, harassed, held up, or denied passage. My father had been detained on several occasions. One time, when he was returning home from a photo shoot in West Germany, border guards asked him to wait in a small trailer without food, water, or communication. After sixteen hours, they let him go. "We doubted your birth date," was all they said.

In November 1958, Soviet leader Nikita Khrushchev had given the Western Allies an ultimatum. "Within six months," he had said, "I want you to sign a peace treaty relative to Germany and to turn West Berlin into a demilitarized 'free city.'" In case of Western noncooperation he had threatened, Moscow would unilaterally sign a treaty with East Germany and turn over all access rights to West Berlin to the East Germans. The possibility terrified West Berliners. Under this scenario, the Western Allies would be required to cross East German borders if they wanted to defend us. That could mean war—possibly nuclear war. If they decided not to defend us, it could mean that West Berlin would be absorbed by the East.

Khrushchev had warned time and again of his plan to modify West Berlin's status. And by March 1961, the worrisome incidents began to multiply. When President John F. Kennedy reiterated that the United States was bound "by treaty and conviction" to maintain the freedom of West Berlin, his assurance initially calmed our fears. America, the super-power, was going to protect us.

But a month later, when the Russians put the first man, Lieutenant Yuri Gagarin, into space, we wavered. Even though Gagarin had entered the cosmos for only a few hours, the Soviet achievement suggested a much greater military potential than we had imagined. Was America still capable of protecting us?

A few days later, we learned of the unsuccessful attempt by the United States-backed Cuban exiles to overthrow the government of Cuban dictator, Fidel Castro. Confidence in our protectors slipped another notch.

Then Ulbricht tightened his grip on West Berlin again. For the first time, East Germany required that diplomats, accredited to West Germany, seek permission from East German authorities to enter the East. Border agents even turned back Walter Dowling, the US ambassador to West Germany because he could not produce a permit.

I was fifteen years old, and the pervasive feeling of panic snuck up on me as well. Throughout my childhood, I had listened to stories about how difficult everyday life had been during the blockade. But during those days, the airlift had kept West Berlin alive. Now, the only alternative seemed to be war. Was it likely that the Allies would risk war to save us? Would we find ourselves behind the *Eiserne Vorhang*—the Iron Curtain? Was war even a realistic option?

In early June, Kennedy and Khrushchev met in Vienna. West Berliners put all their hopes in Kennedy's ability to appease the Soviet leader. But our dreams were quickly dashed when the meeting produced less than desired results. Khrushchev again made it clear that he intended to end all occupation rights in Berlin by the end of 1961. He insisted that his decision was "firm and irrevocable."

When Walter Ulbricht repeated the results of the Vienna Summit on East German television the following day, more refugees fled East Berlin than on any other day of the year, despite Ulbricht's assurance that, "*Niemand hat die Absicht, eine Mauer zu errichten*—No one has the intention of building a wall."

The charged atmosphere became a nail-biting one. Something was in the air, but what? Discussions about leaving West Berlin became commonplace. People wanted to leave before the Iron Curtain cut them off from the West. "I wouldn't mind moving to Hamburg," my father said more than once, but my mother would not hear of it.

In the middle of July, The USSR conducted a massive exercise in the Arctic Circle, involving nuclear missiles, capable of reaching even American territory. Now, it appeared clear that the Soviets were preparing for the possibility of war—nuclear war.

At the end of the month, Kennedy appeared on television saying, "America will make good on our commitment to the two million free people of the city." His words no longer sounded as reassuring as they once had. But convinced or not, our ability to lead normal lives depended wholly on John F. Kennedy and America. Was he willing to go to war over Berlin?

The East German exodus reached critical levels. With the tightening of restrictions on movement between East and West Berlin, *Torschlußpanik*—literally the fear of closing the gate—spread throughout East and West Germany. West Berlin seemed to throb with danger.

But all that changed for me on August 7, when Marilyn, Scotty, and Sharon Kelly arrived in Berlin for a four-day visit. Marilyn's mother, Mary, accompanied them. Granny Mary was unlike any grandmother I had ever met. She did not wear sensible shoes or old-fashioned clothes. To the contrary, she was divorced, fashionably dressed, wore makeup, and had a job. And what a job! She was a member of the state of Connecticut's House of Representatives. I was in awe. This lady defied all stereotyping.

The anxiety I had harbored for the past six months vanished in a flash. I no longer worried about West Berlin's safety or about having to live behind the Iron Curtain. Being once more in the fold of the Kelly family took away all of my fears. *Everything will be all right. America will protect us. AMERICA.* The word sounded almost sacred.

Pre-Wall

UNAWARE OF THE IMMINENT DEVELOPMENTS, the Kellys returned to Wiesbaden on August 11, two days before the Cold War once again focused on Berlin. With a teen's uncanny facility for changing moods quickly, I quit worrying about Berlin's political situation, now that I felt protected again by the superpower, America. My generation had grown up in a Cold War environment. The endless communist threats had produced a numbing effect akin to commercials. "You know," I told Christina, "political slogans remind me of sitting in church during Latin mass. You hear the words but have no idea what's being said."

After the Kellys' Berlin visit, I took it for granted that America would protect us and stopped worrying about the crisis. I had a bigger concern: a recent development at school.

My two girlfriends, Doris and Christina, had started to exclude me from their after-school activities. There had been no quarrel, there just did not seem be room for me in our threesome anymore. I felt hurt and dejected. When no one was watching, I allowed my tears to run freely. Belonging meant everything to me.

Making new friends became my primary objective. Aside from one-on-one friendships, there were several cliques in class that loosely linked girls with shared attitudes and interests. The athletes were drawn to kids with physical prowess; the fashion-conscious enjoyed dressing and talked about the newest fads; the achievers valued academic excellence. And then there were the popular girls, the leaders, who were liked by everybody. They were self-assured, outgoing, and set the tone in class.

Being brought up to compliance and submission, I had never made it into the popular clique. I fit in with the achievers, called *Streberleichen*, literally "achiever corpses." We were respected for our academic achievements but sometimes also poked fun at for our blind pursuit of scholastic success. Would the popular girls accept me into their circle?

I was positive that Mutti would not allow me to befriend any of these girls once she learned of their backgrounds. To satisfy my mother's criteria, a friend of mine had to come from a good home and excel in school. That meant she had to have two parents. Single, absent, or divorced parents were out of the question. And a child from a bad neighborhood did not qualify either.

Unfortunately, most of the popular girls had only average grades and lived in marginal settings. One girl was raised by a single mom; another lived with her family in Berlin's red-light district where rents were cheap; a third was a "foreigner" from the Middle East; the group leader was involved in a relationship with a man almost ten years her senior. Only two of the girls potentially met my mother's standards.

I was desperate for friends and could not hold out for a girlfriend who satisfied my mother's norms. Working hard at befriending these popular teens, I lied to my parents about my new companions. Since my mother did not encourage my bringing friends home, and since she did not socialize with other parents, my evasions and lies went undetected.

Joining the group of popular girls with backgrounds so different from my own unlocked a new world for me. With one exception, we were all only-children, born after World War II when economic constraints made it nearly impossible for families to support more than one child. Without siblings, we became extremely close and shared every detail of our lives. Many of the others' experiences differed radically from mine. Our conversations centered not only on who went with whom, what acne medication worked, or what was in fashion, but they also included disclosure of details from the most mundane to the intimate. Everything was hashed out; notes were compared; trivia was shared. I was thrilled that they accepted me into their circle.

"I've always wanted a *Stupsnase*—a pug nose," I admitted one day.
"Your nose looks fine."
"I don't like it. I tried to turn it into a pug nose a few years ago."
"How?"
"I figured if Chinese women can bind their feet and turn under their toes, I could tie up my nose and make it a pug nose."

"You're kidding." The girls laughed. "You bound your nose?"

"Sort of. I rolled some hair into two curlers and anchored them with curler picks to the top of my head. Then I tied a scarf around the tip of my nose and knotted it between the two curlers."

"And?"

"Nothing. I did that every night. When I woke up in the morning, I always had a deep crease across my nose. But thirty minutes later, my nose was down again."

Between laughs, we shared many personal stories like this. My girl-friends became the most important people in my world.

Along with my new friends, I adopted new study habits. The six of us swapped assignments and often completed them just before class. I lost my compulsion to do homework altogether. It was a new way of life. Exciting. Free. I acquired a sense of humor, I told jokes, I performed skits. Thanks to my solid foundation, I stayed in the top five percent of my class so that my parents remained oblivious to the changes in my life. It remained my little secret.

In the afternoons, I liked to watch American sitcoms on television. My favorite show was *Vater ist der Beste—Father Knows Best.* Betty, Bud, and Kathy could always turn to their parents who enjoyed their children's friends and offered help when asked, but otherwise held back. Their loving family interactions made me envious. Those were the kind of parents I longed for.

Along with sitcoms, I adored everything American: fashion, music, and movies. Unlike Germans, Americans appeared to appreciate youth. That seemed evident by their recently elected young president, John F. Kennedy, and his stunningly beautiful wife.

Visiting the Kellys the previous summer had started to unlock a door. My new friends helped to open it even more. I now wanted my parents to stop hovering and began to openly question their values, to challenge their opinions, and to debate their rules. I looked for a rationale behind every request and no longer accepted arbitrary rules without protest. At times, I even felt the urge to oppose whatever they proposed, "just be-cause" as my mother liked to say.

My parents did not intend to put up with my antics and immediately called me to order. "Don't you dare TELL me what you're going to do. I'm not going to tolerate that sort of behavior. Let's not forget that you're the child here, and we're the parents. You ASK for permission," my mother said.

A tug-of-war ensued. I set out on a crusade of silent resistance by visibly ignoring my parents. Without saying a word that could possibly offend, I would make plain by my actions that so far as I was concerned, my parents did not exist. There were a hundred ways of doing this: I would engage in an ever-so-subtle whistle while my parents lectured me. If questioned, I'd say, "Wh-a-a-t? I'm just hot." Or I would roll my eyes to show what I thought of their fossilized attitudes. "Wh-a-a-t? I was just looking up." Sometimes, I would address myself to others, completely ignoring my parents' presence. But all I really wanted was to be allowed to find my own path and to have the freedom to make my own mistakes. I craved acknowledgement that I had come of age.

Barbed Wire Fence

THE SUN WAS UP ALREADY. The time was six o'clock in the morning on Sunday, August 13, 1961. I usually had this early hour to myself. Reaching for my small transistor radio, a gift from the Kellys, I popped in earphones. Then I turned the dial to the American Forces Network, aware that I was violating a standing house rule.

"Turn off that dreadful noise," my parents routinely commanded at the first English-sounding word. "Why can't you listen to something that all of us can understand?" Mutti and Pappi hated AFN. But in the early morning hours, when they were still asleep, I often enjoyed a clandestine hour of forbidden listening.

Turning the dial to AFN, I caught the last words of Egon Bahr's news brief on RIAS, Radio in the American Sector.

. . . MAYOR WILLY BRANDT . . . RETURNING TO BERLIN . . . EXPECTED TO ARRIVE AT 8:00 A.M. . . .

I continued turning the dial and, unintentionally, picked up the typical party line drivel of the East German *Deutschlandsender*. Used to endless communist propaganda, I tended to ignore it and, therefore, picked up only bits and pieces:

... AGITATION BY FASCIST ELEMENTS ... PEACE-LOVING WORKERS AND PEASANTS STATE ... INCREASE BORDER SECURITY ... WILL NOT AFFECT THE ACCESS ROUTES BETWEEN WEST BERLIN AND WEST GERMANY ...

Then the Young Pioneers sang, "*Die Partei hat immer Recht*—the Party is always right."

I almost resumed dialing AFN, when something inside made me wonder, what did they say would not affect the access routes between West Berlin and West Germany? My thumb paused on the controls, then returned to RIAS.

. . . EAST GERMAN POLICE . . . BLOCKING BORDER STREETS WITH TRUCKS AND TANKS ...

Tanks? I leapt out of bed, opened the connecting door to the living room where my parents slept and yelled, "Mutti, Pappi, there is something weird going on at the border! There are tanks there!" Still in my nightgown, I turned on the full-sized radio in the cherrywood cabinet beneath the window.

. . . SENTRIES ARE POSTED AT TWO-METER INTERVALS ALONG THE ENTIRE BORDER BETWEEN EAST AND WEST BERLIN.

I glanced at my parents, eager for reassurance, but their faces looked pasty and somber. My mother mangled her handkerchief; my father's arms were tightly crossed in front of his chest, his six-foot-something frame erect as a candlestick. Their tense body language and empty stares spelled danger.

A menacing feeling rose from the pit of my stomach. During the past few weeks, I had been far more occupied with myself than with the world around me. Now, I got a panicky feeling. Weren't the communists bluffing again? Wasn't this just another creation of their propaganda machine, I wondered.

My parents' crumpled outlines, silhouetted against the neatly embossed white wallpaper looked worrisome. Normally, my father, a stickler for decorum, insisted on getting fully dressed first thing in the morning. "Robes are for loafers," he maintained. At this moment, Mutti and Pappi looked far from imposing in their nightgowns. *Are we at the brink of disaster?*

Despite being fifteen, I continued to be a child in my parents' eyes, a little girl that must be protected from the real world. Political events were not among the subjects we discussed as a family. The inability to talk openly only raised my anxiety level.

For the first time ever, I became totally engrossed in a newscast. Station bulletins and eyewitness reports sounded grave. There appeared to be consensus that extraordinary border activities had begun under the cloak of darkness, around one o'clock in the morning. A bus driver recalled streetlights on the East side of the border going off shortly after midnight and remaining off during the entire night. Other reports described large amounts of barbed wire being unloaded.

Details were murky, but a troublesome picture began to emerge. "They're closing the border! There's going to be war," my mother's panic was thinly veiled. "I just knew something like this was going to happen." Her words hung in the air like a chilling fog. Naked fear tightened my chest. It grew more pronounced to the point where my heart began pounding with such force that I wondered whether the dull thumps were audible. *War? As in World War III?* I was born six months after World War II had ended, but its consequences were still evident throughout the city. Many families were without a father, a brother, or a son; ruins remained on most streets, housing was still scarce, and Berlin was still divided.

My father moved to the green velour couch; my mother sat slumped into one of the stuffed armchairs. They did not speak. Only radio announcements pierced the silence in our flat. Despite summertime temperatures, I felt a chill.

News bulletins were updated in fifteen-minute intervals. Was "Spitzbart'" really going to close the access routes? The well-known derogatory term poked fun at East German Party Chief Walter Ulbricht's goatee. At last, my father broke the silence. "Don't worry; the Western Allies aren't going to take this lying down."

A huge weight lifted off my shoulders. His words provided the respite I needed. I relaxed. But wait! Was there an undertone in his voice?

Did he really believe it, or were his words only intended to ease Mutti's and my fears?

My father opened the cabinets' veneered sliding doors and exposed our television set. Shortly after pushing the button, black-and-white flickers began to run across the screen. Apparently, the station was still off the air. Not at all unusual because programming was still in its infancy. Wordless, we continued to listen to the radio.

During most of my life, West Berlin had been a dying town. My parents knew a different Berlin. Before World War II, it had been the lively capital of the country. When the war was over, forty percent of its buildings were destroyed and in its center scarcely a structure remained standing. Still, my parents decided to remain in the heavily damaged metropolis because it was their home. Seeing Mutti and Pappi slumped into the furniture now, I wondered if they regretted that decision.

. . . MAY BE SEALING OFF THE BORDERS TO PREVENT THE SO-CALLED "PROFITEERS" THAT LIVE IN THE EAST FROM COMING TO THE WEST, a commentator speculated.

"Profiteers." That's what the Communist Party called the fifty thousand workers who crossed the border every day to work in the West, where wages were high, and lived in the East, where rents were cheap. In one afternoon's work in the West, a border crosser could earn the equivalent of an entire week's salary in the East.

"That must be it," my father exclaimed in a flash of recognition. "The measures are only temporary."

My fists unclenched, my jaw relaxed; I let out a sigh and felt the warmth return to my hands. *Thank God*—But wait! What about the exodus of scientists, doctors, engineers, and skilled workers? Ulbricht couldn't stop their stampede to the West with a temporary border closure. My anxiety returned. Didn't I read recently that since the end of World War II an average of 150,000 people left East Germany every year? That would be close to 2.5 million over the past sixteen years.

The news turned more ominous by the minute. Now, eyewitnesses reported that the *Volksarmee*, the East German militia, used picks and pneumatic drills to tear up sidewalks and roads on the east side of the border. Passengers on the East-West elevated train, the *S-Bahn*, were prevented from continuing to the West, and East Berlin's station entrances to the subway, the *U-Bahn*, had been barricaded. Work details were sealing the border between East and West Berlin with concrete poles cemented into the ground and barbed wire strung from post to post, reports said. The intent of the wall of wire was becoming clear: It was to keep East Germans inside East Berlin.

I pulled up a hassock and listened to the news with growing concern. Why didn't anyone speak out? Where were the West Berlin police? Where was Mayor Willy Brandt? Where was our chancellor, Konrad Adenauer? Where were the Allies, the ultimate authority in Berlin?

Reporters and eyewitnesses gave their accounts of the situation, but, so far, no formal explanation has been provided. Journalists described how West Berlin police and British, American, and French military officers briefly appeared on the scene, conversed among themselves, and drove off again. No statements were made; no actions were taken.

At 10:00 a.m., nine hours after the start of these bizarre activities, the three Western commandants and their staffs finally gathered at the four-power Allied Kommandatura. But their official statement was limited to, "Our respective capitals have been informed."

I was flabbergasted. Wasn't anyone going to launch a protest with the Soviets? Could Walter Ulbricht violate the Potsdam Agreement and block free access between the four sectors without any sanctions from the three Western Allies? Didn't the Western powers always assert their authority as occupiers against the actions the West Berlin government wanted to take, and now they meekly accepted the rules laid down by Ulbricht?

Although drained by the morning's developments, my parents attempted to maintain our Sunday routine. I was dispatched to pick up the breakfast rolls. At the elevator, I bumped into Herr Höthmann, our neighbor, who was on his way to purchase a newspaper. We exchanged brief greetings. As the lift descended, he muttered, "They won't risk a war for our sake. Just wait, they're going to hand us over to the Communists."

His words sent icy shivers down my spine. *Is he talking about America?* Wordless, we reached ground level. Gloom seemed to have replaced the blood in my veins.

Upon entering the bakery, the pleasant whiff of freshly baked breads and rolls of every color, from the deepest brown to the snowiest white, tantalized my nostrils. For a moment, I allowed myself to bask in the warm, familiar aroma. As usual, the shop was crowded, but I did not recognize anyone. Most customers spoke in hushed tones, except for one older man with thin, gray hair and a bulbous nose. In a booming voice he shared his startling discovery. "I wouldn't have believed it if I hadn't seen it with my own eyes," he kept repeating, not speaking to anyone in particular.

"Seen what?" A young woman hollered across several heads from the other side of the shop.

"Barbed wire with English labels. That's what!" the man yelled back. "I drove to the border this morning to have a look for myself, and sure enough, it's true what they're saying. There they were: rolls of barbed wire with English stickers. BRITISH tags, not Russian." he emphasized. Heads turned in his direction.

"British? Really?" another man questioned.

"If you think the Allies are going to fight for our freedom, you're in for a surprise," the old man continued. "They made a deal under the table, I tell you. They knew this was coming—all of them. That's why they aren't doing a damned thing. Haven't you wondered why nobody has said so much as a 'peep' all day?"

I stood rooted to the floor like a statue. *He's right. Why haven't the Allies protested?* Had they known all along? Would they turn us over to the Russians? Would we have to become Communists and live behind the Iron Curtain?

A tall, slender woman, holding a little girl by the hand, whispered to the middle-aged housewife in front of me, "I pray to God we aren't headed for war. If it comes to a nuclear war, we'll all be wiped off the map. Maybe some of the USA and USSR will be left standing, but my guess is the rest of us will all be gone." She pulled the little girl a little closer.

I shuddered. Collusion, British labels, under-the-table deals, nuclear war—the images raced through my head until I was dizzy. Without listening to further discussion, I bought my buns and hurried home. The rumors I had heard added a whole new dimension to the situation. I clutched my sack of rolls and wondered if the bakery, too, might be behind the Iron Curtain next time I came to purchase rolls—or if there even would be a next time.

Because of Berlin's four-power status, Willy Brandt, our governing mayor, had no power to intervene. Neither did our chancellor, Konrad Adenauer. But what about the Western Allies? As long as I could remember, they had mocked the communist regime and called it "bogus." Only two days ago, John F. Kennedy had said that America was committed to protecting the freedom of West Berlin. Had that been mere rhetoric to counter communist propaganda? I had always believed the Western Allies, and especially the Americans. I had thought they were the good guys, and the Russians were the bad guys. Was the man in the bakery right about collusion?

When I returned home, the table was set, and we proceeded with our Sunday morning breakfast ritual. But no one was in the mood for food. Having forced down a few sips of coffee, we cleared the table.

At noon, my father suddenly announced, "I'm going to fill the tank with gas. Get our passports, insurance papers, and phone numbers together," he told my mother.

"Pack a change of clothes for everyone," he instructed me. "If things get worse, we'll jump in the car and drive straight through the border checkpoints. No matter who or what blocks our way."

My mouth went dry. *Leave Berlin? Go where?*

"But . . . but . . . but . . . the borders are manned by armed guards. There are concrete road blocks," my mother cut in tearfully.

"What choice do we have? We'll have to take our chances. Or do you want to end up behind the Iron Curtain?"

His words brought the picture into full focus and stifled further questions. Wordless, my mother and I prepared our Volkswagen Beetle for a getaway. Her panic also snuck up inside of me. I had visions of dying in the back seat from gunshot wounds as we powered through the border.

Silently, I prayed for a peaceful turn of events and took inventory of my small bedroom. Suddenly, I valued everything in it. I looked at the Sputnik-shaped ceiling light my parents had given me after the Soviets had launched the world's first artificial satellite into orbit four years earlier. Six bare candle bulbs shot in symmetrical arches from a triangular base. The thought of space travel had placed so much hope on the future then.

Turning around, my eyes fell on my small cosmetic table. I had built it by converting an old storage box with Pappi's handsaw, hammer, and nails.

I opened the little red poetry album on my dresser. It contained inspirations from my high-school friends.

I glanced at the couch pillow I had made the previous year by pulling thick red wool threads through the rough weave of two ordinary scouring rags. I had been so proud of my creation.

Everything would have to stay behind now. If only I had known, I could have appreciated it so much more.

By early afternoon, the car was ready. We cowered anxiously in front of the television for updates on border developments. Although my parents feigned some self-control, their nervousness was very much apparent. I tried to speculate what action might trigger our decision to leave but could not fathom the answer.

At 3:00 p.m. Scotty Kelly called from Ramstein Air Base. "Are you all right? What's going on there? We have only sketchy details. Do you want to come and stay with us for a while, Utah? Until this thing blows over?"

"I'd love to, really, but I can't. We're packed and ready to leave if we have to. I have to stay," I whispered, wishing I could say otherwise.

During the six o'clock evening news, I watched my father closely. His knuckles looked white against the hardened skin of his hands. I could tell by his stiff back that he weighed every word. He looked like a tiger ready to sprint.

On the screen, we watched armored cars and water trucks inch through the archways of the Brandenburg Gate, stopping behind the demarcation line, just in back of a string of East German *Vopos*, the People's Police. East Berlin radio stations broadcast warnings to West Berliners,

"Do not come within one hundred meters of the border, or we will employ countermeasures."

The threat spread like wildfire. Angry crowds formed on both sides of the border. *Vopos* warned through megaphones, "If provoked, our men will shoot."

I sensed my father was getting close to give the dreaded command and held my breath. West Berlin Mayor Willy Brandt called for restraint. Just in time, escalation of hostilities stopped, and the crowds began to disperse. We all exhaled.

Then we watched as construction brigades continued to put up more barbed wire and concrete blocks. In some areas, they ran barbed wire down the middle of street, separating neighbors who lived on opposite sides of the street. Although the barrier was no more than a few feet high yet, it severed major East-West arteries. On television, we saw people dash to the West through remaining openings in the fence. Others looked resigned, waving to their relatives on the other side, holding up small children and pets. Reports said that some East Berliners had swum across the Teltow Canal or the Spree River, two waterways that flow between East and West Berlin, and were not yet heavily guarded. Others had sneaked across the wooded portions of the border between West Berlin and East Germany. One thing became clear: By nightfall Berlin was split into two, separating families and friends.

The Wall

MONDAY, AUGUST 14

I slept in fits and starts, but mostly, I stared into the darkness, eyes wide open. We hadn't fled West Berlin yet. Would we be safe now or was the worst yet to come? If the Ulbricht regime could cut Berlin into two without Allied reaction, then what was to keep the Soviet Army from taking over the West? Were we trapped? Would we be forced to become Communists? On the other hand, the barriers had been erected just inside East Berlin, not on the border itself. Any Western attempt to remove them might be considered an invasion of Soviet-occupied territory. The thoughts rolled through my mind like tumbleweeds in a windstorm.

As soon as the stores opened, my mother and I got in line with bags and our shopping nets to stock up. "Just in case," my mother said. Apparently, many housewives shared her fears because the stores were mobbed. People bought all the staples and canned goods they could get their hands on. No one said it out loud, but there were whispers everywhere, "Oh Lord, please let this not turn into World War III."

"I heard on the radio that our illustrious chancellor is campaigning in Regensburg instead of rushing over here to help," our neighbor, Herr Höthmann, sneered. "I think good ol' Adenauer, the 'Apostle of the Cold War' is afraid that the Russians will throw him in the slammer if he shows his face in Berlin. He'd rather hand us over to the Russians."

"Those Bastards. As I've always said, those damned politicians are all the same. All they care about is their own butt," my father added.

In the evening news, Washington carefully played down the events in Berlin. The word "wall" was not mentioned once. Instead, the monstrosity was called "measures designed to halt the flow of refugees to the West." Wasn't that the same double-talk Ulbricht was known for? Didn't anyone dare to speak out?

The United States hinted that the Allies would not undertake any military countermeasures as long as access to Berlin was not threatened. What will they consider a threat, I wondered?

By Monday night, the wall of wire separating East and West Berlin was largely completed. The East Germans had closed the Brandenburg Gate. Their actions looked less temporary by the hour, and we slowly began to realize that Berlin's division might be permanent. But I still could not imagine what that would mean for the future.

TUESDAY, AUGUST 15

On the third day of wall construction, the East German government prohibited its barges from using waterways that passed through West Berlin.

East Berlin pedestrians were now prohibited from entering the free part of the city. With appropriate identification, West Berliners were still allowed to cross the border. But when rumors spread that "Workers' Fist" gangs roamed the streets of East Berlin, hoping to embroil Westerners into arguments and street fights, border crossing by Westerners dropped off sharply.

Until now, the Soviets had limited their administrative actions to their sector, leaving the city's infrastructure more or less intact. Although direct telephone communication had been cut in 1952, gas, electricity, transportation, and sewer, had remained largely unaffected. Now, everything was severed.

"Pappi, if the phone lines were cut so long ago, how come we were able to reach Frau Mandel when Mutti was sick last year and didn't want her to come?" I asked. Frau Mandel had cleaned our apartment almost ever since I could remember. She lived in East Berlin and had many jobs in the West. "Our call went through even though she lives in the East."

"True," my father admitted, "but we called her via Copenhagen. We couldn't have called directly. Those lines were cut nine years ago."

We were lucky. All of our family members lived in the West. Frau Mandel was the only person in the East we regularly associated with. Now, she would no longer be able to come to clean house. Not only would my mother have to find another cleaning lady, but Frau Mandel's two sons worked in the West and lived in the East. They crossed the border daily. Where were they now, I wondered?

Then something happened that made a much deeper impression on me than anything so far. A nineteen-year-old East German soldier, by the name of Conrad Schumann, leapt over the barbed wire barrier he was supposed to guard and escaped to West Berlin. A professional photographer captured his jump in midair, and within minutes the image was wired around the world. It was inconceivable. Instantly, Schumann became a hero in the West and a traitor in the East.

We read in the paper the next day that Corporal Schumann was supposed to have guarded the Bernauer Straße boundary where the Soviet and French sectors met. Along with two comrades, he had been stationed at the corner of Ruppiner Straße since August 13. The three armed guards were to stop anyone from crossing the border when, for the third day in a row, pedestrians accosted them from the Western side. People were pressing for explanations for these border-sealing activities. But Schumann and his comrades had no information themselves. They simply followed orders.

Eyewitnesses reported later, that Schumann smoked one cigarette after another that day while pedestrians kept yelling, "*Komm rüber,*

Komm rüber!—Jump across, jump across!" He appeared tense and then suddenly, slung his machine gun to the side and jumped across the still only knee-high barrier. On the Western side, a police car stood ready to whisk him away. It all had happened within minutes.

Conrad Schumann was only four years my senior. I admired his courage. Would I have had his guts? I had so many questions: Did he really think it through, or did he act on impulse? Was he glad he had done it, or did he regret his action? Of course, he could never go back. Desertion was punishable with death in East Germany. Would there be repercussions for his comrades, his parents, or his siblings?

WEDNESDAY, AUGUST 16

Early in the morning, my parents sent me to pick up a *Bild Zeitung*, one of West Berlin's major newspapers. Its bold headline shouted, "Kennedy is silent!" The cover story claimed that the Allies were tipped off in advance of Ulbricht's plans to construct a barrier. Supposedly, Field Marshall Ivan Stepanovich Koniev had informed Allied military leaders of Ulbricht's border-sealing plans three full days before it had actually happened and had assured them that their rights would not be affected.

Berliners were livid. On this fourth day of unchallenged border-closing construction the atmosphere was ripe for rumors. People were willing to believe anything that seemed to validate what they suspected. My reverence for America was also shaken.

A mass protest against the violations of the Potsdam Agreement, which outlined Allied occupation policies, was scheduled for 3:00 p.m. in front of Schöneberg Rathaus, West Berlin's town hall. Over half a million citizens participated. My parents would neither allow me to, nor did I wish to attend. I watched the demonstration on television.

Protesters carried banners of disillusionment with national and international leaders that read:

BETRAYED BY THE WEST

NINETY HOURS AND NO ACTION!

ENOUGH PROTESTS—LET DEEDS FOLLOW!

WHERE IS OUR CHANCELLOR—VACATIONING IN ITALY?

THURSDAY, AUGUST 17

Morale plummeted to a new low. Ulbricht's regime had succeeded in stemming the outflow of workers. A serious shortage of skilled labor was evident in West Berlin, while East Berlin experienced a glut for the first time. East Germans were now employed constructing their own prison. I wondered if Frau Mandel's sons were among the workers, conscripted to build the wall.

FRIDAY, AUGUST 18

Apparently convinced that the Allies would not interfere with the construction of the wall, work crews began to replace some of the provisional wire barriers with concrete slabs. They started in the heart of the city. Slowly, the monstrosity was turning into a wall with a capital "W." I still could not fathom that this hastily erected mishmash of barriers would over time turn into a demoralizing Wall that would divide the city for decades.

SATURDAY, AUGUST 19

British Prime Minister Harold Macmillan returned from grouse shooting and immediately left for a second holiday. Obviously, he did not care. His lack of concern sent a clear message to Berliners.

Then, that same afternoon, US Vice President Lyndon B. Johnson arrived together with General Lucius D. Clay in West Berlin. The sidewalks between Tempelhof Airport and the US military headquarters in Dahlem were packed with cheering crowds. The visit instilled a new ripple of hope.

Clay, who was riding in the second limousine, received as much, if not more, attention as the vice president. The people of West Berlin extended a warm welcome to the man who had organized the 1948/1949 airlift. We prayed that he would save us a second time.

SUNDAY, AUGUST 20

There was hardly an inhabitant of West Berlin who did not know that Johnson and Clay had arrived the day before. Both gentlemen offered words of support from US President John F. Kennedy. The turnout was even greater than on the previous afternoon. Hundreds of thousands of men, women, and children lined the avenues and streets as their motorcade passed.

I, too, stood in the crowd along the curb of the Kaiserdamm and threw one yellow rose into Johnson's open black sedan. "They are Johnson's favorite," people said. "At least the *Amis*—the Americans— came," reverberated throughout the crowd. Tears of joy streamed down my face. My faith in America was restored.

"I think Johnson looks a little like Robert Young of *Father Knows Best*," I said to Tina who stood next to me at the curb. "He has that fatherly look, doesn't he?"

Because of Johnson and Clay's visit, morale surged. Even though the Wall was getting higher and more impervious by the day, we saw for the first time in seven days evidence that someone outside of Berlin cared.

TUESDAY, AUGUST 22

Following Johnson and Clay's departure the previous day, German Chancellor Adenauer finally paid West Berlin a visit. He was greeted with catcalls and boos by scattered groups along the roads. I did not join them. I shared the crowd's sentiment that mocked his late arrival in our beleaguered city with slogans like, "IT'S ABOUT TIME!"

Late that evening, when solid concrete barriers began to snake along the border between East and West Berlin, the East German Ministry of the Interior issued three new decrees:

- West Berlin pedestrians, like motorists, would be required to obtain special permits to enter the Soviet sector. (People suspected that, in reality, no one would qualify to obtain one.)
- Border-crossing points were reduced from twelve to seven: Four for West Berliners, two for West Germans, one for all non-Germans and diplomats. (The last one would eventually become Checkpoint Charlie.)
- Westerners were ordered to stay one hundred meters behind the border.

In response to these decrees, the Allies finally reacted by hammering out a joint protest, stating that they had no intention of being told by the

East where the West sectors began and ended. "We will send our troops at any time and to any place we wish in our area of responsibility," the statement read.

At 1:00 p.m. troops from three Allied garrisons moved to the border. We were fearful and grateful at the same time. We wanted to see Wall construction stopped, but we did not want war. East Germany responded by also positioning several armored cars but refrained from escalating the conflict into a show of strength.

In the days that followed August 13, escapes became more and more difficult. East German workers were dispatched to seal holes in the makeshift barrier and to brick up doors and windows of houses facing the border. They also devised long-handled mirrors to catch refugees, hidden under trains or cars. By the end of August, the barbed-wire wall had been reinforced with large concrete and granite blocks, bricks, and steel stakes, separating East from West Berlin. The outer perimeter of our city was sealed off to East German citizens with barbed wire stretched between seven-foot-high concrete posts. Still, 45,000 refugees had found a way to escape and had registered at the Marienfelde camp in West Berlin since August 13.

Harz Trip

WE ALL HUNGERED FOR RELIEF from the fear that held us in its grip. Since the day the Wall had gone up, many East Berliners had jumped over or snuck through the newly erected barriers. To foil further escapes, the East German government had hastily relocated residents who lived adjacent to West Berlin streets and bricked in their apartment windows and doors. Their homes became part of the Berlin Wall.

In the Bernauer Straße, the sector boundary was drawn in such a way that the six-story apartment buildings on one side of the street were located in the Soviet sector and the ones on the opposite side in the French sector. Both sidewalks and the street were part of the French zone. In last-ditch efforts, some East Berlin residents fled to the West by jumping out of their windows just prior to being relocated. They jumped into nets held out by West Berlin police and firemen. Not all attempts were successful. It was mainly the young who tried to escape. Unwilling to leave loved ones behind, many elders resigned themselves to life behind the Wall.

My father no longer talked about the possibility of moving to West Germany. Along with scores of others, he had begun to accept the Wall as a new reality. The West called it the "Wall of Shame," and the East referred to as an "Anti-Fascist Protective Rampart." We liked to believe that the Communists would not have built a Wall, had they intended to occupy West Berlin. It made us feel safer.

I had never looked forward to the start of school following summer vacations more than in 1961. Earlier in the year, my class had been approved for a two-week holiday in the western part of the Harz mountain range in the central part of Germany. Part of the 866-mile *Zonengrenze*, the inner German border, divided this range into East and West as well.

Our class was scheduled to stay in youth hostels in the West German towns of Altenau and St. Andreasberg. Frau Brunk, our homeroom teacher, would accompany us. Following the events of August 13, however, we were informed that our trip was in jeopardy. Although both destinations were in the free part of Germany, school officials became apprehensive about taking us to an area that brought us almost as close to the East German border as we were in Berlin.

Then, fate dealt a second blow. Frau Brunk was diagnosed with a serious illness and requested an extended leave of absence. Our eager anticipation turned into disillusionment.

"I think we can forget about the trip," I lamented. "First the Wall, and now Frau Brunk."

But to our surprise, Herr Bartsch, our math teacher and avid hiker, enlisted the assistance of a female substitute instructor and agreed to chaperone our class.

"We're going, we're going," reverberated from the school halls where the twenty-six of us danced up and down, squealing with delight.

Our hostel stays were confirmed. Herr Bartsch put together an extensive program of day hikes, sightseeing, and cultural enrichment.

And before we knew it, it was time to board a charter bus to mountainous Altenau. For the best part of the 180-mile trip we sang "Ninety-nine Bottles of Beer on the Wall" and "*Eisgekühlte Coca Cola*—Ice Cold Coke."

Clad in *Bundhosen*—trousers gathered at the ankles, a Bavarian felt jacket, and a Basque beret, Herr Bartsch greeted us with a broad grin on the first morning of the trip. With a well-worn rucksack on his back and several trail maps under his arm, he waited for us, leaning casually on his walking stick. His soft, brimless cap covered the top of his head like an upside-down bowl and concealed his grey, bristly hair.

"I hope no one sees us with him," Gina murmured under her breath.

Herr Bartsch was close to retirement and indifferent to fashion. Anxious to open our hearts and minds to nature, he insisted on early breakfasts and departures. With an enthusiastic "*Morgenstund' hat Gold im Mund*—morning-hour has gold in her mouth," he greeted us each morning at 7:00 a.m. for breakfast. Still drowsy at the early hour, we routinely replied, "*Morgenstund' hat Blei im Hintern*—morning-hour has lead in her posterior."

Being city girls, most of us did not own hiking gear. Instead of sporting sturdy shoes and rain gear, we assembled in street shoes and city clothes, carrying umbrellas and flimsy plastic ponchos. Like a row of ducklings, we followed our fearless leader through dense fir forests to mountaintops, springs, dams and meadows. Rain or shine, we traipsed through knee-high grass, up and down rocky paths, and returned to the hostel with rubber knees and muddy shoes. Despite umbrellas, we were soaked to the skin on rainy days.

But on each hike, we were rewarded with vistas we had never before encountered. We trekked to two dams that offered breathtaking panoramic vistas. One day, we even climbed the peak of the three-thousand-foot-high *Achtermann*, the fourth highest mountain in the region. On other days, we hiked to abandoned mines that had once produced silver, copper, lead, iron or salt. And every day, we laughed, sang, and enjoyed each other's camaraderie.

Sightseeing was a novel experience for many in our class. Although I enjoyed a family holiday at the seaside every year, my parents never made it a practice to visit nearby attractions. They considered vacations much deserved opportunities for rest. This trip was different. Aside from day hikes, we smelled the stench of sulfur dioxide for the first time when we visited a sulfur spring. In the historic town of Goslar, we visited the Kaiserpfalz, the eleventh-century medieval palace that served the emperors as their summer residence. We also explored Clausthal-Zellerfeld, the birthplace of Nobel Prize-winner Robert Koch, who isolated the tuberculosis bacillus.

Each evening, we returned to the hostel, washed up, dried our clothes, and squeezed onto narrow wood benches that flanked long family-style pine tables. Dinner was served in large tin bowls that could easily have doubled as washbasins. They were always heaped full with interesting concoctions. After dinner and before bedtime, we tried to strike up friendships with the other hostel guests. Some of them were all-boy classes. New friendships were followed by good-byes, address exchanges, and promises to stay in touch. Next morning, without mercy, Herr Bartsch called 6:30 reveille again.

House rules called for lights out by 10:00 p.m., but that did not mean we went to sleep. Often, we told and retold silly incidents that had occurred during the day. Whispering across bunk beds, we shared our experiences until the wee hours of the morning. On moonlit nights, we signed to each other. We had not forgotten the unique sign language we had acquired in Storzeln three years earlier.

My pinecone encounter was one of the stories that produced endless giggles, stifled beneath the covers to keep the housemother at bay. It had happened several hours into our *Achtermann* climb when I could no longer postpone urgent business. Along with Tina and Doris, I intentionally fell behind to be able to step unnoticed into the tall grass to the side of the trail. My friends stood watch.

My rucksack deposited on a nearby tree stump, I loosened critical articles of clothing and squatted on the spongy, needle-covered forest floor. Still damp with morning dew, decomposing leaves and needles released their earthy scent.

No sooner had I settled into action, when I heard Tina issue a hushed warning, "Someone's coming!"

"Right." I giggled. Not having run into a soul for several hours, it was unlikely that a hiker shared out path this very moment. Tina was undoubtedly trying to play a practical joke on me. Unruffled, I proceeded with the business at hand when, all of a sudden, muffled murmurs turned into audible speech. Then two backpackers materialized like Fata Morganas. I froze.

Too late to recover from my position without drawing further notice to myself, I continued to squat, bare bottomed, by the side of the trail and feigned a keen interest in the scattering of pine cones around me.

The trekkers passed within inches, barely noticing—or kindly ignoring—my compromised position. My friends stood rooted to the trail. As soon as the hikers had disappeared around the next bend, the three of us broke into gut-wrenching laughter.

Each night we dropped into bed filled with exhilarating new experiences. During the entire two weeks, none of us thought even once of the Berlin Wall. We wanted to forget, and we succeeded.

Dance Lessons

TENTH-GRADE BOYS TOOK WOODSHOP. We girls were taught to cook and sew. Although I had fun preparing *Grieß Flammerie*, a creamy wheat pudding, and sewing a linen apron with hemstitch border, I also wanted to enroll in woodshop.

"Forget it!" Our principal waved me off. "You girls need to get ready for married life." The allure of marriage hit a new low.

But my disappointment was soon forgotten when my mother allowed me to sign up for *Tanzschule*, a three-month stint of dance lessons. During the last year of high school, basic private dance lessons were a traditional coming-of-age pursuit. It represented the first sanctioned event in which boys and girls met socially. In ninety minutes on Friday nights, we learned to move gracefully across the parquet to the rhythms of fox-trot, Vienna waltz, slow waltz, rhumba, cha-cha, boogie, samba, and tango.

I was astonished to discover that many of the guys trembled as much as I did when we were made to stand paired-up in dance position, just prior to the start of the music. As my forearm rested lightly on my partner's elevated upper arm, I often felt that support quiver inside its sleeve. And when the guy placed his hand tentatively on my shoulder blade, it sometimes felt like ice; other times like a damp sponge.

Along with dance steps, we were taught proper table manners and etiquette.

"Imagine yourselves arriving late at the movie theater. The film has already started." Our dance instructor, Herr Finck, painted the image for us. "The theater is packed with patrons, and your seat is in the middle of the row. How will you get there? Should you face the patrons as you make your way to your seat, or should you face the screen?"

Sixty pairs of eyes studied the floor.

"Come on," Herr Finck prodded. "You'd have to decide. What would you do?"

Still no response. "Think about it. If you sat in your seat already, and someone else tried to squeeze by you—what would you rather look at? Someone's face or someone's derrière? Well, there's your answer."

On the first day of dance lessons, the young men, in suit and tie—often the first and only ones they owned—congregated uneasily in one of the corners of the rectangular ballroom. The equal number of ladies, wearing their finest Sunday dresses, buoyed by petticoats, clustered in the opposite corner. Each group sized up the other.

In our corner, winners and losers on the other side of the room were quickly identified. On subsequent evenings, a young man, initially relegated to a lower rung of the popularity ladder, could improve his position by demonstrating superior aptitude on the dance floor or a disarming personality. The boys used their own yardsticks.

Since the young men were given the prerogative of selecting their dance partners, my girlfriends and I were forced to covertly influence their choices. That meant we flirted. I loved to test the effectiveness of my flirtations. *Pick me! Pick me!* I would will a young man across the room, and then I would pray that he would not turn out to be a klutz.

Once I had succeeded in attracting him, however, I would immediately lose interest. After the first rendezvous, "Mr. Interesting" invariably turned into "Mr. Tiresome." And should he ask for a second date, I would hedge, "I think I'm busy that night."

It was a game of catch and release. Both sexes played it with delight. My girlfriends were still the most important people in my world. While some of them began going steady already, exclusive relationships held no interest for me. I enjoyed playing the field and meeting as many different boys as possible.

My young suitors quickly became my mother's adversaries, however. Relieved that I didn't pursue long-term relationships she, nonetheless, leapt into a protective mode. If she picked up the slightest hint that I wanted to wiggle out of a date, she jumped into action and shielded me from persistent young men by eagerly meeting them at the front door with the pretense that her daughter was out. Out of town. Gone for an indeterminate length of time.

In conversation with relatives and neighbors, my mother belittled my dates. I pushed back by placing an embargo on the subject. I played it cool, despite aching to ask her, "What in the world does one talk about on a date?" or "Is it okay to wait until the end of the week to accept an invitation, in case a better offer comes along?"

FIVE

SAILING WITH PREVAILING WINDS

High-School Graduation

MONTHS BEFORE GRADUATION DAY in March 1962, my classmates and I were already bursting with anticipation. We looked forward to the freedom from classes and tests. An *Abschlußball*—a prom—was scheduled for the weekend following ceremonies. The word literally meant "closing ball" and implied a strange finality.

"Why don't we burn our tests in a huge bonfire on the last day of school," Monika proposed.

"Perfect! We'll reduce them to ashes," the rest of us agreed.

"Let's do it in our *Schrebergarten*," I proposed. If my mother and father let us, I thought. Lately, it had become difficult to predict my parents' reactions. It seemed I could do anything I wanted within their color palette, but not from the entire spectrum. Sometimes, my parents were agreeable; other times, they acted like prison wardens. The rules, once so clear to me, had become fuzzy. While other parents had eased restrictions as time went by, mine had multiplied the constraints. Why were my parents so obstinate? I earned good grades. All I wanted was to do what my friends did.

Despite feigning indifference, even joyful anticipation, toward graduation, I struggled with the uncertainty that loomed ahead. Most of my classmates would enter three-year administrative apprenticeships in government or insurance; some expected to join the family business; others prepared for nursing school. Three girls in class had decided on a two-year business-school program. I was still clueless and felt embarrassed about my lack of plans.

College was not an option. Higher education called for a seven-year high-school curriculum, the *Gymnasium*, which included Latin and all general collegiate classes. My classmates and I were graduating from a four-year school. I was stymied about what kind of work I might be fit for. There was no family business to join. "Becoming a photographer? Over my dead body," my mother had said. And the thought of an administrative apprenticeship did not stir my passion. Clerical work smacked of dusty files, dictation, and phone messages. Secretly, I still had set my sights on becoming a stewardess, awed by the mystique of foreign travel and smart-looking uniforms. But airlines required a minimum entry age of twenty-one, and I was only sixteen. Maybe business school would be a way of spending two out of those five years in a holding pattern until I reached the required age. In my eagerness, it escaped me that both business schools and apprenticeships prepared their graduates for identical occupations: administrative work which I loathed.

At home, we did not discuss my career options. For as long as I could remember, it had been tacitly understood that the occupation I would pursue would be unimportant as long as I was employed by a respectable organization. Neither my mother nor my father could conceive of a lower-middle-class girl becoming a doctor, lawyer, or a business executive. To the contrary, my mother took it for granted that I would want to choose a feminine path—maybe that of hairdresser or saleslady in a fashion boutique.

All my mother said on the topic of life after graduation was, "Once you are working, we expect you to pay one hundred marks per month for room and board."

Her announcement shocked me. It amounted to close to one-third of the income I could expect. "Then I'll sublease a room somewhere," I said defiantly, assuming that if I lived somewhere else, I would, at least, be able to come and go as I pleased.

"Are you naïve," my mother laughed, "rooms are expensive, if you can even find one. And then you'll have a landlady to please. Don't think she'll be as lenient as your father and I. Besides, you'll still have to pay for food. And who do you think will be doing your laundry? Go ahead, figure it out. You'll end up paying more renting a room than what you have to pay at home. And at home laundry and meals are free."

I said no more and vowed to check out my prospects. But I had a sinking feeling. This was 1962. Housing was still scarce. Roughly 600,000 apartments had been destroyed in World War II. Few had been replaced. This year, construction of several large housing projects was scheduled to start. But these were only the first large-scale efforts to ease the housing shortage. Often, even married couples were forced to live with their parents for several years before they found an apartment of their own. What chance would a jobless sixteen-year-old have?

"Hanni, Ursula, and Fee are going to business school," I announced a few days later, in hopes of advancing my plan to kill two of the five years before being able to work as a stewardess. "Can I go, too?"

Oblivious to my dislike for administrative work, my parents consented without further discussion. I, on the other hand, could not guess that the reason my mother so willingly approved my choice was that she assumed I wanted to become a receptionist in one of the many medical and accounting offices in our neighborhood. The six-story buildings that lined the major streets in our community housed retail shops at ground level, small offices on the first and second floors, and residential flats above. My mother looked forward to my returning home for lunch and dinner while I dreamed of flying to faraway places and visiting my parents on holidays.

The day came when my classmates and I closed the high-school gates behind us for the last time. Flying into the apartment, I waved my report card.

"Mutti, look! I graduated at the top of my class. I got a '1' in typing, a '2' in German, French, English, math, biology, geography, art, handwriting, and home economics, a '3' in history, physics, chemistry, music, and shorthand, and one '4' in physical education," I rattled off.

Grades ranged from "1" to "6," with "2" to "6" corresponding roughly to American grades "A" to "F." We were not graded on a curve. Grade "1" represented perfect test scores, conduct, and attendance throughout the school year.

"Pappi owes me thirteen marks!" I announced.

Throughout high school, my father had paid five marks for each "1" and one mark for each "2." In turn, I owed him one mark for each

"4," five marks for each "5" and ten marks for a "6." No money changed hands for a "3" (satisfactory). I considered the bargain a fair one and worked hard for good grades.

Thirteen marks were no fortune, but they bought four admissions to the Riverboat, a popular dance club, or six large chocolate bars. It was the knowledge that I had graduated at the top of my class, not the money, that filled me with pride.

With her usual reserve, my mother praised me for my good grades. Fully expecting my father to be ecstatic, I was shocked to find that he was not at all impressed. Scrutinizing my report card, he pointed to the "4" in physical education and to the five "satisfactory" grades. Rather than offering praise for graduating at the top of my class, he berated me for my less than perfect performance.

"I got that '4' in PE because I couldn't clear the pummel horse," I protested. "How about the '2s' in German, French, English, math, biology, and geography? Don't they account for anything? Besides, I got the best report card of all four graduating classes!"

Outraged and disappointed, I recoiled. An overwhelming feeling of disgust washed over me. What was the point of studying hard if nothing was good enough? Shouldn't my parents be thrilled that their daughter graduated at the top of her class?

That afternoon, as planned, five classmates and I boarded the No. 55 streetcar to the district of Spandau where our family garden plot was located. Dressed in parkas to stave off the March chill, we scrunched up piles of test papers and constructed a sizeable mound on the still partially frozen soil. The northern breeze made it difficult to start a fire. After numerous tries, we teased thin swirls of smoke out of the stack, and finally a hesitant flicker. Far from the raging inferno we had imagined, the flames leapt up lazily and soon fizzled out. The result fell far short of our expectations, and we returned home in subdued moods. I felt particularly disappointed. The botched blaze added to the morning's debacle over my grades and resulted in acute disillusionment.

Off and on throughout the year, I had felt disconnected from my classmates. After having jetted with stellar speed into early adolescence just two years earlier, I now felt that my progress had come to a halt.

Two years earlier, in 1960, I had appeared on television and arranged a German-American student exchange. Now, life seemed to recede like a subway train that pulls away from the station: All of my classmates were on board while I was still standing on the platform.

Our *Abschlußball* was an elegant affair that did not include parents. We danced to popular tunes in a ballroom with crystal chandeliers and a large dance floor. The girls wore chic prom dresses; the boys were in suits and ties. On the elevated stage, the four graduating classes performed skits that highlighted the best and the worst of growing and learning together. Still, I could not shake my vague gloom. It didn't even help that I was the envy of my girlfriends when Rudi Stevens, the principal's stepson, didn't miss a dance with me.

Business School

AFTER GRADUATING FROM HIGH SCHOOL in March of 1962, Fee and I immediately entered a *Handelsschule*—business school. Two other girls from my class chose a different business school. The core curriculum consisted of business practices, accounting principles, economics, political science, literature, business English, French, German, and Spanish. Typing and shorthand rounded out the groundwork for careers in administration.

The class consisted of seventeen girls and four boys. We were sixteen years old and now addressed by our surnames. I remained a good student and excelled in foreign languages, Spanish being the newest addition.

Since elementary school, Fee and I had occupied adjacent seats. This time, we sat in the second row along the windows until the day when our class discussed food production in the African marshland. Bored, I whispered, "Did you know that the human hair is a marsh plant?"

"The hair?" Fee looked confused.

"Yeah. It grows only on a hydrocephalus," I mumbled.

Silence. Fee was processing the information. Then she started to snort like a piglet and finally broke into unrestrained laughter.

"Would you mind sharing with the rest of the class what you find so funny about marginal cultivation practices, Miss Löffler?" Herr Durek inquired in his stern demeanor.

"It's nothing—it was just a joke," Fee replied.

"We'd all like to hear a good joke. Please, Miss Löffler, fill us in." Herr Durek pressed.

"Well," Fee struggled, "I have this thick hair, and Jutta has fine hair. We always kid each other. She just said that hair grows well on a hydrocephalus," she continued, glancing in my direction. "She implied that I have nothing but water . . ."

"Enough, Miss Löffler," Herr Durek interrupted. "If that comment strikes you as funny, I feel sorry for you."

"Miss Umbach, you should be ashamed," he continued, turning to me. "Hydrocephalic disease is a condition that only a completely immature person would joke about."

Fee and I lowered our heads. I think even my ears blushed. Why did I have to make such a stupid comment? I was just trying to be funny. *God, please, don't let him tell my parents. They'll ground me again.* House arrest had lately become one of my mother's newest disciplinary tools.

Herr Durek didn't tell my parents; he separated us instead. Fee was allowed to remain in her seat while I was moved to the last row, next to a girl named Lorena.

Sitting in the back of the class turned out to be a whole new experience. I had always sat in the first couple of rows. Here, in the last row, I could get away with all kinds of mischief without being noticed. We passed notes to each other and sometimes slipped answers to test questions into our panty hose, to be revealed with a quick hike of the skirt. During my entire elementary and high-school careers I had never been aware of the opportunities in the back of the class.

Lorena and I soon became best friends. Along with half a dozen others we formed a clique that included one boy. His name was Axel. He had red cheeks, impish blue eyes, liked to laugh and dance, and was an excellent storyteller. We suspected he was a 175er.

Paragraph 175 of the German Criminal Code addressed homosexuality. The terms gays, lesbians, or homosexuals were almost never used. We spoke of 175ers. Our clique was not at all concerned with Axel's sexuality. To the contrary, it was easy to enjoy his company without having to posture, which was so often the case in relationships with the opposite sex. In a pinch, Axel even filled the role of a protector.

Of course, I was careful not to mention our suspicions to my parents. That would have meant terminating the friendship at once. A 175er was not the kind of person my parents expected their daughter to be exposed to, much less befriend.

After school, we gathered without fail at a small, nearby coffee shop. Here, we discussed the day's events over a cup of *Tchibo* coffee and a cigarette while crowding around one of the three or four small pedestal tables. I was not allowed to smoke and would have been grounded with certainty had my mother found out. However, there was something enticing about holding a cigarette suspended between the second and third fingers, six inches from the chin, and taking a deliberate draw. It made smoking look attractive, even though I did not care for the taste and never inhaled. Still, I was committed to my favorite brand, *Kent*, and puffed it with delight. On the way home, I chewed mints and gum to freshen my breath and blamed secondary smoke for the smell in my clothes.

Lorena and I soon discovered that each of our mothers owned a sewing machine, and we decided to redesign our wardrobes. Although our combined sewing abilities were rudimentary, we excelled in enthusiasm. Two or three times each week, we cut, basted, and sewed in the afternoon, usually at Lorena's home. An old dress was reworked into a skirt; a skirt became a blouse; a blouse a bikini top. We also traded garments and before long had doubled our wardrobes.

Lorena's father was a streetcar driver, her mother a factory worker. Her parents carefully budgeted their household income. Yet, whenever we sewed at my friend's home past mealtime, I was invited to join the family for supper. My girlfriend, on the other hand, an only child herself, was never invited to dinner when we worked at my home.

Lorena's room was a nook in the hallway that her father had lovingly walled off with plywood and outfitted with an entry door to provide privacy, a notion my parents thought ridiculous. During our sew-ins, I noticed that Lorena's parents, like the Kellys, did not order us about; they listened more than they talked, and they respected our opinions. Whenever I spoke of my visits with Lorena's family, my mother quickly terminated the conversation.

After spending several afternoons each week sewing with Lorena or knitting with Evi, other entertainment venues opened up. Axel was able to come by inexpensive theater tickets and Fee, whose parents were opera singers, supplied us with opera tickets. I promoted these evening outings at home as educational enrichment and secured parental permission to participate. This way, I got to enjoy at least one night out with my friends each week.

Soon, our clique looked for other forms of entertainment. Having completed dance lessons, we decided to go dancing on Friday and Saturday nights at a local dance club. But that plan made my mother's cup overflow. She put her foot down which turned into a long-lasting conflict during which our mother-daughter relationship continued to erode.

"You're staying home," my mother said unceremoniously when I asked to join my friends on Saturday nights at Club 100. "What your friends are doing doesn't interest me. Your father and I are responsible for your well-being. We believe it's far more important that you spend the time on your homework and get plenty of rest than to amuse yourself in some hole in the wall."

"But it's Saturday. I don't have any homework. My grades are excellent. I can sleep in tomorrow. The Club 100 is a dance studio. Besides, everyone else's parents are okay with it," I argued.

"It doesn't make any difference what other parents do. It seems that you're not keeping good company. It's high time you picked some nice friends."

"But they are nice friends. I'll be home no later than twelve-thirty. Lorena is allowed to go!"

"If I hear the word 'Lorena' one more time, you're going to be grounded for the next month," my mother said.

Life became more complicated. Indeed, I was forced to let my English and my French books take the place of much more enjoyable afternoon and evening activities. I no longer talked about my friends at home; in fact, I seldom spoke at all.

Struggles for Freedom

WEST BERLINERS HADN'T VOLUNTEERED to become the eye of the Cold War. We longed to return to our former lives that had revolved around family, work, and play. But it was impossible. Disturbing events continued to profoundly affect our lives and routines.

By the end of 1961, more than five hundred East Germans had fled to West Berlin, despite the Wall. Initially, they had escaped through the city's canals, its subway system, or by crossing the provisional Wall. Now, people dug their way to freedom by building tunnels. Most of the excavations started in the West, often led by men who had fled the East and hoped to bring the rest of the family across the border. Some of the tunnels flooded, collapsed, or were discovered before they had served their purpose; others became celebrated passageways to freedom. Nearly every month that year, someone lost their life at the monstrosity that now snaked through the city.

In June 1962, East German authorities erected a second wall, one hundred ten yards into East German territory and called it the *bordermarker*. By erasing all housing between the original Wall and the new barrier, they created a closely monitored no-man's-land that allowed a clear line of fire. This Death Strip, as it would later be called, was planted with mines. A road running parallel to the Death Strip was covered with fine, loose gravel and raked smooth so that defectors' footprints could easily be spotted and lax guards identified. They also built a series of thirty-foot-high watchtowers from which guards looked down on the Death Strip with orders to shoot to kill any East German who tried to cross.

Several tunneling attempts remain edged in my memory. While the *bordermarker* was under construction, Siegfried Noffke and Dieter Hoetger were surprised by East German police when they tried to flee through their newly completed tunnel. Noffke was killed and Hoetger badly injured.

A week later, another man, Rudolf Müller, tried to lead his family to the entrance of a passageway he had dug from the basement of the West's biggest publishing house, the *Axel Springer Verlag*. As the group approached the tunnel's East Berlin opening, they were stopped by a young East German guard who was armed with a machine gun. In the ensuing scuffle, the soldier was shot to death. Müller and his family escaped to the West. Details of the event remained murky for years. Although hearts poured out to Rudolf Müller and his family at the time, following reunification, he would be tried and convicted for murder.

We had barely assimilated the attempted escapes of Noffke, Hoetger, and Müller when, in August 1962, Peter Fechter, a young East Berlin construction worker, made international news. When he tried to make his escape through no-man's-land, East German guards shot him. Lying mortally wounded on the ground behind the Wall on the East Berlin side, he cried for help for more than an hour while slowly bleeding to death. Neither East Berlin sentries nor West Berlin police dared to approach him for fear of escalating hostilities.

Finally, there was some good news. Hasso Herschel brought his sister and twenty-eight others to safety in September when he dug a tunnel from a West Berlin bakery to a cellar in East Berlin, passing under two streets and one entire block of houses. He became the most successful tunnel digger.

Within the weeks, months, and years that followed the initial makeshift wire obstacle would morph into a formidable barrier. Once East Germans could no longer leave for the West, their regime concentrated on austerity policies and consumer cutbacks. When finished, the Wall around West Berlin extended for almost a hundred miles, thirty of them dividing East from West Berlin. East and West Germany were divided by 866 additional miles of wire and concrete barriers. It would be overseen by watchtowers and manned by guards with orders to shoot. The no-man's-land between East and West would be equipped with alarms, self-activating searchlights, antivehicle trenches, and beds of nails. For the next twenty years, it would continue to be fortified, until its unexpected fall in 1989.

Thirty-seven years after the rise of the Berlin Wall, Conrad Schumann would be in the news once more. Following customary refugee processing, he had been flown to West Germany on an Allied plane. There, he had started a new life in Bavaria. Although content with the way his jump had turned out, he never relinquished the dream that one day he would be able to reunite with his family. Soon after the Wall fell, Schumann visited relatives and friends for the first time in many years. But not all of them were willing to readmit him to their circle. By deserting, they said, he had given up his right to belong. Unable to cope with the rejection, he became severely depressed and committed suicide in 1998.

The Move

"HE WHO LIVES ON AN ISLAND should not make an enemy of the ocean," East Germany's propaganda machine warned, reminding us that our lives lay in the hands of those who ruled the Communist sea around us. The words struck a chord with me. I felt like I now lived behind two walls: Ulbricht's Wall with a capital "W" and the wall with a lower case "w," the one my parents had erected with their multitude of restrictions. Lately, my mother had grounded me on several occasions, hoping to redirect my interests to what she considered "wholesome activities" such as homework. I suspected she wanted to permanently separate me from my friends.

My circle of girlfriends was still the most important thing in my life. All I wanted to do was to join them in whatever they did. Why did my parents object to our pastimes? They were innocent ones. We liked to skate in winter, swim in summer, throw occasional parties, and hang out together. What was so terrible about that? My friends' parents did not voice any objections. Did my parents expect me to admit to my friends that I was grounded much of the time? Or worse, did they want me to confess that I had to stay home to get plenty of rest? Did they not know that there was shame in having parents who wanted their offspring to move in lockstep with them? I would quickly become the laughing stock of my peers. Trying to save face, I continued to invent excuses whenever my friends invited me. But I was getting desperate.

Several unexpected events made me put my woes on temporary hold and rechannel my energy. When Sharon Kelly announced her return to the United States to start college in fall of 1962, she also invited me to spend one more summer vacation with her and her family in Ramstein. My parents did not object, and I was overjoyed at the prospect. During my visit, their black-and-tan dachshund, Mr. Poops, fathered a litter of the most adorable pups. Being an ardent lover of anything four-legged, I devoted every free minute to the five cute little fur balls that reeked of milk and puppy chow. Upon my return to Berlin, I talked of nothing but puppies, fully aware that we could not keep a dog at home because pets were not allowed in our building.

"Guess what? We're going to move!" My father announced the day I returned from Ramstein.

"Move? When? Whereto?" I was shocked and surprised. After having shared the same room with my parents for thirteen years in the Knesebeckstraβe, we had moved to our current location less than four years earlier. Our building was newly constructed and beautifully situated. Opposite a lovely park and lake, the Lietzensee, it was within a short walking distance of school and my friends' homes.

Although our flat was small, it was considerably larger than the apartment I had grown up in. I finally had my own bedroom, although it also held my father's bookcase, my mother's sewing machine, and the two armoires containing everyone's clothes. Our living room continued to double as our dining room and my parents' bedroom. My father's office was set up in the small study. Still, we lived in luxury compared to Knesebeckstraβe.

"Will I be able to keep my room?" I inquired, fearing the worst.

"Don't worry. You'll have your own room again." My father assured me.

"When are we supposed to move? And where are we going? Why are we moving anyway?"

"In about three months. To the new building that's going up down the street," my father said.

Thank God. We were staying in the same neighborhood. Actually, we were moving only two blocks away. I would stay near my friends and wouldn't have to share my room. I felt relieved. Over the course of the next hour, I learned that in our street, on the other side of the lake, a subsidized housing project was under construction. I knew the building because I had walked by the site many times.

"They're selling twenty *Eigentumswohnungen*," my father said. "They're a new form of housing. The walls belong to everybody. The buyers purchase only the air space," he explained.

I was puzzled. "We'll only own air space? How can we hang pictures if we don't own the walls?"

"We can do anything we like, as long as it's on the inside of our walls," my father enlightened me.

I was still baffled. How could anyone own air space and the inside, but not the outside, of the walls? But my father went on, "We won't have to pay rent anymore." The whole scheme began to sound like a practical joke. I looked him square in the eye.

"We'll purchase the apartment instead of renting it," he said. "In lieu of rent, we'll have to take out a mortgage and pay installments to a lender. We'll also have to pay a maintenance fee to a management company."

I was speechless. *We'll be property owners!* "If this is such a good thing, how come 'we' got to buy one of these ownership apartments? Wouldn't everyone want to buy one, too?"

"Lots of people wanted to," my mother cut in. "Pappi had to bribe everyone from the secretary to the project manager to clinch the deal."

Slowly I learned that, aside from the inevitable bribes, strict income limits, and occupation criteria applied. The five largest units in the building consisted of a bedroom, a living room, a small study, kitchen, bathroom, and a powder room. Only households of three or more persons, like us, were eligible to occupy one of those units. We had already been approved for the purchase and were scheduled to move on October 31, 1962.

"Can we keep a pet there?" I wondered out loud, thinking of the Kellys' adorable pups.

"I don't know," my father said absentmindedly, his mind already occupied with the mechanics of the move.

Tapsi

SIX WEEKS BEFORE WE MOVED into our new condo, my parents and I went on holiday to Marina di Massa on the Mediterranean. Sharon had left for the United States already, but Scotty and Marilyn Kelly joined us. My parents and I traveled in our new chocolate-brown BMW to Ramstein Air Base where we linked up with the Kellys who then followed us in their Volkswagen Beetle across the Alps and into Italy.

Putting the three hundred fifty miles between West Berlin and Ramstein behind us was far more time-consuming than traveling twice that distance between Ramstein and Marina di Massa. Since construction of the Berlin Wall, car travel through East Germany had become even more tedious than on my first trip abroad when I was seven. We were reminded once again that, although we lived in the West, we were by no means free.

As in 1952, a trip from West Berlin to West Germany required passing through four controls: one each at the Western and Eastern borders of Berlin and two more in reverse order upon entering West Germany. But inspections had become much more sophisticated since the construction of the Wall. As before, our first stop occurred at *Dreilinden*, the last outpost in the American sector of Berlin. Here, passenger and vehicle information were collected to insure safe passage through East Germany. Then, a few yards down the road, at the East German checkpoint *Drewitz*, the real tedium began:

"*Ausweise bitte*—identity cards please," the guard demanded, reaching into the car. Squatting down to our eye level, he carefully compared faces with our photo identifications.

"*Brille abnehmen*—glasses off," he barked, studying my father's features.

"*Alle aussteigen*—everyone out of the car. *Hauben auf, vorne und hinten, alle* Türen *und Handschuhfach*—Open the hoods, front and back, all doors, and the glove compartment."

As instructed, we unloaded our luggage and opened each bag to prove that we did not carry subversive literature, microfiche, or other illegal items. Carrying a Western newspaper could be considered a dissident act and lead to serious trouble. At times, the guards even required travelers to remove the car's front seats for further inspection or to have the vehicle partly dismantled by an inspection unit. But we were lucky.

My mother took a seat in the car again while my father and I walked to a group of pale yellow, abandoned-looking barracks to join the long line of travelers that was queued up in front of one of the trailers. Its doors were closed, and the interior of the windows were completely covered with cardboard or plastic. When it was our turn, my father slid the required documents through the small opening underneath one of the windows. The hole was the size of the letter slot in a mailbox. I saw a hand reach for the documents; its owner remained invisible.

Then we waited. Since there was no seating, travelers milled about until their name was called. The wait could take hours. Conversation was kept to a minimum because no one wished to draw attention. Being noticed might lead to additional inspections or to being asked into an interrogation room where family members were often cross-examined separately.

When our name was called, another faceless hand returned our identification cards through a slot under a different window. Then, my father and I had to walk to a second trailer to pay our *Autobahngebühr*, the fee for use of the poorly maintained East German highway. When all formalities were completed, we joined my mother in the car.

Upon receiving a hand signal from the guard, we slowly entered the East German autobahn and drove toward the checkpoints Marienborn (east) and Helmstedt (west), observing the strictly enforced speed limit of 100 kilometers per hour (60 miles per hour). If we took less than two hours to reach Marienborn, we would be penalized for speeding. Fines were costly and meant to infuse Western currency into the Eastern economy. If the trip took considerably more than two hours, we would have some explaining to do because no Westerner was allowed to detour into East German towns or the countryside. It was even dangerous to converse with East German citizens at designated rest stops. Spies in disguise often tried to embroil Westerners into arguments that could be interpreted as hostile to the East German Democratic Republic and lead to detainment.

In Marienborn, the East German control point at the border to West Germany, the inspection process was far more rigorous than upon leaving Berlin. Now, guards were on the lookout for vehicular modifications that might have created sufficient space to smuggle a fugitive into the West. Border patrol agents carried rods, calibrated to measure the dimensions of almost all vehicles. The exception was a small car made by BMW, the Isetta. The calibrated rods did not reference this tiny car because it was judged clearly too small to hide a refugee. But two years later, in 1964, that assumption would be disproved when nine people escaped in Isettas. With the car's heating system and battery removed, one person could successfully be hidden, although it was a tight fit.

On this trip to Ramstein, the guards carefully scrutinized our car's chassis, seats, trunk, and engine compartment. Then they stuck a rod into our fuel tank and compared the depth of its reservoir with factory measurements. Tank depth of each make and model was marked on the stick. The three of us were still watching our car's inspection progress when my mother suddenly tilted her head in the direction of a black hearse, parked to one side, and exclaimed under her breath, "Look at that!"

My father and I turned our heads in the direction she had pointed to, just in time to see border personnel take a peek into a coffin that extended from the hearse's open doors. "They're checking if the occupant is really dead," my father said in disgust. "It's legal."

Since we had not stopped in East Germany and had obeyed all traffic laws, the sentry waved us on, after checking our vehicle and travel documents. We then zigzagged through heavy concrete buttresses that were chain-anchored to both sides of the road. In case of an attempted getaway, they could be released to smash the runaway vehicle and its passengers.

Our last brief stop was at the allied *Kontrollpunkt Helmstedt* before continuing to Ramstein. Even without extraordinary delays, the trip from Berlin to Ramstein which should have taken five hours had expanded into a nine-hour travel experience. But we had put the most difficult one hundred twenty miles of the trip behind us.

Having stayed overnight with the Kellys, we caravanned to Italy for the next day and a half. During the two relaxing weeks that followed, the five of us basked in the warm sun and played in the gentle waves of the Mediterranean. Each day, we worked on our suntans; each evening, we strolled along the promenade. On Sundays, we visited the local open-air market to purchase chic and inexpensive leather goods and table linens. Toward the end of the vacation, we visited Pisa and the marble and granite quarries of Carrara where Scotty and Marilyn purchased a slab of granite to be shipped to the United Sates. Throughout the holiday, I acted as our interpreter and thoroughly enjoyed myself.

On the return trip, we again spent one night with the Kellys in Ramstein. All but one of the dachshund puppies had been sold. The remaining little pup had black eyes, a black nose, and a fawn coat with black markings. Her short legs made all of her movements look particularly uncoordinated. I called her Tapsi, an affectionate term for waddling. The little wiener dog was full of mischief and, within the first thirty minutes of our arrival, had ruined the tips of my mother's pumps. Although Mutti's shoes never quite looked the same, she only said, "Is okay." My father's suspenders acquired a new look as well when Tapsi dragged his pants across the bedroom floor, digging her sharp baby teeth into the elastic. But no one could get mad at her. She rolled and jumped and licked and kissed. Her tail rotated in full circles.

"Bitte, bitte, Pappi," I pleaded with my father, despite the pet restriction in our apartment. "Can we take her home? We're moving to that new condo. Maybe they'll allow dogs." My father could be an easy touch, and the little pup knew how to wiggle herself into everyone's heart, including his. He reluctantly agreed. On our trip home I was ecstatic. Sitting next to a big bag of Purina Puppy Chow that looked like a fourth passenger, I cradled Tapsi in my lap, her chew toys strewn across the backseat of our BMW.

The little dog soon became my best buddy. Unless I was in school, Tapsi was my constant companion. I fed her and taught her tricks. We took long walks together; my friends were her friends; and she slept in my bed. If I wasn't allowed to join my peers in the evenings, it did not bother me so much. I now had Tapsi. And for a while, I forgot all about the restrictive walls my parents had erected around me.

Independence Denied

IN 1963, MANY OF THE STONE PORTIONS of the Wall were replaced with concrete, and a second front in the Cold War opened up: mine. Later, I would remember the year as the first in a series that provided a dark background to the many colorful images of my life. It was a time when my peers began to whisper behind my back, "Poor Jutta—her parents keep her locked up behind *Schwedische Gardinen.*" Swedish curtains were a colloquialism for prison, because the bars in penitentiaries were often made from Swedish steel.

"If not now, then when will I be able to make my own decisions?" I pressed my mother, eager to establish new guidelines for joining my friends in their daily activities. I felt a broadening of parameters was in order. I was still required to ask permission whenever I left the house, whether it entailed window shopping with the girls, walking Tapsi, taking in a movie with a date, or attending a party at a classmate's home.

My mother's voice was calm, but firm, when she replied, "When you turn twenty-one. Until then, you live by our rules."

I swallowed hard. *Twenty-one!* That was four years away! I was willing to accept not being entitled to complete independence, but I also thought it reasonable to be allowed the freedom to go out on weekend evenings. As long as I communicated to my parents where I went, whose company I was in, and returned at the designated time, I saw no problem. I also believed that I should be permitted to hang out with my girlfriends in the afternoons once my homework was done.

It wasn't that I objected to strict discipline. To the contrary. I had been brought up to respect and abide by parental decisions. I favored clear guidelines, even rigid ones. If I was supposed to be home at midnight and didn't return until two minutes after, I accepted punishment without complaint. But I loathed arbitrary rules.

"*Wo Du hin willst, da komme ich schon lange her*—I have long been down the path you're about to take," was one of my mother's favorite lines when she wanted to end a conversation. And she used it often. "Until you turn twenty-one, your father and I are responsible for you. There's plenty of time for you to date when you get older. You won't understand that now, but some day, you'll thank us."

Ja klar—fat chance, I thought, and held back tears.

My parents refused far more requests for permission to go out than they approved. If a young man was involved, I could expect a veto. Even if the activity involved a girlfriend, consent was by no means in the bag. I was no longer able to pretend to my friends that I was making my own decisions, not even token ones. It was humiliating. In vain, I pointed out to my parents that all of my friends socialized under the same basic rules. It was like a battle with the Titans. My mother would not budge on the subject, and my father backed my mother. They acted like two boots of the same pair.

So that's it then, four more years of prison. It was only February, and my parents had already made me turn down a number of invitations, even a birthday party at the home of my former high-school homeroom teacher, Frau Brunk. The reasons for refusal varied:

"Helga isn't the kind of company we'd like you to keep,"

"It's too dangerous to take the bus late at night,"

"You just went last week. That's enough," or

"Who's going to take Tapsi for a walk while you're out gallivanting?"

My mother reminded me often that I had asked for a dog and had promised to take care of it. Other times, she scheduled sewing projects that required my assistance and could not be postponed, even by a few hours.

My friends asked, "Why don't you stand up to your parents? Are you afraid of them?"

Why didn't I stand up? I had no answer. Maybe it had something to do with the concept of honoring thy mother and thy father. Maybe my strict upbringing precluded disobedience. Maybe I just had not learned how to fight yet. As often as not, I responded to my parents' rules by falling into sullen silence. Away from home, I faked cheerfulness. But my parents' stern stance had a confidence-busting, resentment-fostering, personality-changing effect on me that I had not anticipated. I felt like a pawn on a chessboard. The battle of the wills took a heavy toll as both sides dug in. In a timid attempt at showing independence, I feigned indifference toward the restrictions imposed on me. *Fine. See if I care!* I liked to show a total lack of interest in any alternatives my parents might present. *Go to a coffee house as a family? Forget it. I'd rather stay home.*

But the resulting isolation got to me. I needed to find something to do with my time. Remembering the fun I had had in my art classes in high school, I initially turned to crafts and painting. I constructed a magazine rack for my room and covered it with wine-bottle labels; I converted a wooden box into a small vanity table and draped a light-blue curtain around it that matched my drapes. The activities felt rewarding at first, but soon I felt empty again. I missed the camaraderie of my friends.

Next I joined International Pen Pals and began corresponding with two French-speaking young men my age: a Parisian, named Jean Paul, and André in Québec, Canada. I was in my fifth year of learning French, and since both young men lived far from Berlin, my parents voiced no objections. I spent hours in my room composing letters in French. There were rough drafts, lots of revisions, and then a carefully penned final version on my light-blue stationery. We swapped photos, described our hometowns and lifestyles, and talked about family and friends. Sometimes, we used reel-to-reel tape recordings to share local history. Jean Paul and André also recorded the latest hits in their countries. In lieu of real-life dates, I fantasized about my pen pals.

I was still allowed to sew with Lorena, and once every fortnight, Tapsi and I marched to her home to alter our existing clothes or to create new pieces. Some alterations presented opportunities to provoke my parents' ire while feigning innocence. My navy-blue summer dress was an example. The garment came with an enormous white collar that made my head look like an afterthought. Tentatively, I removed the collar and studied the dress.

"Lorena, how do you think it would look if I made a cut below the bra line and put white lace over the bosom? I could sew on spaghetti straps."

"Why not? But how are you going to do that?" We conferred for a while, and then Lorena helped me mark the cuts with tailors' chalk. Boldly, I cut into the fabric and returned home with no more than a skeleton of the dress.

"How do you like this?" I asked my parents as I strutted into the living room during the news hour. Clad in the navy-blue outfit with a very scanty top that was held up by nothing more than two thin ribbons framing my bra, I said, "*Oben Ohne*—going topless." It took several minutes for my parents to recover.

My afternoons with Lorena also provided a welcome chance to prattle about my secret crushes and her latest dates. Despite these efforts at keeping busy, however, I often felt lonely and depressed. I hated my curtailed life. But I was looking forward to the month of May, a huge reprieve waiting on the horizon.

England

DURING OUR SECOND AND LAST YEAR of business school, Herr Zellmer, our English teacher, took the entire class on a study tour to Great Britain. It was May of 1963 when my bells of freedom rang.

Following an eight-hour train ride, we reached Hoek van Holland Haven on the western coast of the Netherlands. There, we boarded an overnight ferry and crossed the English Channel to Harwich on the British Isles. Since the sea passage was going to be an all-nighter, we were sent to our cabins soon after dinner. Each berth accommodated four or five students.

"Look! Isn't that cute," Evi said and pointed to a rail along the leading edge of the beds, "They decorated in a nautical theme." The ship rocked gently back and forth as we giggled with excitement, getting ready for the night ahead. Curlers and clips placed strategically for a stunning bouffant hairdo the next morning, we pulled the blankets to our chins and wished each other sweet dreams.

Less than two hours later, the ferry no longer rocked softly. It rolled powerfully from side to side. Afraid of accidentally falling out of bed, we held on to the bed rails which apparently were more than decorative.

"I feel a little woozy. Are you guys okay?" Evi whispered after a while.

"I'm getting nauseous, too." Rita sounded subdued.

Although each one of us had pretended to be asleep, we were in fact wide-awake and now confessed to queasy stomachs. Recalling Tante Michen's advice, "Always look at the horizon when you feel seasick," I persuaded Lorena to get up and go topside with me. We removed our curlers, got dressed, and climbed to the upper deck.

The night was black. The deck was wet and slick. A stiff, frigid breeze slapped our faces, and with each swell, the ship bolted high and fell back hard. Holding on to the bulkhead, we could make out the shapes of Fee and several other classmates alongside the rail, their collars turned up. They, too, had come topside to keep from getting sick. When we joined them, wobbling over like drunks, we learned that more than half of our group was ill. Lorena and I did not return to our cabin until the oyster light of dawn exposed the horizon, and then only to gather our belongings. Seeing Rita's and Evi's greenish faces and smelling the diesel had sufficed to send us topside again.

As soon as we debarked, everyone felt better. A bus took us to Luton, a town that had partnered with West Berlin in the Sister City program, and was located about thirty miles north of London. Close to noon, the coach disgorged its fare at a youth hostel, our home base for the next two weeks. From the moment we arrived in Luton, days were filled with new and exciting impressions. We started by venturing into nearby villages. Then we explored several of the colleges and churches in nearby Cambridge. On a trip to London, we visited Trafalgar Square and the famous clock tower that houses Big Ben. We also watched the changing of the guards at Buckingham Palace, photographed London Bridge, and visited the Houses of Parliament. The famous Luton millinery invited the girls to tour their facility while the boys were whisked off to Vauxhall

Motor Factory. On another day, we were paired with local host families for a firsthand encounter with British life. My hosts lived in a single-family home in the suburbs and introduced me to shepherd's pie at lunchtime and tea and crumpets in the late afternoon. While we chatted, Cliff Richard's newest hit, "Lucky Lips" played on the gramophone. "Please, please play it once more," I begged over and over. I wanted to commit the song to memory before my parents could put the kibosh on my listening to popular music again.

In a quiet moment I wondered if Onkel Asa, the British soldier who had wanted to adopt me shortly after the blockade, lived near Luton. I would have liked to meet him, but unfortunately, I neither had a surname nor an address.

Evenings were spent at the hostel and filled with games and dances put on by area youth groups. When it was the local boys' turn to plan the night's entertainment, they picked a game in which only the girls got to participate. We soon found out why. We were asked to form two teams, made up of the seventeen of us plus a few of the English lasses. The girls at the head of each line were handed a key on a long string. At the sound of a whistle, the game began. As fast as we could, we were to drop the key inside our tops, thread it through our skirts, and pass it to the girl behind us until the last team member had strung the key through her clothing. By that time, each team was short of rope. The more the girls at the end of the line pulled, the deeper the necklines of the ones in the front plunged, and the higher their skirts rose. Holding tops and skirts in place, we crouched, huddled, and squealed. The English chaps, along with our four boys, cheered us on with cameras ready to shoot.

One afternoon during the last week of our stay, our class was invited to a reception at city hall, given by the mayor of Luton. The visit included a brief talk on England's political system, its borough, councils, and wards.

On the way to the function, Herr Zellmer, chatting with the driver in the front of the bus, suddenly turned around and declared, "I was going to address the mayor myself, but I think it would be much nicer if one of you did it." Waving his notes through the air, he looked at me.

"How about it, Jutta? You're our top English student, aren't you?" He winked, making fun of my exposure to American English.

Chest swelling with pride, I swung my feet into the aisle. I felt as if I had just received a personal invitation to dine with the queen. For a moment, I shamelessly basked in the honor about to be bestowed on me.

"I jotted down a few words here," Zellmer said, waving his notes and bringing me back to reality. "You can use them if you want." He handed me his draft and turned back to the driver.

I looked at the paper. I looked again. *I can't read this!* Tripping over a word in every line, I mouthed, *it is a great honour and pleasure . . . f . . . what?* "Herr Zellmer, excuse me, what does this say?" I tapped him on the shoulder.

He glanced at his notes and read aloud, "It is a great honour and pleasure for me." "Oh, okay, thanks." I reread the passage, "It is a great honour and pleasure for me . . . having . . . been ordered . . . to . . . what?" My progress was foiled again. "Herr Zellmer, I can't read this either."

It quickly became obvious that I had serious trouble deciphering his scribbles. But since I wanted to give the mayoral address badly, I hung in there.

"How much time before we'll get there?" I asked.

"Five minutes at the most. Don't try to memorize the speech. Just use it as a crutch," Herr Zellmer said.

Use it as a crutch? I can't just give a speech off the top of my head, I thought, and asked a few more questions. But the more I asked, the more revisions he suggested, and the more confused I got. Some words I had never even heard of. Running out of time, I did the one thing Herr Zellmer did not want me to do: I tried to memorize the speech. Just rattle it off whether you understand it or not, I told myself.

In the interim, our English teacher had redirected his attention to my classmates. "Can you guys sing a song at the reception? How 'bout one of those folk songs you sang on the way to Holland?" He asked. Suggestions were shouted; melodies whistled; jokes cracked. Throughout the general joviality, I rehearsed my speech, plugging my ears with both fingers.

The majestic, dark-paneled council chamber of Luton embraced centuries of history. As we filed into our seats, we could almost feel the connection to the past. Then the mayor welcomed us from the dais. His wife and young daughter sat in the front row; we huddled together several rows back. I rehearsed my speech in silence during his opening remarks until Herr Zellmer motioned me to the front with a flick of his head.

I rose. As the metal taps of my heels echoed on the hardwood floor, I felt my knees go weak. My thoughts still racing through the speech one last time, I tried to commit every word and every line to memory.

The walk seemed endless. Only my heels broke the silence. All eyes were on me as reporters with cameras, cables, and lights were poised to the side of the dais, ready to capture the moment. With each step ahead, my courage oozed farther away from me. By the time I had arrived in the front, my mind was blank.

"Mr. Mayor, Mayoress," I began. "It is a great honour and pleasure for me having been ordered . . ."

Darn! I was supposed to say "asked."

". . . to return your address. Far or less, it is our first visit to a . . ." I tried to visualize Zellmer's paper. *What is the next word?* His scribbles failed to come into focus. In desperation, I started from the beginning.

"Mr. Mayor, Mayoress, it is a great honour and pleasure for me having been ordered . . . uhm asked . . . to return your address. Far or less, it is our first visit to a . . ." Still nothing. Blank. Cameras flashing. Chaos.

"Mr. Mayor, Mayoress . . ." I began a third time.

God, you got me into this. Now get me out of here. If there had been a trapdoor, I would have liked to have fallen into the abyss below. My mind completely blank, tears rolled down my cheeks.

With warm and heartfelt words the mayor rushed to my assistance and thanked me. On cue, my classmates began to sing. Head hanging, I returned to my seat, heels clicking on the hardwood floor all the way back. Herr Zellmer apologized on my behalf and gave the speech himself. My classmate, Joachim, squeezed my hand and whispered, "It's all right. Zellmer should've given you more time." Then he put his arm around me. His kind gesture felt so good. Still breathing in small hiccuppy spurts, I leaned against him. *He's sticking up for me.*

On our final night in Luton, the local teens threw a farewell party. The dance floor was crowded with English and German youths when suddenly the lights went out. Power failures were not uncommon in the old building. Within minutes, the lights were restored, but not before I felt someone grab me by the shoulders from behind, turn me around, and plant a kiss onto my lips. When the lights came back on, I saw a faint grin on Joachim's face. He stood next to me with his British partner. My heart jumped. It had been my first kiss, this kiss in the dark. I was seventeen.

The Man, the Myth

REINER. MY CRUSH ON HIM was my secret. No one knew; not even the object of my adoration. The delicate fabric of this romance was spun of nothing but tender dreams. He was my hero; I was his heroine. Lying in bed late at night, I conjured up innocent encounters. In my mind, he had the physique of Adonis, eyes the color of a fawn, and the persona of a saint. Occasionally, I caught a glimpse of him riding his bike to and from school. Two years my senior, he prepared for university entry. At first, we nodded shy greetings to each other; then added bashful smiles. The nods and smiles continued for months until an opportunity for a formal introduction arose.

Late one early summer afternoon in 1963, only a month after our class trip to England, my mother asked me to dash to the grocer for a half dozen eggs, essential for that evening's meal of *Strammer Max*—stiff Max. This quick repast, popular since the 1920s, consisted of a slice of buttered bread, topped with smoked ham and a fried egg. Folklore had it that this simple meal strengthened the sexual prowess of the person consuming it. Had my mother been acquainted with the myth, *Strammer Max* would undoubtedly have been stricken from the Umbach menu. Neither did she seem aware that sometime during the past forty years, the name "Max" had also acquired a colloquial meaning akin to the American name "Dick."

Pleased with myself for being "in" on the vernacular of the day and light-years ahead of my mother, I sauntered down the street. Turning the corner, I almost bumped into Reiner who cradled two large bags of groceries.

My heart jumped. My vocal cords tightened. My mouth went dry. There it was—the moment I had waited for. *Does my hair look okay? My outfit?*

Reiner stopped midstride, smiled and said, "Well, hullo there. I'm Reiner. What's your name?"

My tongue felt like a dehydrated sponge. My lips stuck to my teeth. I searched for a witty reply but, instead, felt only a powerful dip in articulating ability. I barely managed to squeeze out a faint "Hullo." Painful silence followed. *Verflixt*—shoot—I had rehearsed this moment over and over. Where did the poetic lines go I had memorized?

Reiner took the lead again, "You've moved, haven't you? Where do you live now?"

"We moved down the street." I felt my voice shrivel as I pointed in the direction of our new condo. I wanted so much to impress him but I couldn't think of one clever response. A wave of heat made its way from my chest, past my neck and ears, to the roots of my hair. I began to tremble. Unable to advance our conversation, Reiner soon bade me good day, and we continued on our separate missions.

How could I act like such an idiot? I blew it. I hated myself. On the way back from the grocer, I went over and over the few words and glances we had exchanged and concluded that Reiner would never speak to me again.

A couple of weeks later, I took Tapsi for a walk through the Lietzensee Park. Its gardens surrounded a body of water that was part of a chain of small lakes, dating back to the Ice Age. Countless willow, poplar, birch, and maple trees provided serenity to this otherwise bustling central neighborhood. Weeping willows formed canopies over the water's edge. Swans and ducklings made their homes in the thick grass. Benches under idyllic arbors of fragrant vines lined footpaths of decomposed granite. Until my family's move to the new condo, Reiner and I had lived in the same apartment building, on the other side of the lake.

And there, on a path merging with mine, Reiner approached. "Hi there. What's your dog's name?" He asked.

"Tapsi."

"What are you doing here?"

"I'm taking Tapsi for a walk."

We strolled side by side. At last, I was composed enough to walk and talk at the same time. My feet barely touched ground. The subject of our conversation was immaterial. I was walking and talking with Reiner—the man, the myth, the legend!

We approached a spacious circular area. Secluded benches lined its perimeter. A life-size sculpture at the center depicted a nude male youth untying his sandals. The plaque on the stone base read: *Sandalenlösender Knabe*—sandal-binding boy—by Fritz Röll. I knew the bronze had won a major award. Since its recent installation in the park, I had studied it carefully and concluded that it was anatomically correct. Now, as I was walking toward this representational art piece in the company of a living specimen of the same sex, I grew apprehensive. Presumably, there were similarities. *Can he tell what I'm thinking?*

My eyes darted to the ground, to the sky, anywhere. As soon as I got up my nerve to look at Reiner, I felt the heat rising. My voice began to shrivel again; then it petered out altogether. We soon parted and went our separate ways.

A few more weeks passed. The *Volkshochschule*, an evening school for adults, offered a class in conversational English. Given my prior exposure to everyday American English with the Kellys, I decided to give it a try. Under the guidance of Mr. Blackburn, we took turns reading and translating from current British newspapers. Although I found it difficult to work without a dictionary, I enjoyed the class.

Every few minutes, a female student in the seat in front of me dabbed an alluring fragrance behind her ears. "What's the name of that cologne?" I finally asked.

"It's not a cologne, it's an eau de toilette," she corrected me. "It's Nina Ricci's L'Air du Temps." She showed me the bottle. From that day forward, L'Air du Temps became my fragrance, too.

One evening, I arrived in class, trailed by a cloud of my new delicate scent, when I saw Reiner seated in the back row. While thrilled to see him there, I dreaded having to reveal my ignorance with pitiful translations. *Shall I make a quick exit?* But Reiner had already caught my eye, and I took the chair next to him. All went well until it was my turn to translate the day's piece. Then, the print turned into hieroglyphs, and I could not make out a single word. Only with Reiner's help did I manage to get through the text. For the few minutes we collaborated, I lost track of past, present, and future and was filled with only one overwhelming thought: He likes me.

Still the Little Girl

"DON'T YOU HAVE ANY PRIDE?" my mother asked, inspecting an old dress I had just updated by making a few tucks here and there. "It looks pretty nice until one takes a closer look!"

I hated the ubiquitous "one," the apparent keeper of the code of conduct who refused to entertain opposing views.

"You should've overlocked the seams so they won't unravel. The inside is just as important as the outside, even if no one sees it. 'Made in Germany' stands for quality."

"I guess I'm doing turn-of-the-century work then," I chuckled, "because in the late 1800s, 'Made in Germany' stood for inferior merchandise."

My mother looked at me in disbelief, but said nothing.

"Honest!" I went on. "The Brits invented the label. Their government wanted to discourage imported goods and marked German merchandise. Seeing the stamp implied, 'Watch out. This product might be inferior.'"

"Do you always have to have the last word?" my mother asked, ignoring my diatribe.

"It's true," I defended myself, "we just learned it in school."

Mutti had apprenticed as a seamstress and expected perfection from herself and others. She could and would hand sew a dress with such tiny stitches that they looked machine made. I, on the other hand, was impatient. I wanted my work to look stylish and did not care about the inside. Chic and speed were my motivators.

My mother turned away. Derailed conversations infuriated her. She had meant well, but as it happened so often these days, we had talked past each other. Our disagreements had escalated in recent months. Now, we even quarreled over the sliver of light that escaped from underneath my bedroom door.

One night I had read in bed, long before midnight, but past my parents' bedtime, when my father suddenly opened my door. "*Mach' sofort das Licht aus*—Turn off that light immediately," he thundered.

"Why? I'm reading."

"Number one, reading late at night is bad for your eyes, and number two, your mother and I can't sleep. We can see the light shine through the glass in our bedroom door, and it keeps us awake. We have to work tomorrow."

"But my door is solid wood and it is closed. How can the light bother you?"

"Well, it does. So, please . . . no arguments."

Annoyed, I quit reading and turned off the light, but the next evening, I read again. This time, I hunkered down under my eiderdown comforter holding a flashlight. Still, my father noticed the light and made me stop.

We disagreed on my appearance as well. One sunny afternoon, Fee and I promenaded through the park, dressed in high heels and our Sunday finery. Over a tailored grey skirt I had fashioned during one of my sew-ins with Lorena, I wore my new Wedgwood-blue knit pullover and buttoned sweater set, and a pair of matching clip-on earrings from Woolworth. To further enhance my appearance, I had painstakingly experimented with black eyeliner and white lipstick, the current fads.

As Fee and I strolled through the park, we happened upon my parents who also decided to take in a breath of fresh air. We briefly greeted one another and continued on our separate paths. Upon returning home, however, my father received me with a stern, "Take off that war paint at once. You look like a whore." I was shocked. I had thought my makeup rather attractive.

A few days after reflecting on the event in my diary, a small hardcover book with a simple latch, I became aware that my mother seemed strangely familiar with my notes. I knew she routinely read my mail. But had she read my journal as well? I'll code my commentary in the future, I decided, and came up with a crude set of symbols. The sign language we had used on class trips served as my model. *See if you can read this,* I silently dared my mother a few hours later after I had perfected the code. Would she approach me about the meaning of an entry like "ꝋ‖ 8ΛΘλⅉƐ⧣"? But my mother never mentioned my secret language, and I began to encrypt all intimate thoughts.

My requests to be allowed to participate in social events remained a major issue. If the occasion included young men, permission was routinely denied. For consent to attend girls-only functions, it helped to get the friend's mother to extend the invitation. Even then, the answer could go either way. Longing for relaxation of restrictions, I asked my favorite aunt and godmother to intercede on my behalf.

"Tante Michen, please talk to Mutti and Pappi! All I want is to do the things my friends are allowed to do."

A polio survivor, and less than five feet tall, my aunt had lots of spunk. "Your parents aren't easily convinced, but I'll try."

"They'll listen to you." I said full of optimism.

One afternoon, my mother and aunt chatted in the living room where I was absorbed in a school project when Mutti suddenly demanded, "Jutta, please go to your room." I suspected that the touchy subject of house rules had been broached. Without a word, I scampered next door and pressed my ear against the wall. Although I could make out voices, I could not catch the words. After my aunt left, I waited for a proclamation of new, more lenient rules. But nothing happened. My parents' strict stance remained unchanged. Disappointed, I pressed my aunt a few days later, "What did Mutti say?"

Tante Michen sighed, "Jutta, there's nothing I can do. Your mother has her own ideas about what's best for you."

Then, something unexpected happened. Scotty Kelly and his father, Frank, came to Berlin for a few days. Together, the five of us toured the city's attractions. On the last day of their stay which was also Grandpa Kelly's 72nd birthday, my dad arranged to take all of us to a famous Berlin nightclub, the *Ballhaus Resi*. To my surprise, he included me. It was my first time in a nightclub, and I definitely wanted to act grown-up. But the magic of the establishment was somewhat intimidating. First of all, the *Resi* was huge. Tall sprays of water swayed to live music, emulating graceful dancers while the band played one popular tune after another. People dined and danced. But the most incredible feature of the house was the table décor which included telephones and pneumatic mail tubes. Red posts were mounted to each table with a dial that incorporated the triangular foot of the handset. At the top of each post, large numerals indicated the table number. Patrons wanting to request a dance simply lifted their receiver and dialed the number of the desired table.

Soon after we were seated at table number 26, the light on top of our post flashed. My father picked up the phone and momentarily handed me the receiver. "Here, it's for you."

Confused, I grabbed the phone. A man's voice said, "Hullo, I'm Klaus at table 54. Would you care to dance that twist?"

I flushed and looked around the room. There, at the other end near the wall, a young man waved. *Kinda cute!* Wide-eyed, I looked around our table. Scotty smiled and nodded, "Go for it."

I cast a questioning glance at my father. He also nodded. My mother smiled.

Really? No objections anyone?

"Sure," I said into the phone. "I'd love to."

When I returned to the table, still panting from the twist, a message was waiting in the mail tube.

"How about the next waltz?" It was signed, "Andreas."

I was in heaven. Throughout the evening, I waltzed, boogied, bopped, and twisted with various partners. Even Grandpa Kelly proved to be an excellent dancer. Everyone, including my mother, had a wonderful time. *Hurrah!* Tante Michen's talk had worked its magic after all.

But by New Year's Day, I was back to brooding. My mother, father, and I had celebrated New Year's Eve at the *Palais am Funkturm*, a beautiful dance pavilion next to the radio tower. I suspected that I was the sole reason for this extravagance because my parents rarely went out or danced. Although I would have preferred to attend a party with friends, I appreciated the gesture.

Two levels of comfortable booth and table seating surrounded a humungous dance floor. With few breaks, a live orchestra played dance music from nine o'clock in the evening on New Year's Eve to five o'clock in the morning on New Year's Day. Following midnight well-wishes, partygoers enjoyed a brief display of fireworks in the cold night air and then hurried back onto the dance floor. I danced every dance until closing time, alternating between two or three good dancers. Meanwhile, my parents sat at the table, sipped champagne, and watched the crowd. I did not see them take more than one or two turns around the parquet. Nonetheless, they seemed to enjoy the evening and had no issue with my partners. However, when I agreed to a date with one of them for the next day, my parents scowled and put their foot down. "Haven't you danced enough tonight? Give it a rest. No dates for a while, okay?"

I was baffled. Were we are back to the old restrictions? How could it be okay to dance with a guy all night and then totally unacceptable to go out with him the following day? I racked my brain for answers. *Do my parents want to chaperone my dates? Do they still not trust me after seventeen years?*

John F. Kennedy's Berlin Visit

MY PARENTS WERE STILL SNOOZING when I slipped into a skirt and sweater at 5:00 a.m. on June 26, 1963. Shortly after noon that day, US President John F. Kennedy was expected to speak in front of Schöneberger Rathaus, West Berlin's city hall. Because his visit was likely to bring out unprecedented numbers of Berliners, my friends and I wanted to arrive early. We hoped for a spot near the podium.

At 6:00 a.m. I arrived in the plaza in front of city hall, carrying a full-size American flag, a present from Grandpa Kelly. To our surprise, we were by no means among the first ones to arrive. Large numbers of people had camped on the sidewalk overnight.

"They expect the biggest crowds ever," Joachim said.

It was only the second political rally I had ever attended. When I came to see Robert F. Kennedy speak the year before, I had come because Bobby was "cute." This time, I came to hear the message. I wanted to know where America stood on the Berlin question. JFK was the first American president since Harry S. Truman, Soviet Premier Joseph Stalin, and British Prime Minister Clement Atlee had attended the Potsdam Conference in the outskirts of Berlin in July 1945. Young, athletic, and charismatic, President Kennedy embodied a new breed of politician. He motivated and inspired. By comparison, our German statesmen came across as bores with poor oratory skills.

After Germany's surrender and occupation by the four victorious powers—the United States, the Soviet Union, Great Britain, and France—tension had developed between East and West. That tension had turned into conflict. The conflict had produced a Cold War, and the Cold War had heated up until the East German government built a wall.

My friends and I were lucky. We resided in West Berlin's district of Charlottenburg. Our movements were unrestricted inside the three Western sectors, but beyond that, we lived like islanders within the large Communist territory. A trip to any other Western destination was limited to air travel within three designated corridors or to highway travel on four specific roads. The latter was synonymous with long border delays and harassment by East German guards. Since the construction of the Berlin Wall, men and women were dying trying to cross it, and West German and international heads of state had avoided visiting our city. Even our West German brothers had been heard to whisper, "Why not simply hand West Berlin to the Russians? Then we'll have peace." If our fellow Germans couldn't be bothered, why should the rest of the world care?

With our isolation came a sense of abandonment and fear of communist takeover. This insecurity had spread like a cancer. We now looked to America for peace and protection. And to us, John F. Kennedy was the face of America.

Our small group of friends claimed a spot about six feet from the podium and passed the time watching people tie ladders to light posts and traffic signs, hoping to create first-rate viewing platforms. Shortly after 9:30 a.m., Joachim turned on his transistor radio. "The presidential Boeing 707 has landed. President Kennedy was received with a twenty-one gun salute," the commentator said. We followed the slow progress of Mr. Kennedy's motorcade as it proceeded to Congress Hall, the Brandenburg Gate, Checkpoint Charlie, and the Airlift Memorial. "Tens of thousands line the streets," the reporter said. I knew that even my father, a totally apolitical man, planned to stand with his camera at the corner of Joachimstaler Straße, hoping to snap photos of Kennedy, Adenauer, and Brandt as they passed by in Kennedy's limousine.

An hour before the president was scheduled to arrive, the Rudolph-Wilde-Platz in front of city hall, where we stood, was already packed. Still, more people pushed into the area. About 450,000 now squeezed together in the small square and its narrow feeder streets. Balconies, trees, rooftops, statues, streetlights, and traffic signs, all had become prime viewing stands.

Berliners of all ages and economic status—students like us, seniors, blue-collar workers, professionals, men and women, young and old—pressed shoulder to shoulder. The pulsating mass seemed to take on a life of its own. My small group had been pushed to one side and ended up about twenty feet from the podium. We no longer held the only American flag in the crowd. Two others had appeared. One was even hand sewn, each star appliquéd individually.

Tension mounted. When Kennedy finally stepped onto the podium shortly after 1:00 p.m., applause gathered speed like an approaching storm. The president of Berlin's House of Representatives, Otto Bach, spoke the opening words. Next, Chancellor Konrad Adenauer fueled our emotions by reminding us,

"TODAY, FIFTEEN YEARS AGO, ON THE TWENTY-SIXTH OF JUNE, THE FIRST PLANES OF THE AIRLIFT LANDED AND SAVED BERLIN."

Cheers turned into a roar. Tears blurred my vision for a moment when I considered how lucky I was to be standing in the crowd at this very moment. If it hadn't been for the US-conceived airlift in 1948, after the Russians besieged our city, who knows whether I would have survived? Without coal, we might have frozen to death; without food, we might have starved to death during those worrisome 324 days when I was less than three years old.

Finally—finally, John F. Kennedy reached for the microphone. For a brief moment, a hush fell over the crowd. We listened to his voice echo across the sea of his fans, followed by the interpreter's translation:

"I AM PROUD TO COME TO YOUR CITY TODAY AS GUEST OF YOUR MAYOR.

I AM PROUD TO HAVE VISITED THE FEDERAL REPUBLIC OF GERMANY TOGETHER WITH YOUR CHANCELLOR. . . I AM PROUD TO HAVE COME IN THE COMPANY OF GENERAL CLAY WHO HAS COME TO THIS CITY DURING ITS GREAT MOMENTS OF CRISES AND WILL COME AGAIN, IF EVER NEEDED."

We went wild. General Lucius D. Clay was the military governor of the US occupation zone from 1947 to 1949. It was Clay who gave the orders for "Operation Vittles," the code name for the Berlin Airlift. Air supply started only two days after the Soviets had blocked all access routes. Now, General Clay stood humbly to one side of President Kennedy, who continued,

"TWO THOUSAND YEARS AGO, THE PROUDEST BOAST WAS: 'CIVIS ROMANUS SUM.' (I AM A ROMAN). TODAY, IN THE FREE WORLD, THE PROUDEST BOAST IS: *ICH BIN EIN BERLINER.*"

At this moment, I was so proud to be a Berliner. Was I proud! I waved the American flag with abandon. "Joachim, can you hold the flag for a while?" I shouted across several heads. My arms were getting numb. Throughout the speech, they had been stretched way above my head. Now, I could not get them down. People pressed shoulder to shoulder. The crowd held up my body and made it impossible for me to bring down my arms. My feet barely touched ground. Kennedy continued,

"THERE ARE MANY PEOPLE IN THE WORLD WHO REALLY DON'T UNDERSTAND, OR SAY THEY DON'T, WHAT IS THE GREAT ISSUE BETWEEN THE FREE WORLD AND THE COMMUNIST WORLD. LET THEM COME TO BERLIN."

We cheered.

"THERE ARE SOME WHO SAY THAT COMMUNISM IS THE WAVE OF THE FUTURE. LET THEM COME TO BERLIN."

We cheered. *Yes, let them come to Berlin, and let them look over the Wall. Let them see what it looks like on the other side.*

"AND THERE ARE SOME WHO SAY, IN EUROPE AND ELSEWHERE, WE CAN WORK WITH THE COMMUNISTS. LET THEM COME TO BERLIN."

The roar increased. It was deafening. We cheered from the tops of our voices.

"AND THERE ARE EVEN A FEW WHO SAY THAT IT IS TRUE THAT COMMUNISM IS AN EVIL SYSTEM, BUT IT PERMITS US TO MAKE ECONOMIC PROGRESS. *LASST SIE NACH BERLIN KOMMEN* (LET THEM COME TO BERLIN)."

Now, tears streamed down my face. It was the most emotional moment I had ever experienced. Had I succumbed to mass hysteria, or did Kennedy really understand what it was like to be a Berliner? He was on our side. We waved and shouted in unison "Kennedy, Kennedy!" Much of the world seemed to have written us off, but Kennedy was with us. He was our man. He continued,

"FREEDOM HAS MANY DIFFICULITES AND DEMOCRACY IS NOT PERFECT, BUT WE HAVE NEVER HAD TO PUT A WALL UP TO KEEP OUR PEOPLE IN, TO PREVENT THEM FROM LEAVING US."

"Kennedy, Kennedy!" We yelled. We had lived with the monstrosity for almost two years already. It separated families and friends. And he understood.

"I WANT TO SAY ON BEHALF OF MY COUNTRYMEN… THAT THEY TAKE THE GREATEST PRIDE THAT THEY HAVE BEEN ABLE TO SHARE WITH YOU, EVEN FROM A DISTANCE, THE STORY OF THE LAST EIGHTEEN YEARS.

I KNOW OF NO TOWN, NO CITY, THAT HAS BEEN BESIEGED FOR EIGHTEEN YEARS AND THAT STILL LIVES WITH THE VITALITY AND THE FORCE, AND THE HOPE, AND THE DETERMINATION OF THE CITY OF WEST BERLIN."

I felt so proud to be someone to be admired and respected. I felt so proud to be someone with such courage and resilience, to be a Berliner! Kennedy's words comforted and uplifted us all.

"Kennedy, Kennedy Kennedy!" We shouted. Konrad Adenauer stepped forward and took a little bow. He assumed we yelled, "Konny, Konny, Konny."

"Booooooo," we screamed. "This isn't your show, Konny. Where have you been the past two years?" The crowd surged forward.

"WHILE THE WALL IS THE MOST OBVIOUS AND VIVID DEMONSTRATION OF THE FAILURES OF THE COMMUNIST SYSTEM . . ."

Kennedy talked about freedom and the right to choose, but I could no longer focus. I was exhausted. Never before had I experienced such intense feelings. He concluded by saying,

"ALL—ALL FREE MEN WHEREVER THEY MAY LIVE, ARE CITIZENS OF BERLIN. AND THEREFORE, AS A FREE MAN, I TAKE PRIDE IN THE WORDS *"ICH BIN EIN BERLINER."*

His words were swallowed by deafening cheers. Kennedy had spoken from the heart. We wanted to hug him, to kiss him, to keep him, to adopt him. The crowd pressed toward the podium and carried me forward. I was nothing more than an insignificant molecule in an untamed sea of Kennedy fans.

Mayor Willy Brandt spoke the closing words. Kennedy signed Berlin's Golden Book while the freedom bell rang and the roar calmed to spine-tingling silence.

Then the rally was over. As people pushed and shoved to break away from the pack, I became separated from my friends and almost got thrust into a subway tunnel. Instead, I was propelled over a knee-high wall. By the time I arrived at home, I looked like a weary soccer fan in a shredded skirt and pantyhose, carrying my torn flag. But I was filled with joy.

I turned on the television and watched the replays of the confetti parades in the Rheinstraße and Schloßstraße, Kennedy's review of the American troops stationed in Berlin's district of Dahlem, his speech at the university, and his departure shortly after 5:00 p.m. Before the day was out, 1.5 million West Berliners—equal to three-quarters of all of West Berlin—had been on their feet to get a glimpse of the boyish Mr. Kennedy.

"ICH BIN EIN BERLINER," Kennedy had said in his delightful foreign tongue.

Yes, you are, Mr. Kennedy, we feel honored that you want to be one of us. I want to see your land. Maybe I will some day. Maybe I will.

Turmoil

IN EARLY JULY, when the forecast called for a rare stretch of sunny and warm weather, my father unexpectedly proposed, "Let's go to Borkum for a week." An island in the North Sea, Borkum is part of an archipelago that extends from the Netherlands, along the northern coast of Germany, all the way to Denmark. In short order, we headed for the largest of the seven inhabited landmasses in a string of twelve, collectively called the East Frisian Islands.

To reach Borkum, which is part of West Germany, we drove by car through East Germany and took a ferry from Emden at the northern shore of West Germany. Because of the usual border delays, the five-hundred-kilometer (three-hundred-mile) car trip took most of the day while the ferry ride took only two and a half hours. Upon arrival at our destination, we connected with several of my father's colleagues who worked summers on the island, photographing beach-going vacationers. Each summer, tourists quadrupled Borkum's year-round population of 6,000 and created demand for holiday mementos. Personal cameras still remained an unaffordable luxury for many.

During the first two days of our stay, my mother was sick, something my father and I had come to expect. *Luftveränderung*—change of air—Mutti called it whenever we traveled. Years later, I came to realize that it was her inability to adapt to change that made her sick.

Following her recovery, we lollygagged on the beach, window-shopped in town, or enjoyed the late afternoon sun from the chairs of various outdoor cafés. In the evenings, we joined my father's colleagues at a restaurant where the men had a beer or two and outdid each other telling tall tales from the photography business. The wives listened over a glass of wine, while I danced every dance with strangers. Everyone had a good time.

Were these the same parents, who objected to my dating in Berlin, I asked myself? Had I exaggerated the severity of their restrictions? Shouldn't I be grateful to have parents who took me to nice places? Guilt crashed down hard on me again. I had been unfair, I was convinced. Suddenly, I came to believe that I could broach any subject with my parents and get a fair hearing. And there was a topic that weighed on me heavily.

"Why don't you come and live with us for six months after we get back to the States?" Scotty and Marilyn had suggested on numerous occasions. I would have loved to spend several months in America, discovering the country and its people, but I had never repeated these conversations to my parents out of fear of being rejected. Vacationing on Borkum, I felt encouraged to ask my parents for permission and decided I would bring up the subject immediately upon our return to Berlin.

The vacation flew by. During our absence, the mailman had dropped the post through a slot in the door, so that we had to sweep aside a huge pile of correspondence upon our return. Buried among stacks of business dispatches was a small white envelope, edged with the familiar red-and-blue airmail markings—a letter from Scotty and Marilyn.

Filled with anticipation, I ripped it open and read Scotty's carefully penned letter. Still struggling with the English language, I had to reread it several times. Surely, I had misunderstood. Scotty and Marilyn were dividing something? I consulted Cassell's New German Dictionary.

Stunned, I realized that they had separated and that Marilyn had returned to the United States to join her mother. "I will remain in Ramstein for the remainder of my service obligation," the letter went on to say.

I was devastated. What could have gone wrong? Scotty and Marilyn had treated each other so lovingly. Why on earth would they want to separate? I had been convinced that theirs was the ideal marriage. Could I have been wrong?

"What does the letter say?" my mother asked.

"Marilyn and Scotty have broken up," I said almost tonelessly as the envelope fluttered to the ground.

My mother's jaw fell open. "Read me the letter," she pressed. Quietly, I complied. I was heartbroken. Scotty's letter did not sound angry. It placed no blame. It gave no reasons. It simply stated a fact. Over and over I read his words that day until it finally sank in that my two most favorite people had parted. The news had created a giant hole inside of me that made me feel empty. There was no longer any need to ask my parents if I could stay six months with the Kellys in the United States. Their separation had put an end to my dream.

Troubled by Marilyn and Scotty's impending divorce, I felt glum for weeks. To add to my grief, my parents sold our garden plot in Boxfelde where my girlfriends and I had burned our high-school tests. Although I had rarely visited our *Schrebergarten* anymore, I now felt like the foundation of my life was crumbling, and I did not know how to regain my balance.

By September, I was glad to be back in business school after the disturbing events of summer. My parents looked forward to their annual seaside holiday in Marina di Massa in Italy. This year, another couple would be joining them. Since my parents liked to vacation in fall when school vacations were over and the crowds had thinned, I was to stay in Berlin with my aunt.

One evening, Scotty, now a bachelor, called us at home. "Utah, ask your parents if it would be okay for me to join them in Marina di Massa on their holiday. I have a ten-day vacation coming up." The Kellys had vacationed with us in Marina di Massa the year before and had fallen in love with the small seaside community.

"You wouldn't be able to join us, would you? We could use an interpreter, I'm sure."

My chances were slim, I knew. In order for me to go on holiday this time of year, I would have to skip school. Nonetheless I yelled full of excitement, "Pappi, Mutti . . ."

My father was delighted to have Scotty's company. Since our two families had first met in 1960, we had visited each other every year, and Scotty had stopped by whenever he was in Berlin on military business. To my surprise, it didn't take long before my father consented to let me join them as well.

"You won't miss much in school in ten days," he determined. "It'll be okay. Your mother and I will stay for three weeks. You can drive back with Scotty and fly home from Frankfurt."

I was overjoyed. Pappi could be so generous.

We caravanned to Italy. Scotty and I surfed the gentle waves of the Mediterranean all day, while my parents and their friends sunbathed. In the evenings, we all shared a bottle of Chianti in the balmy night air or went for long walks.

Ten days later, I returned to school with a curious tan, considering I had officially nursed a serious and persistent cold at home. My classmates knew the truth. All but one of my teachers pretended not to notice, but Herr Zellmer sneered, "Will you be able to make it to the blackboard on your own, Miss Umbach, or do you need assistance? You look terribly weak."

Throughout the summer, Lorena and I had spent many afternoons at her family's garden plot. Sunbathing on their small rectangle of grass avoided quarrels with my parents over what to do with Tapsi. My little buddy loved to prowl the perimeter of the plot, while Lorena and I absorbed every single ray of sunshine. She had become my very best friend. But all that changed when she fell in love with Peter, her first steady boyfriend. Suddenly, my company was no longer welcome. I was deeply hurt. We had been close since we met in business school, and all of a sudden, I did not count anymore? I could accept that she preferred her boyfriend's company to mine outside of school, but I could not understand why Lorena barely wanted to talk to me in school. "Peter and I talk about everything. There isn't much left to say," she told me. My favorite couple had separated and my girlfriend had ditched me. My world was coming apart. I felt like a ship without a rudder. Everything I had built on seemed to fall away. I felt utterly alone again.

Looking around me, I befriended a girl in class I had previously associated with on no more than a casual basis. Her name was Sonja. Her parents were divorced, and her mother had immigrated to the United States when Sonja was a young teen. Since then, Sonja had lived with her father in various parts of Germany and had moved to Berlin about the time we started business school. Sharing a common interest in the United States, we formed a friendship that would turn into a lifelong bond.

My eighteenth birthday fell on a Thursday. I didn't celebrate until the next afternoon, on November 22. Three girlfriends came for a *Kaffeeklatsch* and had barely left when the phone rang. It was Scotty. I assumed he wanted to wish me a happy birthday. Instead he asked, "Have you heard the news?"

"What news?"

"President Kennedy has been shot!"

A long silence. I tried to comprehend.

"President Kennedy? When?"

"Less than half an hour ago."

"Shot at? Or shot dead?"

Scotty shared what he knew. "Go and turn on your television set," he said. We quickly said good-bye, and I flicked on the set. In disbelief, my parents and I watched as the tragedy in Dallas unfolded. Although the shooting had occurred shortly after noon Texas time, it was already evening in Berlin. Within hours, thousands of Berliners gathered at the Rudolph-Wilde-Platz in front of city hall where John F. Kennedy had spoken only five months earlier. In a broadcast, the mayor of West Berlin, Willy Brandt, read,

"EINE FLAMME IS ERLOSCHEN. ERLOSCHEN FÜR ALLE MENSCHEN, DIE AUF EINEN GERECHTEN FRIEDEN HOFFEN UND AUF EIN BESSERES LEBEN. DIE WELT IST

*AN DIESEM ABEND SEHR VIEL ÄRMER GEWORDEN.—*A FLAME HAS GONE OUT. GONE OUT FOR ALL PEOPLE WHO HOPE FOR A JUST PEACE AND A BETTER LIFE. THE WORLD HAS GROWN CONSIDERABLY POORER THIS EVENING."

The following afternoon, my friends and I joined the 15,000 students who walked in silence from the Airlift Memorial to the Schöneberg Rathaus. We marched behind a banner that read "*Wir haben einen Freund verloren*—We have lost a friend."

On the day of Kennedy's state funeral at Arlington National Cemetery, 250,000 gathered in front of our city hall. The Rudolph-Wilde-Platz was renamed "John-F.-Kennedy Platz." In West Berlin, where the East-West confrontation could be felt more than anywhere else in the world, the grief for Kennedy was particularly deep. Our loss was personal.

During that second half of 1963, I had learned an important lesson. With childish simplicity I had held on to the fantasy that life was predictable. It wasn't, as I found out. Now, Kennedy, my hero, was gone; Scotty and Marilyn had separated; my friend Lorena had dropped out of my life; and my American dream had evaporated. My plans for the future seemed to unravel, and I could not fix any of it.

Life Begins in Earnest

JUST A COUPLE OF WEEKS LATER, and quite unexpectedly, East German authorities indicated a willingness to talk about temporary day-passes that would allow West Berliners to meet their relatives in East Berlin during the upcoming Christmas and New Year season. The Allies, West Berlin's governing mayor, Willy Brandt, and West German Chancellor Ludwig Erhard immediately agreed. East Berlin prepared for 30,000 visitors. 800,000 came. The total figure was closer to 1.2 million because many came more than once. Although West Berliners were limited to visiting family members in East Berlin, relatives from all over East Germany joined them for jubilant reunions. It was a win-win situation.

East and West Germans joyfully, although only temporarily, reunited, and the East German head of state, Walter Ulbricht, was pleased with the amount of incoming Western cash.

Similar agreements were reached over the next three years. But in 1966, Ulbricht stopped the agreements again.

Since my family did not have relatives in the East, we were unaffected by Ulbricht's unexpected Christmas bonus. I was thinking about my upcoming graduation from business school instead. It was approaching in March of 1964 and my employment prospects became of paramount importance. By January, the majority of my classmates had landed contracts. I remained stymied about what kind of work I might like to do. In February, I made application to my top two contenders, Pan American Airways and British European Airways. The allure of travel and foreign language opportunities, not to mention the chic uniforms, had steered me toward the airline industry. Disqualified from becoming a stewardess until age twenty-one, I penned into the "area of interest" box, FOREIGN CORRESPONDENT. I had no clear concept of the nature of the work, but the title sounded intriguing.

Ten days later I received my first rejection. It came from BEA. Pan Am's response arrived two weeks later: "We do not have a suitable position at this time but will keep your application on file." It was now the beginning of March, less than three weeks to graduation, and I was still without a job offer.

"How's your job search going?" my parents inquired.

"I'm working on it," I mumbled.

The next day, I applied to my second choice employers, Air France and Lufthansa, second choice because I was less competent in French than in English, and Lufthansa flew internationally but not to Berlin. Under the postwar occupation statute, only four airlines had Berlin landing rights: Pan Am, BEA, and Air France in West Berlin and Aeroflot in East Berlin. Lufthansa served West Berlin by maintaining reservation offices and by partnering with the three Western airlines for airfreight shipments.

I considered myself to be in dire straits. My longtime friend, Fee, had secured an entry-level position at a bank; Sonja had accepted a secretarial post at our local electric company. Most of my classmates talked of nothing but their impending first job. *What is wrong with me?* Why didn't I have anything lined up yet?

On March 19, I graduated at the top of my class and was presented with a scholastic achievement award. Although still without firm prospects, I was relieved to learn that Lufthansa had invited me to a group examination with the potential for further interviews.

I was one of seven girls, all recent graduates, who were invited to the airline's city offices. In a battery of tests that lasted most of the day, the company psychologist assessed our individual abilities to solve grammatical and mathematical problems, tested language aptitude, and conducted a lengthy IQ test. None of my classmates had undergone such extensive assessment or had landed jobs with national firms. I felt my star to be on the rise again.

Next day, my parents and I drove to Ramstein Air Base to bid farewell to Scotty Kelly who had completed his European tour of duty and was returning to the United States. With his departure, another important chapter of my life had come to a close. The friendship with the Kellys had opened my eyes to new ways of thinking, often to the chagrin of my parents. But even my mother and father had opened up a little during our four-year friendship with the Kellys, and Scotty's send-off touched each one of us in a different way.

Upon our return to Berlin two days later, my glum spirits got a lift when I spotted an official-looking letter from Lufthansa in the mailbox. I had been scheduled for a follow-up interview with the company director, Herr Schröder. The meeting went well. I was hired on the spot to fill a position in Lufthansa's freight department, directly at the airport. I was thrilled. *Soon, I'll be right in the middle of the sizzle that airports are known for.*

The two-year contract called for a monthly salary of three hundred fifty marks ($87.50 at the time). My parents insisted on one hundred marks for room and board, leaving me a whopping two hundred fifty marks. Obviously, entry-level employment would not lead to riches. However, the contract contained a clause that clinched the deal for me. I was not only encouraged, I was obligated, to complete a four-week training course in Hamburg. Lufthansa would pay for training, accommodations, transportation, and meals. I was ecstatic. I hadn't even started to work yet, and already a travel opportunity presented itself. *I'm going to like this job!*

"What's your title going to be?" my mother asked when I got home.

"Foreign correspondent," I said with confidence.

I was to report to work six days later and leave for Hamburg three days after that. During the few days preceding the start of my employment, my mother insisted, "Put your things in order. Time is short. You're not in school anymore. *Der Ernst des Lebens beginnt*—Life begins in earnest."

She was adamant that I wash, iron, and repair my clothes, clean my room, start packing, and forego all social engagements. *Things will change soon*, I consoled myself, *Once I work, my mother won't be able to rule my life like that anymore. I'll be gone most of the day.*

The first day on the job, my boss, Herr Fischer, with horn-rimmed glasses, white shirt and no tie, introduced me to my coworkers, partner airline personnel, and shipping agents. Lufthansa occupied three office spaces on the first floor of the freight hangar. I was to share an office with Herr Fischer and an "Acquisiteur." *A who?* I didn't ask. I did not want to appear stupid.

Their desks stood in the middle of the room, back to back. The third desk, mine, adjoined theirs along one side, creating a rectangle. One black rotary phone cradled in an expandable chrome arm, the only phone in the room, was installed in such a way that it served all three desks. A manual Olympic typewriter took up most of the space on a small table in the corner, next to the room's only window. It overlooked a covered hangar so that virtually no natural light was available.

A second door opened into the adjoining conference room which also served as Herr Fisher's private office. But the real hub of freight operations was located across the hall, in Lufthansa's third office space. Here, two dispatchers and one administrative clerk booked and coordinated shipments. All three wore the chic airline uniforms. How I wished I could have dressed in that stylish navy-blue airline suit and turquoise blouse. But as support personnel, I was relegated to wearing civvies.

When I returned home that evening, still dazzled by the day's impressions, my mother handed me a message from Pan American. It was a job offer. But I had already committed to two years with Lufthansa. I was devastated.

I few days later, I boarded a company-paid flight to Hamburg, proudly presenting my grey employee voucher at the gate. Training felt much like an extension of school. Our class of thirty, mostly women, spent all day in an instructional facility before breaking into small groups to dine in town each evening. Afterwards, we returned to our hotel to study for the next day's exams or pop quizzes. For two weeks, we trained together. Then we separated according to spheres of duty. Participants came from all over the world, and we struck up friendships across the globe.

Soon, we fell into a work/play rhythm. Following our evening studies in the hotel, we went dancing late into the night. Young men swamped our hotel reception with calls and messages. On weekends we toured the town. A "must" on everyone's list was the red-light district, the *Reeperbahn*. In one notorious mile, bordellos, law and order, sex shops, streetwalkers, drunks, and hundreds of customers and tourists quilted into a crazy patchwork. *If my parents only knew.*

During the entire four weeks of training, I barely rested. *Who needs sleep?* It was the life I had dreamed of. I loved it.

Upon my return to Berlin, I became more than ever aware of my confinement. Nothing had changed, except that I now went to the office every day between 8:00 a.m. and 5:30 p.m. Every other Saturday, I worked an additional half day that could be banked for vacation. Factoring in the hour-long bus ride each way, there was little time for leisure. I soon realized that I often had far more fun at the office than away from it. When shipments were safely dispatched, the freight staff would invite me to a game of *Mau Mau*, a card game similar to Uno. The previous day's loser treated the players to a bottle of wine.

Although I had memorized freight routes, rates, city codes, and connections and knew the freight manual like the keyboard of my typewriter, there was little call for my newly acquired expertise. Most days, I sat alone in the office with nothing to do but daydream until

Herr Fischer or the *Acquisiteur* entered, threw their papers on the desk, and called out, "Fräulein Umbach, get ready for dictation." More often than not, they did not return until shortly before quitting time. I slowly realized that my job was not that of a foreign correspondent or that of a freight dispatcher, but that I was a secretary. I had been hired to take shorthand, type, file, and relay messages. The job offer had sounded so glamorous that I had failed to ask about my responsibilities. The promise of travel had eclipsed everything else.

During those lonely hours in the office, I cracked the meaning of *Acquisiteur*. He acquisitioned new customers; he was a salesman. It was one of my duties to schedule his daily appointments and poke corresponding color-coded pins into a huge wall map. While he never failed to thank me for my efforts, he rarely paid attention to them. In truth, he did not give a hoot about my dots on the map.

I liked my colleagues but hated the job. I would much rather have been a freight dispatcher or an *Acquisiteur*. My parents showed little empathy. "When I was your age I worked twelve-hour days," my father said. "And no one asked me how I liked it. Your generation is spoiled."

My mother repeated, "Life has begun in earnest. The real world isn't a playground."

A couple of weeks into it, the airline job had lost its patina altogether. My new girlfriend, Sonja, related similar feelings relative to her job with the electric company. Looking for mental stimulation, we visited the Maison de France, the Amerika Haus, and the British Center and signed up for free lectures. Then, three months later, she announced that she had quit her job and planned to study in the United States where her mother and stepfather lived. Her tentative departure date was in September. She would sail to New York and continue by plane to San Diego in California. I was stunned. My best friend would be thousands of miles away while I was stuck in Berlin with a two-year contract?

"Look at the bright side," Sonja said, "While I'm in San Diego, maybe you can come and visit me."

Remote Possibilities

"MUTTI, MUTTI, SONJA SAYS I CAN STAY with her in San Diego!" I stormed through the front door, all keyed up. The words tumbled from my mouth in rapid succession, betraying the enormity of my excitement. "Sonja's mom and stepfather just bought a new house. All of us can live there. Isn't that fantastic?" Returning from a Sunday afternoon visit with my girlfriend, I flew into the kitchen where my mother was busy cracking eggs into a bowl.

"Will you calm down?" My mother halted the flow of my animated prattle with an upward flick of the elbow, suspending an egg in midair. "Sonja's on another continent. She's lonely. She's looking for a friend. Do her parents know that their daughter is planting a flea in your ear? Her mother and stepfather have never even met you. Think for a moment, Jutta, think! Didn't you say that Sonja's mother just remarried? Don't you think the last thing she and her new husband would want is two teenagers underfoot? One of them not even related? Her parents are still newlyweds, for heaven's sake."

She paused, added milk to the bowl, and vigorously blended the ingredients with a fork.

"Besides, who do you propose would pay for this excursion of yours?" she continued. "Didn't you just sign a two-year contract with Lufthansa? Get America out of your head, young lady. You're only eighteen. Some day, when you earn plenty of money, you can take a trip around the world if you like. Until then, you belong home. You belong here with us, your parents."

"I could get a job in San Diego," I interjected meekly, but my words sounded as deflated as I felt. Blindsided by hope, I had not thought it through.

Sifting flour into the mixture, my mother paused and looked up, "Get a job—yeah, right," she chuckled. "Just how do you expect to land a job? Don't you think that the people in San Diego need jobs, too? And who, do you think, they're going to hire? Someone who speaks their language or Jutta who just flew in for a little fun?"

"America isn't waiting for you, my dear," my mother began again, pouring the viscous blend into the heated frying pan on the stove. "Get that crazy idea out of your head once and for all. Now go and wash your hands and get ready for dinner. We're having potato pancakes. And I don't want to hear another word about America."

I slunk down the hall to the bathroom while my mother continued her meal preparations. Deep inside I knew that she was right, but I refused to believe. Soaping my hands, I glanced into the small mirror above the sink and saw a pale, grim face stare back at me. Don't give up, not yet, not until you have investigated all possibilities, I told myself and continued to search for a weak link in my mother's reasoning.

True, Sonja's parents didn't actually invite me . . . but I can get my own apartment.

True, I haven't saved up enough money to support myself . . . but I can get a job.
My optimism grew again.
How and where will I find a job? What can I do? Down I plummeted.
Does it really matter what I do? It'll only be for six months.
Up, my emotional roller coaster went.

My Lufthansa contract presented a serious problem. Breaking it would be expensive. I'd have to pay back the training costs. That would wipe out my entire savings and leave me in debt. I concluded that the airline contract represented the biggest stumbling block to my plans. But seeing and exploring the land of the people who had conceived of the Berlin Airlift, the land that was home to the only American family I knew, the Kellys, and the land of John F. Kennedy and Lucius D. Clay, was my greatest wish. Until Scotty and Marilyn's divorce, I had counted on visiting them. Now, I tied my hopes to Sonja and her family.

I'm not going giving up my dream—not yet.

During the weeks and months that followed, I became a regular visitor at the local library. After several weeks of research, I came across a Fulbright Commission brochure that read, "Our program promotes international good will through the exchange of students. Its purpose is to bring together young people of different backgrounds to share experiences, ideas, and knowledge. Participants serve as Youth Ambassadors to their native countries and are chosen for their leadership potential."

The thin trifold fueled my imagination. As a Youth Ambassador, I would be able to experience different cultures and different ways of life. It definitely beat pushing pins into a wall chart. Forgotten was the Lufthansa contract again. In a fit of runaway optimism, I sent away for an application.

"Here we go again," my mother sighed when the forms arrived in the mail. "How can I get it through to you that you're too young to travel alone to a foreign country? You're eighteen. How many times do I have to point that out to you? Your father and I are still responsible for you. You're not going anywhere, not until you're twenty-one."

I flinched. Three more years. That meant I was not going anywhere soon. It would probably be best if I faced reality and quit dreaming big dreams. America was not for me.

In the meantime, Sonja prepared for her departure to the United States. With her grandmother as a chaperone, the two of them looked forward to a sea passage to New York, followed by a flight to San Diego via Los Angeles. Their imminent transatlantic crossing evoked in me images of sizzling adventure and mystery.

Since luggage was limited to two suitcases each, Sonja had to decide what to leave behind. I became the grateful recipient of her dresses, skirts, blouses, sweaters, shoes, purses, and jewelry—anything that did not fit into her luggage. It felt like Christmas in August. For a while, I even forgot that I would not see Sonja again, possibly not for years to come.

Although originally scheduled for September, my girlfriend's departure had to be postponed until mid-October, some time after my parents' return from their annual fall holiday in Italy. Ineligible for vacation during my first year of employment, I would be unable to join them this year. I was glad, but it left my parents in a serious quandary. On one hand, they did not want to forego their trip; on the other, they did not want to see me getting into mischief during their absence. Following a lengthy debate, they decided to stick to their original plan. They went on holiday, secure in the knowledge that Sonja's father, another strict disciplinarian, would keep a watchful eye on his daughter and thereby prevent both of us from getting into trouble. Wrong. Mutti and Pappi were unaware that Sonja's father had also booked a vacation in September, assuming that my folks would be there to keep both of us in line. Neither parent bothered to check with the other.

We did not consider it our job to enlighten either set of parents and took full advantage of this rare opportunity for independence. We partied until the dance halls closed. Since I worked full time and Sonja had already terminated her employment, we coordinated our activities. I handed her the key to our flat, and she prepared a quick bite to eat before I got home. All I had to do was to jump into the shower, change into a dance dress and shoes, wolf down a sandwich, and off we went to the Riverboat, our favorite dance club. There we danced the evening away. At closing time, we returned by bus to our respective homes. I jumped into bed for a short snooze and rose again four hours later. An hour after that, I sat on the bus to the airport, ready for the ten-hour workday. For almost three weeks, Sonja and I repeated this routine, except on weekends when we did not come home until 5:00 a.m.

Each morning, we checked in with each other. "I don't think I can manage another night out, Sonja. I'm so tired, I'm sleepwalking." But by evening, we agreed with renewed vigor, "Hey, let's do it. Let's go dancing. It's a once-in-a-lifetime opportunity."

We bonded like identical twins.

My parents returned from their holiday and suspected nothing of their daughter's recent social activities. In the middle of October, Sonja and her grandmother left for Bremen and ultimately San Diego. My existence returned to dull and predictable because my best friend and partner in crime was out of my life.

In mid-November 1964, I received the first letter from San Diego:

It's wonderful here. You'd love it. We've had sunshine every single day since I arrived. It's like the middle of summer. Yesterday, my Mom and I went to the beach. I saw pelicans, dozens of them, flying along the shoreline. We live only fifteen minutes from the Pacific Ocean. It's so beautiful!

All the houses in our neighborhood are single story and have yards. We live in a five-room house with a kitchen and bath. No one here walks. Everyone drives, even if it is only a couple of blocks. The sidewalks are empty. I have no idea where the people go.

The plants grow like weeds. We have palm trees and orange trees. Yesterday, my Mom put out a hummingbird feeder. They are tiny little birds that are real fast and feed in flight.

My stepfather wants to enroll me in college, but some papers have to be completed first. I was supposed to start in January, but may have to postpone for one more semester.

They have a big German-American club here. Try to come soon. We have a guest room where you can stay. You'll love it here.

Tausend Grüße

Sonja

P.S. We have mountains, too.

I studied every word as I reread the letter dozens of times. Finally, a picture of San Diego began to emerge: I saw a Bavarian setting with deep green meadows and tall mixed forests rising from the Pacific Ocean. The mountaintops were dotted with Swiss chalets. Single-family brick and stucco homes with steep slate roofs dotted the coast. Country roads, shaded by colorful orange and lemon trees, meandered from the shore to the mountains.

Then, I inserted myself into the landscape. I lived in a sunny apartment on top of a series of undulating hills, covered with juicy green grass and thick patches of wildflowers. From my window, I could see the Holsteins graze beneath my flat. In the distance, gentle ocean waves rolled ashore. I saw myself traveling the country roads in my own small sports car, visiting friends, my red beauty case resting in the back seat for a sleepover. Sunshine, friends, and carefree laughter everywhere. I was independent.

Yes, I'm ready for San Diego.

Herr Zellmer's Draft of the Address
to be Given to the Mayor of Luton, England,
May 14, 1963

Mister Mayor, Mayoress!

It is a great honour and pleasure for me having been ~~ordered~~ asked to return your address. Pure or long it is our first visit to a foreign country and you will, Mister Mayor, quite easily understand ~~here~~ that we were happy just to see your country and your ~~town~~ from which we knew that they part of ... fulness special activity. Let me ... your ... your ... and your words which we greatly appreciate. We are going to have a ... fairly well mixed programme to go round your country and to visit some of your most ~~sister~~ interesting local institutions. More than anybody else ~~me and~~ my and young colleagues welcome this opportunity to ~~know~~ escape from our walled home and to keep up the relation to good friends here as ~~high~~ our teacher never ceased to explain to us.

Let me summarize, Mr Mayor, all our thanks for ~~your~~ this kindness and that of all ladies and gentlemen with whom we are in touch. We have been told that it is strictly almost a tradition to present you one of our German songs ~~I beg to excuse our small group from whom I know that they are~~ ~~sorry to say, no good singers.~~

So do I, but with the excuse ~~that you~~ and statement that our very small group are no perfect singers. Thank you!

SIX

SURGES OF
OPTIMISM

Searching

SIX MONTHS AFTER GRADUATION from business school, my classmates and I met for a reunion. We were eager to reconnect and share in each other's job experiences. "I feel invisible at work," was a complaint that echoed from every table. Looking back, we now deeply appreciated our teachers' attempts at stimulating our curiosity and creativity. Employers were far less interested in our personal fulfillment. We griped about the tediousness of assigned tasks that left us unfulfilled. The only thing the business community seemed to value, we concurred, was compliance. Many wished they could return to the bygone days of school.

During the evening's festivities, I also had a long talk with my ex-girlfriend, Lorena. Our once close friendship had disintegrated when she had fallen in love for the first time. Swept up by the newness of passion, she had bestowed all of her attention on her boyfriend and completely neglected our friendship. I had felt hurt and abandoned. But during the course of the past year, they had broken up, and Lorena hoped to repair the damage to our relationship. We hugged, we cried, and we became best friends again.

One month later, on my nineteenth birthday, my mother surprised me with a welcome, but unexpected, announcement. "From now on, you can go dancing on Saturday nights. But remember, your father and I expect you home by midnight. Don't disappoint us, or we'll have to withdraw this privilege."

Full of enthusiasm, I would have promised anything. *Saturday night? Fantastic. Maybe, over time, it can turn into Friday AND Saturday nights.*

"Don't worry, I'll be home by midnight," I promised and meant it. Reality was a bit more complicated. Since I commuted by bus to and from the dance hall, I had to allow for irregularities in the transportation schedule. That necessitated my leaving more than an hour in advance of the Cinderella deadline unless Lorena, who had obtained a driver's license the year before, drove me home.

For reasons unknown, my mother had developed a strong dislike for both Lorena and her practice of driving me home. On the other hand, the late-night bus alternative did not appeal to my mother either. To my delight, her two aversions worked in my favor.

"How would you like to get your own driver's license and drive our BMW when you go dancing?" my father asked.

"Really?" I was thrilled and ready to sign up for lessons. Obtaining a license was a fairly expensive proposition. To apply for the test required a minimum of twenty hours of classroom instructions and an equal number of driving sessions. Once a week, for the next five months, I took lessons in a Volkswagen Beetle owned by the driving school. The car had an unsynchronized manual transmission which involved double-declutching. It brought back memories of my mother's maiden voyage which had prompted her never to drive again.

During my final driving test, the examiner asked me to back into a parallel parking spot on a cobblestone road, going uphill, in the rain. I stalled and restarted the engine several times trying to double-declutch. With each attempt, I ended up rolling farther down the hill. In the end, I failed the driving test and had to retake it a month later. When I finally held the coveted license, my father kept his word and let me drive the family car to the dance hall on Saturdays. But I continued to use the bus for all other activities.

Since I had discovered at the class reunion that a job, apparently any job, was unlikely to provide much personal satisfaction, I began to take work less seriously. I continued to arrive on time and carried out my assignments, but I aimed at accomplishing no more than required. It was the first time in my life that I did not strive to do my best. Instead of focusing on advancement, I was in search of self. What am I looking for, I wondered? *Do I want adventure, independence, acceptance, variety, stimulation?* The answer eluded me. Only one thing was clear to me: I was not in search of a permanent relationship. Considering the difficulties that liaisons with young men had caused at home, I did not think they were worth it.

Because I could not figure out what it was that I wanted from life, I followed up on every opportunity that came my way. I enrolled in a preparatory program for the Cambridge Certificate of Proficiency in English. Courses were offered through the University of Cambridge in Britain, and the diploma was accepted worldwide. Certificate holders were required to demonstrate competency in written and oral communication. I speculated that a diploma might come in handy should I decide to spend some time in America or become an interpreter at the United Nations, my latest aspiration.

The trip to the United States was no longer one of my primary goals, but neither had I given up on the idea entirely. Out of curiosity, I looked into transportation costs. Icelandic Airlines offered the least expensive travel I came across. The company charged two thousand marks for a round-trip Luxembourg—San Diego—Luxembourg. With a monthly income of only two hundred fifty marks after paying room and board, I figured it would take at least one to two years of serious frugality to accumulate the necessary funds. That was a long time of penny-pinching.

Unwilling to commit to a life of thriftiness, I continued to faithfully attend the certificate courses, studied hard in the evenings, and basked in the praise of Mr. Stone, our instructor. When I located an American service club that offered monthly education programs, dances and social mixers, I joined. All of my energy went into activities outside of work.

In April of 1965, I celebrated my first anniversary with Lufthansa. Following completion of my first full year of employment, I was entitled to four weeks of vacation and a 90% discount on flights to any of Lufthansa's European destinations, space available. It had been a long year in a job I did not enjoy, and I was determined to take full advantage of the position's fringe benefits.

During my first self-earned holiday, I hoped to visit a sunny location as far from Germany as possible. I decided on Greece. A youth organization that promoted low-budget travel offered reasonably priced accommodations. I filled out my request for airline tickets and booked two days in Athens and two weeks on Rhodes, the largest of the Greek islands in the Aegean Sea, southwest of Turkey. Then I announced the fait accompli at home.

"Guess what! I booked my vacation trip to Rhodes today!" I declared over dinner. My parents were stunned. It had never occurred to me to ask permission. I had earned the money that paid for the trip; I had paid for room and board at home; and I had slaved away for a full year in a job I hated. I was entitled to a trip I financed myself, I reasoned.

Upon my mother's insistence, my father paid a visit to the youth organization's head office to verify its legitimacy. "I talked with the manager. Everything appears to be on the up-and-up," my father reported when he returned, but my mother could not warm up to the idea.

"What about the language?" she probed, fingers twitching. "You don't speak Greek. You won't be able to read a street sign, much less a menu or a bill. How will you get around?"

"Big deal. I'll put the alphabet in my pocket," I replied calmly. "Why are you so worried? Going to Greece can't be all that much different from going to Italy. You and Pappi don't speak Italian, and you go to Italy every year."

My mother ignored my comment. "What about hotels? How will you find a reputable place? You'll be all alone, and we know what those Greeks are like. This is crazy. You can't travel by yourself."

The more my mother fretted, the better the trip sounded. I wasn't worried in the least. After all, it would only be for sixteen days. If I didn't like Rhodes, or the hotel, or the Greeks—well, oh well, I would be home again two weeks later. But because of my mother's vehement opposition, I figured the trip had to be an adventure worth pursuing. *I'm nineteen now. Heck, I deserve that holiday.*

I was scheduled to leave for Greece on April 12. My mother had been jumpy for two full weeks prior to my trip, causing me to tread carefully. I was so preoccupied with keeping the peace that her fiftieth birthday slipped my mind. We celebrated birthdays with such restraint at our house that they could easily pass unnoticed. Her fiftieth was no exception. "Birthdays are for kids," my mother used to say. "At my age, you don't celebrate getting older." Though she did not plan a party, she nonetheless counted on my father and me to remember her special day.

Her half-century milestone fell on a Sunday, one day prior to my departure. It wasn't until the morning of the day itself that both my father and I recalled its significance. Stores, with the exception of flower shops and bakeries, were closed on Sundays. I scrambled for a last-minute bouquet and baked a cake but was unable to purchase a gift. Pappi quickly declared, "Buy yourself something nice. That way, it'll be exactly what you want." But my mother could neither forgive our memory lapses nor get used to my impending trip to Greece. I wasn't her perfect little girl anymore, and she had an awful time trying to turn me into an adult carbon copy of herself.

Trip to Rhodes

EARLY NEXT MORNING, I left for Athens via Frankfurt. "Sorry, today's flight to Athens is completely booked," Lufthansa informed me in Frankfurt. "But don't give up. We may have some no-shows." I sat waiting on my cream-colored cardboard suitcase, holding my small, red cosmetic case in my lap as the aircraft's doors closed. "Sorry," the boarding agent said. "Not today. Why don't you try Olympic? They'll have a flight to Athens in a couple of hours from now."

Head held high and back erect, I reached for my luggage and strolled over to Olympic's desk. To me, the unexpected complication was nothing more than fodder for a great story. By resolving this small crisis, I would demonstrate to my parents that I was a skilled problem solver. With a smile on my lips, I approached the Greek Airline's counter.

"Hmmm," said the boarding agent, scratching his chin, "it's close to Greek Easter. Our flights have been pretty full lately." While the passengers for the Athens-bound flight boarded, I sat patiently on my suitcase again. Three destination stickers on my bag proved that I was a seasoned traveler. I'm not going to lose out this time, I told myself, not twice in a row. But I did. I lost out to paying customers again.

My regal bearing began to crack a little at the prospect of having to overnight in Frankfurt. I did not know the city and had not planned on ripping the first hole into my travel budget before reaching my final destination. I thought of my friend, Norbert, whom I had met at Lufthansa training the year before. We had stayed in touch and he had said, "Call me if you have trouble getting on the plane. Chances are I can get you on."

Although I suspected that Norb had exaggerated his clout, I looked for a pay phone.

"Hullo Norb. Guess What? I didn't make Lufthansa's or Olympic's flights to Athens. Do you have any suggestions for an overnight stay, not too far from the airport? And do you still think you can get me on a plane? Maybe tomorrow?"

"Don't worry. I'll get you a ticket," Norbert said with such confidence that I lightened up instantly. "Let me make a couple of calls. Just hang around the ticket counter. I'll be there within the hour."

"Norb, you're worth your weight in gold." I let out a huge sigh and hung up. Then a tiny voice in the back of my head whispered, *what if Norbert proposes his flat instead of a hotel? What are you going to do then?* I dismissed the idea at once. I recognized that voice. It was my mother's.

An hour later, Norb, all smiles, walked toward the ticket counter. After a hearty greeting, he eased my fears. "It's all under control. I made reservations at the Pension Ilona, a small place close by. I'll drop you off tonight. And in the morning, their van will take you back to the airport. And, guess what I have here?" He waved a grey piece of paper high in the air. "It's a confirmed employee seat on Olympic tomorrow morning."

I threw my arms around Norbert. "I don't believe it. How did you do that?"

"My lips are sealed. Let's go and get a bite to eat. We have a lot of catching up to do."

"Aren't you working today?"

"I have the late shift. I have to be back here at eleven."

Arm in arm, we walked out of the airport.

At 11:05 the next morning, the fully booked plane left for Athens with me comfortably seated next to a window. Every cell of me felt alive. I was so proud of myself. I sat on this plane because of Norb's rapport with his colleagues and of my connection to Norb. *I bet my parents couldn't have pulled that off.*

At Athens International Airport, Maria, another Lufthansa training classmate, picked me up. Norb had telexed her with my new arrival time. I exchanged German marks for Greek drachmas after Maria told me where to get the best rate. Then she dropped me off at the Guesthouse Cleo in the middle of the *Plaka*, the oldest section of town which stands in the shadow of the Acropolis. A short, middle-aged Greek woman led me to a teensy room on the third floor. It was no bigger than a closet. French doors opened onto a small terrace filled with potted plants. Helter-skelter rooftops stretched as far as the eye could see; laundry on clotheslines extended from building to building; pungent cooking aromas wafted on gentle breezes; and unfamiliar sounds floated up from open doors and windows. It was April. It felt like summer. Trees barely budded in Germany at this time of year. The charm of this exotic paradise captivated me.

Until nightfall, I wandered alone through the back streets of the *Plaka* and admired the centuries-old buildings. Blue doors and window frames accentuated stark white walls. Crooked stairs, hidden nooks, and picturesque balconies gave the city a strange mystique. Because it was too late in the day to visit the Acropolis, I listened to street musicians.

Next morning, I returned to the airport. I had not noticed the night before how large, rundown, and chaotic it was. Old women lugged around humungous cloth bags and kept small children in line. Poorly dressed men chain-smoked. My eyes stung. I was glad when I finally sat on the plane to Rhodes. Looking at the shimmering Aegean Sea below, I saw countless small islands rise above the surface while their chief landmasses remained submerged beneath the blue-green water.

At Diagoras Airport on the island of Rhodes, I waited until my checked luggage appeared on the carrousel and then exited through large glass doors into the golden sunshine. Looking at the small piece of paper I had taken from my purse I read:

Hotel Ethnikon, King Paul Street No. 3
at the wonderful place of one hundred palm trees
with an excellent view.

Several taxis cued in front of passenger arrival. A dark-skinned, scruffy-looking man jumped out of one of them and flashed a broad smile. In so doing, he exposed several gaps between yellow teeth. Before I could say anything, he grabbed my suitcase and motioned me to his vehicle. All the while, he was yakking in Greek. For a moment I stood there, dumbfounded. Then I came alive. "Wait, wait," I yelled, running after him, "I'm not ready." I was unprepared to summon a cab because I wanted to get an idea of the expected cost first. While the man kept talking and gesturing I snatched my suitcase from his hand and returned to the information booth inside passenger arrival.

Armed with a vague cost estimate for the nine-mile ride to the city, I again exited through the glass doors. Most of the taxis had left by now. I reached for the small piece of paper once more and reread the name and address of the hotel.

A well-dressed Greek man in his early thirties approached from behind and asked in broken English if he could be of service. I showed him my note and explained that I intended to take a cab to this destination.

"You be careful. Very careful," he said. "Taxi cabs scoundrels."

His words confirmed my suspicions. Now, I felt even less at ease. Neither the man's English nor mine were very good so that our dialogue progressed slowly. In the meantime, the kind Greek was gaining my confidence.

"Why not stay at Hotel Akti?" he inquired. "Nicer than Ethnikon." After a slight pause he added, "I own Akti."

"Oh no, no," I replied. "I've already paid for the Ethnikon."

The man kept trying to sway me, but finally, he relented. "I drive you to hotel," he said. "Allow me. Demetrius Papantoniou. My car right here!" He pointed to a blue Opel.

Alarm bells. *He wants to drive me? To MY hotel or his?* With a smile he reached for my suitcase. "You'll drive me to the Ethnikon?"

"Of course, Ethnikon."

Can I trust this man? . . . You know what those Greeks are like . . . my mother's voice again. Although I doubted that I was doing the right thing, I allowed him to place my suitcase in his trunk and got into the car. He slid into the driver's seat, and we pulled away from the curb.

"My wife pass away," he confided soon after we had left the airport. "I look for new wife. German girls make gooood wives," he said.

"Good wives?" I laughed.

"Gooood housewives," he nodded.

I didn't know how to react. The man seemed almost old enough to be my father. I was a guest in his country. Since I did not want to hurt his feelings I stayed mum. *Are we still headed toward the Ethnikon?* How much further was it? Had the trip not already taken an eternity, or was it my imagination? My parents would be horrified. I had definitely put myself in danger. *What am I going to do if he drives me into the backcountry?* After what seemed an eternity, we stopped in front of a small pension. "Hotel Ethnikon" was written on the front of the building in big white letters. A huge weight lifted off my shoulders. Thank God, my naiveté had not gotten me into trouble.

"Dinner tonight," Demetrius Papantoniou said. "I pick up nine o'clock."

"Oh no-no-no. Thank you, Mr. Papantoniou. But I will be too tired."

"Nine o'clock," he insisted. "My great pleasure."

Their interest piqued, some of the hotel guests began to peer through the lobby windows.

"All right, nine o'clock."

Relieved to have reached my destination without major incidents, I rushed inside. Why had I been too cheap to take a taxi? Now I had Demetrius Papantoniou to deal with.

The desk clerk handed me the key to my room. By the time I had unpacked, taken a passing look at the advertised "one hundred palms," hopped into my bathing suit, and headed for the nearby beach, it was already afternoon. In the aftermath of winter, Germans hungered for sunshine and a suntan. In that respect, I was German to the core.

Soon after I had stretched out on my beach towel, a northern breeze picked up and increased in strength until churning sand scoured my pale skin. Still, I refused to be deterred. Having come to Rhodes for the sole purpose of a preseason tan, I foiled the wind by scratching a form-fitting indentation into the sand. Then I matched my body to the trough and soaked up the golden rays with minimal discomfort. As I watched tiny puffs of clouds overhead, I pondered the Papantoniou problem. Despite the Greek man's kindness toward me, I did not intend to spend the next two weeks in the company of an older man. *I'll let him down gently over dinner.*

When I returned to the hotel, sandblasted and chilled, I saw several people my age mill about the lobby. Because the Ethnikon was operated by a youth agency, the ages of its guests ranged between eighteen and twenty-five. I was anxiously looking forward to the company of other young people.

After I had changed into street clothes, I joined the group downstairs. Most of us were single and eager to make new friends. Midway through the usual getting-acquainted rituals, a young couple near the window piqued my interest. They seemed riveted in conversation. Maybe it wasn't so much the couple that mesmerized me as the male half of the duo. Just as Tony focuses on Maria in *West Side Story*, this man drew my complete attention. Unfortunately, he appeared to belong to the stylish blond across from him. With a small sigh I redirected my interests.

Promptly at nine o'clock, my Hellenic suitor entered the lobby. I had hoped he might have changed his mind. "Utahhh," his voice echoed from the foyer, arms stretched for an embrace. Flustered, I allowed my sweater to slide from my arm, retrieved it with a swift sidestep and thereby avoided physical contact. Together, we walked to a nearby taverna. After being seated, he leaned back, lit a cigarette, and flicked for a waiter.

"Ouzo," he pointed as he poured water over ice cubes immersed in a clear liquid. "Watch!" The liquid turned milky. "Very Greek." We nibbled and sipped. The ouzo eased the conversation; yet, in no time, the talk returned to the subject of wives.

"Utahhh, marry me!" His proposal popped like a cork out of a champagne bottle as he reached across the table and seized both of my hands. Stunned, I stared at him. Still clasping my hands, he fixed his dark eyes onto mine and smiled. I lowered my gaze.

"No, no, Mr. Papantoniou," I laughed nervously, pulling my hands away. "I can't marry you." I tried to look casual while stealing a furtive glance. The smoke in the taverna shrouded his face. Pearls formed on my forehead. *Is this the ouzo, or am I trapped? What am I going to do?*

"Demetrius." He corrected me. "Call me Demetrius."

This man addressed me in a way that suggested we had known each other for a long time, and he encouraged me to do the same. During my dating experience, limited as it was, I had always maintained the formal address when I wanted to preserve distance. Now, I longed to wedge the expanse of a continent between us—tactfully.

"Mr. Papantoniou," I repeated, "I'm honored, but I'm not ready for marriage." *There, I said it.*

"I treat you well," he promised.

"Oh, I'm sure. But the answer must be 'no' all the same."

He can't be serious. He doesn't even know me. What did he want? A cleaning lady? *Little does he know that I can't cook and haven't mopped a floor in my life.* I sat there, stiff and erect as a broom. All I wanted to do was to get out of the taverna. The first day on Rhodes, and I had already received a marriage proposal. *Are all Greeks like this?*

When Demetrius Papantoniou saw my discomfort and the futility of his proposal, he agreed to walk me back to my hotel. Over the next few days, he returned on several occasions, asking for me or leaving messages. I never responded and sometimes escaped to the roof garden. Eventually, he gave up.

On my second day in Rhodes, it poured. Most of the hotel guests stayed indoors for the duration of the storm. We played canasta and used the time to become better acquainted. To my great delight, the young man who had caught my fancy the previous afternoon joined us during the second half of the day. His name was Landon. I noted with satisfaction that there was no sign of his blond lady-friend.

As if flipping a switch, I summoned all of my charms. I enchanted, I allured, I beguiled. By the end of the evening, my efforts were rewarded. Landon invited me to accompany him the following day on an excursion to the town of Lindos, one of eleven small villages on the island of Rhodes. I had achieved what I wanted. Our thirty-mile ride on a public bus to Lindos took close to an hour. During that time, I learned that my travel companion was a Harvard student spending his summer vacation traveling throughout Europe. His next destination was Italy where he planned to reunite with his fellow scholars.

I could not have picked a more competent guide than Landon. To my astonishment, he read Greek and knew more about the history of Lindos than I might have dug up at a library. Nestled into a large bay, this village was ancient. Whitewashed houses rose from a sandy beach, and the town's acropolis towered high above the village. "The town was founded by Dorians," he explained. "Its acropolis was fortified first by the Greeks, later by the Romans, then by the Byzantines, the Knights of St. John, and finally by the Ottomans." He described each period in detail. I was awed but also intimidated. I barely remembered these terms from high school. Then, they had been meaningless words. Now, Landon made ancient history come alive with his enthusiasm and vivid descriptions. Where did he learn all this? It had never occurred to me to study the history of the island before I came. My parents and I had traveled to Italy every year, and we had never researched that country's history. We followed the sunshine. The same had been my motivation when I booked this trip to Rhodes. Now, I began to question whether travel would not be better spent on discovery and growth. As we wandered through the ancient narrow streets, poked our heads into churches so tiny they looked like shrines, and stepped over donkey poo on the way to the acropolis, I marveled at Landon's scholarly approach. *How many learning opportunities have I missed in the past?*

Before we caught the bus back to the city of Rhodes in the late afternoon, we relaxed on the crescent bay's white sand. Upon our arrival in the Ethnikon, knowing smiles greeted us. "Where have you two been? Did you have fun?"

"We had a nice time," we said in unison, smiled and left it at that.

The following day, Landon and I explored the old section of town and Mandrake Harbor. Bronze deer statues framed the port's entrance. "The Colossus of Rhodes may have stood here at one time," Landon enlightened me. "You've heard of the Colossus of Rhodes, right? It was one of the seven wonders of the ancient world," Landon said.

I didn't know, but I nodded.

"The statue depicted the Greek God Helios. Fifty years later, it was destroyed by an earthquake," he explained. Landon was a cloudburst of information.

Then, one day later, my extraordinary guide left for Italy. We promised to write, waved good-bye, and I stayed behind with an odd sensation. It had all happened so quickly. In two short days, Landon had come and gone from my life like a white knight. All that remained was my new love for history and discovery.

During the rest of my stay on Rhodes, my new vacation companions and I hiked and biked along the fifty-mile-long island and explored its countless pine, olive, and cypress forests. I returned to Athens two days prior to my scheduled departure to allow for potential delays arising from my standby status. Spending the last of my drachmas, I visited the famous Acropolis and a taverna in the *Plaka*.

When I returned to Berlin I was a different person. I had rediscovered my love for learning.

Herr Schröder

HAVING PROVEN TO MYSELF that I could manage life's quirks, I returned to my airline job. Two days later, I received a phone call from Lufthansa's main office in the city. The chief wanted to see me in his office. I was flattered. My heartbeat quickened. *I bet Herr Direktor Schröder is going to offer me a promotion.* Countless possibilities raced through my mind.

On the designated day, I took pains to look my best. I put on a stylish pale-grey suit with white trim, my own creation and execution; I applied subtle makeup, and arrived far in advance of the appointed time. While I waited in the anteroom, I mentally readied myself to face our legendary chief and accept his offer of advancement.

The director was a man commanding respect. The only time we had ever spoken was during my final employment interview. Since then, I had seen him only from a distance. He sometimes visited the airport, most often in the company of other high-level executives. Prior to Direktor Schröder's arrival, the composure of my boss and freight manager, Herr Fischer, always disintegrated a bit as he fretted over the possibility of having overlooked some essential directive. During those visits, the chief's tall and imposing stature clearly communicated who was in charge. Even from afar he projected authority. His carefully coiffed white mane, tussled by the perpetual draft in the freight hangar, would loom high above his entourage as he issued clear and concise commands in a baritone voice. I understood he could bark orders that caused his staff to scurry for cover. Neither was he known to mince words. I felt both apprehensive and excited about our impending conversation.

When I entered his posh corner office, he directed me to a leather armchair. Despite my valiant attempt at reclining with poise, I found myself plunging far deeper than expected, almost vanishing between the chair's overstuffed armrests. After recovering from my swift descent, I noticed that my nose now barely cleared the edge of the director's desk. In the middle of the highly polished surface of this magnificent piece of rosewood furniture, squared with its edges, sat a blue file folder—my personnel file. The only other items on his desk were a black telephone and a gold-plated pen set.

I felt like a little kid peeking out from the sandbox. To make up for my abruptly reduced height, I extended my torso to its maximum length. Even then, I had to lift my chin to look at the chief. From his massive throne, his clear blue eyes bore into mine. In his dark-blue suit, starched white shirt, and gold cuff links, embossed with the Lufthansa insignia, Herr Direktor looked presidential.

"Miss Umbach," he began glancing at the file before him, "You have the highest IQ any personnel in our Berlin office ever attained." My cheeks flushed in surprise and pleasure. No one had ever mentioned the results of my entry exam. A self-conscious smile formed on my lips. I was pleased beyond words. *The highest score? Promotion guaranteed!*

"Based on your IQ, Herr Fischer and I have been expecting great things from you, Miss Umbach," he continued, "but I hear your performance is marginal at best. How do you explain this?"

My jaw dropped. Unable to marry his words with my expectations, my ability to reason became unhinged, and my thoughts began to ricochet between expected promotion and potential dismissal. The tone of his voice demanded answers. I had none. My lips moved to form words. No sound escaped. Mortified, I lowered my glance and sank further into the bowels of my chair. *What is he talking about? My tardy filing? My reluctance to work overtime? Does he know about the personal letters typed on company time?*

"Miss Umbach, have you been asked to do work you have not been trained to do?""No, Herr Direktor."

"Has anyone treated you with disrespect?"

"No, Herr Direktor."

"Do you want to work for Lufthansa?"

"Yes, Herr Direktor."

"Miss Umbach, we have sent you to Hamburg for four weeks of extensive training, at company expense. In return, we expect an acceptable level of performance from you. If you cannot or will not carry out your duties, I'll have to dismiss you. You understand what a contract is, don't you?

"Yes, Herr Direktor."

"Miss Umbach, you're young. This is your first position. I'll look the other way this time. But in the future, I expect you to live up to our agreement. Do we understand each other?"

"Yes, Herr Direktor."

Intimidated and remorseful, I left his office. I was shaken. How could an expected promotion turn into a near dismissal?

"What did your Direktor have to say?" my parents asked when I returned home.

"Oh, he told me that I had the highest IQ, higher than any of the other employees."

"That was all?"

"Um-mmm, he wanted to talk about stuff in general . . . I've been with Lufthansa for a year now . . . Kind of a recap."

Coming up with a plausible explanation for the conference was tough enough. Sounding convincing was even more difficult. Admission to substandard performance would have grounded me for months. I kept my secret.

However, the brief lecture from the chief had a sobering effect on me. In keeping with his reputation, he had been candid. In doing so, he had touched something in me. Little by little, I began to rethink my attitude toward work. *I signed a contract with Lufthansa. I agreed to do a job. They pay me a salary.* The longer I reflected, the clearer it became that it was my duty, and mine alone, to direct my future. If I did not like the work at Lufthansa, I was free to leave and find more suitable employment. I concluded I would do the best possible job during my two-year obligation. After that, I would seek more challenging work.

Herr Direktor Schröder's scolding caused me to first examine and then to accept the obscure concepts of obligation and reciprocity, and

I began to apply the same principles at home. *To earn freedom from restrictions, I need to reciprocate. Keeping Pappi's business ledgers will buy me the freedom to go dancing on the weekend. Washing the car will get me to the movies.* Indeed, my new mindset affected my parents as well. Without discussion, they eased my restrictions. I assumed we had understood each other.

About my professional future, however, I remained ambivalent. My interest in becoming a stewardess had faded. Although travel still tempted me; the work itself did not. Now, I contemplated the prospect of becoming an interpreter at the United Nations. *If I become fluent in English, French, and Spanish and spend time abroad perfecting each language, I might have a chance,* I reasoned. In addition to the weekly Cambridge Certificate course, I now added Spanish and explored options for spending a year in each country.

Since my return from Greece, most of my energy had gone into work, foreign language studies, and pursuit of opportunities for time abroad. I hoped that my parents would let me spend the year following my twentieth birthday in a foreign country. In part, I wanted to broaden my horizons and acquire the necessary skills to become an interpreter, but I also wanted to escape from my narrow life at home. Upon my return to Berlin, I would be twenty-one and entitled to more freedom. Since my twentieth birthday was only a few months away, I had to make haste.

My first stop was the US Consulate. If I could work in San Diego and live with Sonja and her family, I was set for my first year in an English-speaking country. I entered the embassy with soaring hopes and exited with shattered dreams after learning that a visitor's visa does not permit its holder to work in America. Without a job I would have no means of support. The same rule held true for England as I learned a week later. I did not pursue France or Spain. Undoubtedly, regulations were the same. A year abroad seemed to require either substantial funds or a scholarship. My temporary life in a foreign country would have to depend on the latter.

Investigating scholarship options, I called on the German Department of Education and the Free University of Berlin, aware that my parents would be unsupportive. "College—that's absurd!" my father said when I casually mentioned the subject of higher education. "College is a waste of money. Only people who are too lazy to work choose school. School is for kids. Life is the best teacher." I was accustomed to my father's opinion of book learning.

My little free time I spent with friends. During the weekdays I worked. On weekends, I sewed with Lorena, relaxed at her *Schrebergarten*, or at the Olympic Stadium. On weekend evenings I went dancing. My only responsibility at home was to maintain my father's business ledgers. Because my mother preferred doing things her way, I did not have to help with household chores.

By the time the calendar marked the beginning of summer 1965, I had enjoyed the first two months ever of considerable freedom—aside from my trip to Greece. My parents were still uncomfortable with my emerging need for independence, but I had faith that they would come around to accept it.

Casual Acquaintance

It was Friday evening in late June. As we had done so often since the beginning of summer, Lorena and I met after work at the pool in the *Olympiastadion*. Built for the 1936 Summer Olympics, it was part of a 325-acre sports complex. The tiered spectator bleachers on both sides could accommodate 110,000 spectators during competitions and, along with the surrounding turf, masses of sun worshippers on hot summer days. The area adjacent to the pool was also THE outdoor spot in West Berlin for young people who wanted to see and be seen.

Lorena and I planned to soak up the last rays of the evening sun and maybe enjoy a quick dip before heading home. Both of us held season passes and made frequent use of them. The sky was azure blue. The sun smiled. The place was packed. Because West Berlin's surrounding countryside belonged to the East, the few outdoor venues were always crowded on sunny days.

On impulse, Günter Bayer, Lorena's colleague, decided to join us and brought along his roommate, Dieter Ritter. I had not met either man before. Despite the advancing hour, beach mats and blankets still covered the lawn as far as the eye could see. In search of a spot to spread our towels, we hopped from one grassy patch to the next, trying to avoid other sunbathers' limbs and possessions. For some odd reason, I cherished the days when the stadium was packed like this. Seeing bleachers and turf blanketed with bodies always filled me with a special joy. For me, the sea of humanity represented a refreshing change from my isolation at my home.

Günter and Dieter, however, were taken aback. The two men, our age, had come to Berlin only a few months earlier to avoid the draft. All German males were obligated to serve for nine months in the military or in an accepted alternative civilian service, such as a kindergarten, hospital, rehabilitation center, or assisted-living facility. The easiest way out of conscription was employment in Berlin. Under Allied occupation law, a West Berlin residence card granted immunity from being drafted into the *Bundeswehr,* the West German military service. This made employment in West Berlin extremely attractive to young men. And since many Berliners had left for better employment opportunities in West Germany, the influx of draft-age men was good for West Berlin's economy as well.

Günter and Dieter came from towns in the southern part of West Germany and had requested transfers to their companies' Berlin offices. Although they did not work for the same firm, they pooled their resources by becoming roommates. Still unaccustomed to life surrounded by walls, they were appalled at the close proximity of sun worshippers on the greens and in the bleachers.

Swimming on this Friday evening was, indeed, near impossible because the pool was thicker with steaming bodies than a good Irish stew is with potatoes. It was equally difficult to claim a small spot on the turf. As an alternative, Günter proposed, "Let's drive to Schildhorn for some ice cream." The four of us embraced the idea at once.

In the sixties, it was an anomaly for a young person to own a car. We were lucky if our parents owned a car that we could borrow once in a while. For the most part, teens, and often their parents, relied on public transportation. But Günter represented a pharmaceutical company, and owning a car was mandatory in his line of work. His was a white

Opel Kadett. Owned by General Motors, Opel had introduced the Kadett only two years earlier and aggressively marketed it as the "Anti-Volkswagen" hoping to create a strong competitor to the immensely popular "People's Car."

Schildhorn, a small, picturesque peninsula extends into the river Havel. The narrow tongue of land is located in the Grunewald, Berlin's largest forest. Old-fashioned restaurants and cafés line the water's edge. After the four of us located a vacant table overlooking the river, Lorena and I immediately leaned as far back as we could in our wooden garden chairs and sunbathed arms and faces. No ray of sunshine, no tanning opportunity, was ever lost on us. The men casually leaned back as well. We ordered four tall vanilla ice-cream parfaits, layered with fresh fruit, and savored each spoonful of cool delight while becoming better acquainted.

While Lorena knew both men, I made swift appraisals as we talked. Dieter was of slight build with dark curly hair and brown eyes. Something about him told me that he was only along for the ride and would have preferred to do something else.

Günter, blond and blue-eyed, struck me as the nicer of the two: sociable, attractive, maybe a little arrogant—I wasn't certain. Lorena obviously liked him. I had never seen her more animated. No doubt, she had a crush on him. Since I preferred dark hair and brown eyes, he only interested me in a casual way.

At around 9:00 p.m. Günter drove Lorena and me home. On the autobahn, someone cut us off, and Günter felt the need to retaliate. For a few tense minutes, the two drivers honked, flashed lights, and followed each other much too closely for my comfort. Then we exited the freeway in a sudden move. Lorena and I let out a sigh of relief. How would I have explained an accident to my parents? On my insistence, Günter dropped me off first. Running an hour later than normal, I did not want to invite trouble with my parents.

With more than an hour of summer's long and peaceful twilight left before nightfall, I entered the flat. "I'm home!" I yelled from the hall as I approached the living room. For all I knew, I had stepped into the dim light of a morgue. Only the door from the living room to the balcony was partly open. Windows and blinds were closed to avoid the draft, my mother's mortal enemy. While the sun had turned my skin a light pink to tan, my parents were as pale as farmers' cheese. They sat on the living room couch, wilted by the lingering humidity, and fanned themselves with magazines. Despite the heat, my father wore long pants. He never considered shorts, not even on the beach. A tall glass of sparkling water, no ice, stood in front of each of them as they watched the news. Bangs plastered to her forehead, my mother looked up, "How come you're so late?"

"It's only an hour later than usual. Besides it's still light outside." When my parents did not reply, I continued, "You won't believe how crowded it was today. We decided to drive to a café in Schildhorn for an ice cream. One of Lorena's colleagues has a car."

"I don't like that one bit," my mother looked up after a brief silence.

"We don't want you to ride around the city with lowlifes," my father added.

I felt the hair on my back bristle. *Lowlifes!* Because I had been raised to endure my parents' comments without back talk, I kept my hostility guarded and unexpressed. But I burned up inside. *I've gone out for an ice cream, for heaven's sake. Mutti and Pappi have never even met these guys. I'll turn twenty in November. Can't I even go out for an ice cream?* My parents' words made my blood boil. Throwing my head back, I turned on my heels and prepared for bed.

"In the future, I want you to come straight home from the stadium, no matter what Lorena does," my mother added as I walked out.

The following day, Saturday, the subject of the two young men was not broached. I spent the day at Lorena's parents' garden plot picking cherries. In the evening, she and I headed to our favorite dance club, the Riverboat. Günter and Dieter were forgotten. Sunday was another beautiful day, and Lorena and I met at the Olympic Stadium, shortly after it opened, to stake out a good spot on the bleachers. The perfect location was one from which we could view the entire park. To my surprise, Günter and Dieter turned up again, despite the fact that the stadium was just as packed as on Friday.

Because the run-in with my parents two days earlier was still fresh in my mind, I made it a point to pay closer attention to the automobile owning "lowlife." Aside from the blond hair and blue eyes, I actually found Günter rather attractive and his company quite enjoyable. My mother's criticism had achieved the opposite of what she had intended. Nevertheless, when evening came, I went dancing at the American service club on the military base without giving the two young men another thought. I had become part of a great group of girls, and we always had a good time.

Two more days passed. It was Tuesday evening. "Where did you go Sunday night?" my mother asked in an icy tone when I returned home from work.

"To the club. I always go dancing at the club on the last Sunday of the month, remember?"

"Ohhh? What would you say if I told you that you were seen in Moabit?"

Moabit was a district of Berlin I never visited. It was a long way from home and I knew no one there. "I'd say someone needs new glasses. Why do you ask?"

Usually, a bus from the air base picked us up at the zoo station and drove us to the officer's club. The previous Sunday, however, the bus had not arrived at the appointed time. Thirty minutes later, we had dialed the contact number. "The bus broke down," the operator said. "Can you get here on the subway? We'll have someone meet you at the gate with visitors' passes."

"No problem." We hopped on the underground train, were met at the base gate, danced for a few hours, and then took the subway home. I thought no more about it. Now, my mother was accusing me.

"I know you're lying. You didn't go to the club at all," my mother continued. "I found your subway ticket in the wastebasket. It was stamped Sunday, June 27, 20:36 hours. The bus picks you up at eight o'clock. That means you didn't go to the club. You must think your mother is stupid."

I was beside myself. "The bus broke down, for heaven's sake. We took the *U-Bahn*. That's all." I resented having to defend myself.

"Why didn't you tell me?" My mother asked.

"Because there was nothing to tell. I didn't think it was important."

Nothing more was said, but I knew my mother. I knew what was eating her. She had assumed I had been with Dieter and Günter and was trying to trap me. Had she made up that story about me having been seen in Moabit?

Suddenly, the image of my diary flashed before me. My mother had been familiar with my entries. Although I didn't have proof of her reading my private journal, I now wondered. Wouldn't someone who digs through trash to check on my whereabouts be capable of forcing the shabby lock of my diary, too? I decided to store it in my purse in the future.

The following evening, Lorena stopped by our house to ask if I could go to the *Volksfest* with her.

"Are those guys going to be there, too?" my mother asked.

Dieter and Günter were not joining us. But Lorena's and my assurances did not satisfy her. Without further discussion, my mother forbade me to go to the fair. That evening, Günter moved up several rungs on my interest ladder.

Sticking to the Credo

SUDDENLY, I SAW GÜNTER with new eyes. Where I had seen an okay guy before, now a young man with potentially admirable qualities began to emerge. Upon closer scrutiny, he seemed not only handsome, but intelligent and thoughtful. Thoughtful because he did not carry on with endless drivel about football, cars, and motorcycles. He had mastered the art of conversation with both sexes, unlike some of my previous dates. I also sensed the polite reserve that intelligent people often display. *My parents have no business making groundless accusations. Günter is probably quite nice!*

To my mother's relief, I had never been keen on close relationships with men. Short-term casual friendships were more my style. While the anticipation of that first date with a new guy was titillating, reality invariably disappointed me. And I backed away soon thereafter. Recently though, my lack of commitment had begun to trouble me. Was this normal or was something wrong with me? Did I sidestep permanent relationships to avert inevitable trauma at home? Or did I lack loyalty?

After my Schildhorn escapade, only visits to the Olympic Stadium or chaperoned activities met with my parents' approval. Because my strict upbringing forbade disobedience, I was unpracticed in rebellion and reluctantly abided by the rules—but only on the surface. Secretly, I had no intention of cutting the strings with Günter. As long as he was interested, so would I be.

Against my parents' express instructions, Günter began to occasionally drop by the stadium after work to visit with Lorena and me and to drive us home. Never did I mention these visits or rides to my parents. Neither did I tell Günter about the restrictions imposed on me because I was too embarrassed to admit that my parents still treated me like a small child. The consequence of these omissions was that I became extremely guarded. It became difficult to remember which version of a story I had told to whom.

One sweltering August night, maybe six weeks after Günter and I first met, Lorena held a summerfest at her family's small garden plot in the outskirts of the city. Bright paper moon lanterns hung from fruit trees, candles flickered on small tables, and a traditional fruit and wine punch, called *Bowle*, beckoned to be sampled. All of our friends were invited to this all-night event. Since Lorena's parents chaperoned, I was allowed to join the festivities. Knowing that Günter's presence would cause my parents to withdraw their consent, I did not mention his name.

Everyone was dressed in their summer finery. The girls showed off their colorful short-sleeved outfits; the boys dressed in lightweight shirts and slacks. I noted with delight that Günter paid far more attention to me than to any of the other girls, including Lorena. He even picked up on some of my thoughts before I could turn them into words. When my feet tired, he suggested we'd sit down. When a breeze in the late evening caused me to chill, he proposed a wrap. I felt cared for like a rare diamond on loan. I had never felt like that before. It was both exhilarating and confusing at the same time.

When he looked deep into my eyes under the flickering shade of the paper lanterns, something unforeseen happened. The world around us disappeared. Overwhelmed by the intensity of my feelings, I consciously tried to hold on to my credo:

No steady relationships—they only cause problems at home.
No steady relationships—they only cause problems.
No steady relationships.
No . . .

As he cupped my head with both hands and held it like a valuable vase, I almost lost myself in his embrace. I quivered with excitement at his touch. We looked into each other's eyes. I wanted to fall into his arms and kiss and be kissed, but in a last-ditch effort, I pulled away. Suddenly, I recognized the strange feeling that I felt with every heartbeat. Fear, pure fear, plus the realization: I like him. A lot.

This is not going to sit well at home. I had an ominous feeling. *It's all going to fall apart.* I was scared. Günter would walk away as soon as his advances would not progress as planned, I was sure of that. But what could I do?

To my surprise, he put up with my reserve. He did not insist on a kiss; yet, the twinkle in his eyes told me that I was number one on his mind. *He's got to be the most wonderful man I have ever met.* Before I knew it, I had fallen deeply in love for the first time.

The next morning, the entire group, including Lorena's parents, Herr and Frau Schneider, shared breakfast before disbanding. Although the Schneiders had stayed up all night to chaperone, their job had been an easy one. These were the sixties, people would say later. Not that the thoughts weren't there, but we did not act upon them. Fears of unplanned parenthood were far too great. After breakfast, Günter drove me home. I asked him to stop short of our apartment building and walked the rest of the way. I did not want to be seen with him, and I needed time to come back to earth.

"How was the party?" my mother asked.

"Okay."

"Who was there?"

Careful, this is a trap, my inner voice said. *If Mutti finds out, she won't let me go to Lorena's again.* I named a few names, carefully omitting the objectionable ones.

"Were Lorena's parents there?"

"Of course. They stayed up all night."

I kept the information to a minimum and did not let on that I had reached the zenith of my happiness.

June 1960—
Wall décor assembled
before live television
audience.

December 1960—
From left to right:
Jutta, Marilyn, Scotty,
and Sharon Kelly with
the Brandenburg Gate
in the background.

Fall 1961
in Altenau—
Herr Bartsch stands
ready for the day's hike.

Winter 1961—
In my prom dress
at the end of dance
lessons.

1962—
Fee on the Funkturm,
Berlin's radio tower.

Fall 1962—
Tapsi.

June 1963—
My father snaps a
photo from the corner
of Hardenbergstraße
and Joachimstaler
Straße as Kennedy,
Adenauer, and Brandt
pass by.

1965—
Sonja sends me
a picture from
San Diego.

1965—My father and Tapsi.

*Fall 1965—
From left to right:
Molli, Bubu,
and Yogi hoist
me onto Bubu's
shoulders on
Bulgaria's
Goldstrand.*

*New Year's Eve
1966—
One month
before I leave
for the
United States.*

SEVEN

THE IRON
CURTAIN CLOSES

A Mere Social Call

DURING THE NEXT COUPLE OF WEEKS, Günter continued to join Lorena and me at the stadium on occasion and to drive us home. I never told him that I was strictly barred from associating with him or his roommate. One Saturday, while I enjoyed another afternoon with Lorena at the Schneider's *Schrebergarten*, he tried to call me at home to ask if I wanted to accompany him to the movies the following evening. When my parents refused to disclose my whereabouts, he checked my usual hangouts: the Olympic Stadium and Lorena's family garden plot.

"I thought so," he chuckled when he and Dieter sauntered through the gate. "I called you at home, Jutta, but your parents wouldn't tell me where you were. As a matter of fact, they were rather cagey. Good guess on my part to look for you here, wasn't it?"

"You rang my house?" I felt my heart drop to the vicinity of my toes when Günter mentioned the call. *This'll spell trouble.* Lorena shot a glance in my direction. She knew what I was thinking. Trying to act in as casual a manner as possible, I continued to tease and banter with the rest of them.

Then it was time for coffee and cake, and Frau Schneider placed a mouthwatering *Streuselkuchen*—streusel cake—on the bright flowery oil-cloth that covered the porch table. The freshly-baked aroma caught our attention at once. We were just about to take our seats when I spotted the shadowy outlines of two human shapes through the hedge-covered chain-link fence surrounding the plot: a tall and a petite figure. Both were headed toward the garden gate. *Good God, these wouldn't be my parents, would they?* I didn't think they even knew where the Schneider's garden was located. My imagination seemed to be getting the better of me. But my eyes did not lie.

"Hullo-o-o!" My mother hollered as she pushed open the gate, my father following a couple of steps behind. As both parents came walking down the narrow footpath which was flanked by thick gooseberry bushes, my mother grinned, "We were just in the neighborhood and thought we'd drop by. Nice plot you have here." She flashed a winning smile toward Frau Schneider. "No wonder our daughter likes it here. We used to have a *Schrebergarten* in Spandau. Did she tell you?"

I felt like I had entered the dark forest of a fairy tale where all rules were suspended. Mutti and Pappi weren't in the neighborhood. They lied. *They're here because of Günter's phone call.* I knew the call was going to spell trouble. But this was quickly turning out worse than expected. *And in front of the Schneiders! What is Günter going to think?*

"Come on in," Lorena's mom said with an inviting smile. "We're just about to sit down for a cup of coffee. You'll join us, won't you?" She surveyed the seating arrangements. There were only six folding chairs, and now there were eight of us for coffee. I saw her eyes assess the options and jumped in.

"Why don't we leave the chairs to you and my parents," I proposed, "and we'll go ahead and move inside," pointing to the four of us.

"Oh, no-no—no need for that," my mother cut in. "Surely, we can all squeeze together."

Right, I thought. *I know why you want us to squeeze together. You want to take a close look at Günter.* No doubt, my mother wanted to see what the guy looked like who had the audacity to call me at home after I had been placed under strict orders to stay away from him. Mutti, your nose is getting longer than Pinocchio's, I thought. *No way, I'm not going to give you that satisfaction.*

On my urging, my friends joined me inside. The interior of the tiny cottage consisted of one small room with a kitchen nook. A table and four armchairs stood directly beneath the only window in the cottage which looked straight onto the porch table where my parents and the Schneiders were about to take their seats. The afternoon sun was hitting the glass with merciless intensity. The only fresh air came through the open front door. We were sweltering inside, but opening the window was out of the question. It would have made it possible for my parents to monitor our conversation. And I was bent on foiling my mother's plans.

The unbearable heat was offset by only one benefit, but it was an important one: despite the proximity, the sun-induced glare made it difficult to see inside. Throughout the coffee ritual, my mother aimed several futile glances in our direction. Although I was positive that her fleeting peeks could not have achieved the desired results, I was edgy. *What will Günter think of my parents? What will he think of me? He must be laughing inside.*

Soon after coffee, my parents said their good-byes and left, but the afternoon was ruined. I was nervous about going home and wondered what punitive measures were awaiting me. Furthermore, I resented my parents' notion that I was not entitled to a say in the company I kept. But if I balked at their sly maneuvers for control, my parents were bound to dig in with increased vigor. Any conflict would end up an uneven one. My parents held a cache of disciplinary weapons at their disposal, while I commanded nothing but my poise. By barring me from seeing my friends, and especially Günter, they believed they held the secret to keeping me reined in. *I'm not going to let that happen. Not this time.*

Uneasy, I returned home just before dinner.

"You think your parents are stupid, don't you," my mother began. "Your father and I are rarely ever suspicious, but this knocks the bottom right out of the barrel. The lightbulb finally went on when that *Schnösel*—that impertinent whippersnapper—called. You've been leading us by the nose. '"I'm going to Lorena's.' Right. We believed you, like a couple of fools. You went to Lorena's only to meet up with that lowlife. You used her as a cover. And the Schneiders were in on it, too. If that punk had a speck of decency, he wouldn't put you in a situation like this."

On and on went the lecture. Fearful of my parents' authority, I said nothing and waited for the verdict. But it did not come. Not yet anyway.

The Noose Tightens

I WENT TO BED EARLY THAT NIGHT. Staring at the ceiling, I replayed the afternoon's spectacle. My parents' transparent attempt at spying on me in front of my friends filled me with shame. One of my mother's favorite proverbs popped to mind: *Gleich und gleich gesellt sich gern*—Like and like love to keep company. Would my parents' behavior reflect on me? *Will the Schneiders welcome me in the future or will they keep me at arm's length?*

When I thought of Günter, tears spilled down my face. *I can only imagine what he must think. I'll never see him again.* The humiliation I felt was unbearable. I resented my parents—now my disgust with their behavior veered toward hate. Mutti dislikes Günter because I like him, I concluded. She's jealous. There would never be a man who'd meet my parents' approval, I felt sure of that. I cried myself to sleep.

A week later, Günter and Dieter showed up at the stadium again as if nothing had happened. The intensity of my feelings when I saw him surprised me. Falling in love had catapulted me into an emotional orbit unlike anything I had ever experienced. It almost collapsed my reasoning abilities. But despite my heartbeats doubling up, I greeted the two men with polite reserve. *I can't fall in love. It's going to end badly. My parents will see to that.*

The following morning, Günter called me at the airline. I turned blood red when his melodic Bavarian accent reverberated in my ear. I had not given him my office number. He must have looked it up in the phone book, I thought and wanted to scream, "Life is so wonderful. He hasn't given up on me!"

"I have some business calls to make in the area. So, if you like, I'll stop by during your lunch hour. If you tell me where, I'll pick you up."

Since I had only a forty-five minute lunch break, I normally brought a sandwich to work or ate at the cantina. "I'd love to," I replied without hesitation and described the location of my building. Forgotten was my mother's parchment-wrapped cheese sandwich. "I'll meet you out front at noon."

"See you then."

Following Günter's call, my body no longer required solid sustenance. Steady breathing was my only concern. I was beside myself. It was eleven o'clock and an eternity until noon. Several times during the remaining sixty minutes I ran across the hall to freight operations, our Lufthansa office that overlooked the street. *Not yet.* When the wall clock finally indicated that it was time, nature decided to dump buckets of water from the sky. I stepped out of the building and spotted his white Opel parked at the curb on the opposite side of the street. A gust of wind caught my pocket umbrella and turned it inside out. With the useless implement in one hand and holding the hood of my coat in place with the other, I ran across the street. Günter quickly opened the passenger door from the inside, and I slid into the bucket seat next to him. Rivulets of water trickled down my coat. I was drenched. Almost immediately, the windows fogged up.

It was awkward at first. Both of us were self-conscious and did not know what to talk about. We had never been alone together. I blushed when I met his glance and studied the instruments on the dashboard. Deep inside, I had that same strange sensation that I had first felt at the summerfest. With every heartbeat, something else was beating against the wall of my chest. I could feel electricity. Was it happiness that he pursued me? Was it panic?

After some initial small talk, the conversation relaxed. My forty-five-minute break passed as quickly as a thought. We never left the parking spot and never lunched. But the time was just long enough for him to lock me into his arms and for me to consent to that overdue first kiss. The steamed windows protected us from spying eyes.

All through the rest of that day and night, my thoughts returned to the magical rained-out lunch hour. In fact, I could not think of anything else. Günter hadn't even mentioned the incident with my parents dropping in at the Schneider's *Schrebergarten.* He had come to see me despite everything. My heart sang.

The next morning, I was alone in my office. I stared at the black phone in the center of our three desks and willed it to ring. *Call, Günter, please call.*

He did. Thrilled, I agreed to meet with him during lunch hour the following day. My heart thumped hard when I placed the receiver in its cradle. I barely recognized myself. What was happening to me? Usually, I tried to backpedal as soon as a guy got interested. Why not this time? And there was nothing my parents could do about it. This time, I was not going to let them run my life. *This time, I'm not going to back down.*

In the months that followed, Günter and I worked out a routine. We met during my brief lunch breaks two or three times a week and slowly got to know each other better. Each time, I liked him just a little more. There was something sincere and kind about him. He did not pressure me. He did not ask for explanations. I loved him for that.

At home, Günter remained a nonsubject. Dead-set against him, my parents forbade me all contact. I began to realize that if I wanted to be with him, I would have to take them on. It was clear that my mother would be a formidable opponent. The thought frightened me. Nothing in my life had prepared me for that. And I did not feel ready. When Günter invited Lorena and me to coffee at his shared flat one Saturday afternoon a few weeks later, I invented an excuse again. I could not find the courage to stand up to my parents. Instead, I brooded at home, mourning the good times I was missing out on.

When Lorena asked me to help celebrate her twentieth birthday, my mother's suspicions resurfaced at full strength. "Only if those no-accounts won't be there."

I tiptoed around the truth, hoping to postpone the inevitable a little longer. "All right, in that case, you can go this time," my mother relented.

The Movies

ON A FRIDAY IN AUGUST, shortly after Lorena's twentieth birthday party, Günter invited me to a Sunday movie. *Die Größte Geschichte aller Zeiten—The Greatest Story Ever Told—*played in one of the swanky theaters at the Europa Center.

"I don't know," I hedged. I don't think my parents will let me go," I finally admitted.

Günter was surprised. "It's the story about the life of Jesus Christ. Surely, your parents won't have any objections."

"It's not the movie they object to," I murmured. "It's you."

"Me?" Günter laughed in disbelief. "They don't even know me. We barely met."

"I know. It's not so much you. It's that you are a guy. My parents don't much care for guys." I could have died on the spot. *What man is going to put up with a date like me?*

Günter guffawed with relief. "They can't be THAT bad. We were off to a bad start. That's all. I'll introduce myself properly, and everything will be fine. You'll see."

"No, no, I'll ask them. I promise. I'll ask them tonight or tomorrow." Nervous about new encounters between Günter and my parents, I preferred to take on the task myself. *He thinks my parents will act like normal people. I know better.* I did not want Günter to witness what my home was really like. It would surely kill the tender relationship that was just developing.

When I returned home that night after work, I made several runs at popping the question but never quite garnered enough courage to follow through. My entire body shuddered at the thought. Lying in bed that night, I looked up at the ceiling, trying to read the plaster for an answer. In the end I got mad at myself. I was going to be twenty in three months and was still afraid to ask permission to go to a movie? What was I afraid of? I searched for reasons.

I was not worried about beatings because I had never been beaten. Then what was it? I concluded that I was afraid to oppose my parents' authority. Brought up to humble submission since I was a small child, I had not learned to fight. I didn't know how. Now I had to learn. Somehow.

The next day was a Saturday. I was scheduled for morning duty at Lufthansa. From my office, I dialed our home number. While I listened to the ring tone, I took a deep breath and allowed the air to escape in a long, slow exhale. It would be easier not to have to face my mother when posing the question. After a few courteous exchanges, I said as casual as possible, "Günter has invited me to see *Größte Geschichte aller Zeiten* tomorrow night. That's okay, isn't it?"

I waited for a reply.

Silence.

Then my mother screamed into the phone, "I don't believe it! Are you insane? Your father and I have strictly forbidden you all contact with this jerk. Who do you think you are? Do you think you can hoodwink us? What gives you the right to ignore our rules? Or is this HIS idea? Let's not forget who the adults are here. We are your parents. We make the rules. You don't think we'd allow you to carry on like this, do you? You're not going anywhere. That's that. Once and for all. You're not going. Is that understood?"

She paused.

"I'm disappointed in you," she continued in a calmer tone. "You had such big plans—going to the United States, becoming a stewardess, becoming an interpreter. You want to give all that up and hang around with such a . . . such . . . ?" She could not find a word repulsive enough.

My hand holding the receiver trembled. *I want to go to a movie—not change my career plans for heaven's sake.* But the intensity of my mother's animosity toward Günter had hit me like a brick. I offered no counterarguments and bid a timid good-bye instead.

The receiver back in its cradle, I sat there dumbfounded and stared out the window into the dimly lit freight hanger. After a few minutes, I threw my head back. *If you think I'm going to give him up, you're wrong.*

There was no further discussion on the subject when I returned home from work in the early afternoon. In fact, my parents and I barely spoke. Subdued, I hunkered down in my room. When the phone rang, my mother answered it and called me with a brisk, "For you."

I went to pick up the receiver in the hallway and caught sight of my mother lingering at the other end of the corridor, within a clear view of the phone.

"Hullo-o-o?" I said into the receiver.

"Keep a straight face. It's me. Günter. I told your mother I was Herr Sperling and wanted to speak with Fräulein Jutta Umbach. I made it sound like a call from your office. I had to phone because the movie tickets are selling out quickly. Do you think you'll be able to go? To be honest, I bought the tickets already."

My mother stood planted squarely at the end of the hallway, hands on her hips, watching me with cold steely eyes. Her lips were pressed into thin, straight lines. I did not think she could hear Günter's voice, but she had demonstrated amazing capabilities before. What could I say that would convey my status without giving away his identity? My head spun. Incapable of pulling off a charade, I stammered, "I don't know—maybe," and hung up. I could have killed myself. What a coward I was.

My mother's eyes appraised me from head to toe. Then, she disappeared into the kitchen without a word. *Maybe she doesn't suspect after all.*

Günter's call had shaken me up. I have to let him know that I won't be able to go to the movies, I thought. But how? I decided to call him from a phone booth when I took Tapsi for her walk later that day.

"Do you think your parents will let you visit Lorena?" He asked when I called. "We could meet there and talk."

"I'll try, but I honestly don't know what's going to happen."

"Just give it a try."

When I got back to our flat, I hedged, even more afraid to ask. My chest got so tight, I almost exploded. My mother could get ugly, and I would not know what to do about it. Finally, after dinner I summoned my nerve and warily inquired, "If I can't go to the movies, can I go to Lorena's tomorrow afternoon?"

My mother's response was even more explosive than I had expected.

"You're a disappointment to Pappi and me. We've granted you every freedom in the past. Name another nineteen-year-old who is allowed to travel alone to Greece. We trusted you. What a mistake that was." My mother's eyes bore straight through me. "From now on, you're no longer allowed to visit Lorena; and Lorena is no longer welcome at our house. She's a bad influence on you. From now on, the rules are going to be simple. You won't be seeing those lowlifes, and you won't be seeing Lorena. *Basta.*"

Brows furrowed, my father nodded in agreement.

"But, I . . ."

"There are no buts. Remember, you don't have any rights here. We are your parents. We are responsible for you. We set the rules."

I was devastated. Further discussion was pointless. It would only unleash additional furor. Now, I was completely cut off from my two best friends.

What was I going to do? I couldn't move out. My parents wouldn't let me. And I wasn't twenty-one yet. Besides, there wasn't enough housing. Even young married couples had to live with their parents. *I just might be stuck here until I turn twenty-one. I'm trapped.*

My spirit was broken.

The Introduction

HAVING WATCHED A FEW American movies and countless television sitcoms, I wanted Hollywood-Make-Believe to be reality. I wanted a perfect world. In my romantic fantasy, Günter swept me off my feet, and my parents supported our love for each other. We were all one happy family. In those daydreams, I was simultaneously the producer, director, screenwriter, and cameraman. I swept away any flaws with the airbrush of my imagination and replayed the scenes until they came out right.

After watching Sandra Dee's adventures in *April entdeckt die Männer—Gidget—*I, too, wanted to live as independently as the seventeen-year-old heroine who befriends a group of male teen surfers on the beach of Malibu. I didn't see her parents intervene, and I was already two years older than Gidget! And what about *West Side Story*'s Maria who manages tête-à-tête time with her beloved Tony despite Mama and Papa's vigilance? Not to mention the popular television sitcom *Vater ist der Beste—Father Knows Best—*in which Jim Anderson unobtrusively helps his three teens maneuver out of tight spots. Did he even once give unsolicited advice or wag his finger at Princess, Bud, or Kitten? I wanted MY life to unfold like their movie lives, but my parents continued to defy the Hollywood mold.

On the Monday morning, after my parents had cut me off from my two best friends, Lorena and Günter called at the office. "What happened last weekend? Why didn't you come to the garden plot on Sunday?"

I had to tell them about the newest constraints placed upon my life. I felt like a fool. My friends commiserated and wished me luck, but I alone had to deal with the problem. Depressed, I called my godmother, Tante Michen, and explained what had happened. "Can you stop by the house this evening?" I begged. "It's awful here. The air feels so thick you could cut it with a knife. No one says a word. Please do something." I knew I could count on my aunt whenever I was in trouble. Right after dinner she rushed to our flat under the pretense of some unexpected business in the neighborhood. Since my parents guessed the nature of her call, they gave her the silent treatment. Now, the four of us sat around the table like people engrossed in a difficult chess problem. I would have been grateful for any sound louder than the clinking of a spoon. After an uncomfortable thirty minutes, Tante Michen gave up and left without having accomplished anything.

The following day, Günter came to the airport during lunch hour. Without much of a preamble, he told me that he had made up his mind to pay a visit to my parents. He wanted to formally introduce himself and repair his tarnished image. As much as I tried, he could not be talked out of the plan. The event was to take place two days later, on a Thursday.

"That may be all it'll take. What time do you think would be good? I want to be sure that both your mother and your father will be there."

Panic seized me. *They'll kill him, and then they'll kill me.*

"I don't think it's a good idea, Günter. My parents are—well—they're different. Besides, what am I going to do while you talk to them? Call an ambulance?"

"Very funny. You don't even have to be there if you don't want to," he said. "You get home at six-thirty, right? If I'll get there, say, five-thirty, I'll be long gone before you arrive. Or maybe, we'll all share a reconciliation *Schnaps* by then," he winked.

"Yeah, right! My parents will give you a big hug and kiss you on both cheeks."

"Now, we're talking," he laughed.

I had never confronted my parents head on. I had never had the courage. *Maybe Günter is right. Maybe it's going to work.*

"Five-thirty is too early. It'll disrupt their dinner. They eat at six o'clock sharp. How about getting there at seven? I'll make myself scarce that evening and visit my aunt."

"It's a deal."

That same evening, I informed my parents that I planned to visit Tante Michen after work on Thursday. "I'll have dinner there. I'll be home no later than nine." At least, I was allowed to visit my aunt without much of a problem. My getaway was arranged, but I remained uneasy and off balance. *Günter has nothing to gain by doing this. He's doing it for me!* No one else had gone that far on a limb for me. A gentle wave of warmth pulsed through my veins at the thought. Günter was right. Something had to be done. My mother's desire for control could ruin my life if I continued to allow it to flourish. But what good could come of this meeting? *My parents won't change. They never have. They don't want me to have a boyfriend.*

On the agreed-upon evening, I took the bus to Tante Michen's after work. Despite a nice dinner and her supportive words, my nervousness kept me from fully enjoying our visit. When the grandfather clock struck seven, I jumped. *Is Günter talking to my parents yet? How is it going? What will they say when I get home? Will Günter still be there?*

With a great deal of trepidation, I opened the front door to our flat at nine o'clock sharp. Both parents sat in the living room, engrossed in a television show. They barely looked up. There was no indication that a dialogue had taken place. *Did Günter even make it to our house?* To remain on the safe side, I stayed out of the living room and went to bed without drawing attention to myself.

"So what happened?" I could barely contain my curiosity when I met with Günter at the airport the next day. I had never known him to be anything but even tempered. Now, he was fuming.

"I rang the bell at seven sharp. I was in suit and tie. Your mother opened the door. She almost slammed it shut when I told her my name." Günter's jaw muscles danced in an angry rhythm. "Then your mother planted one foot between door and door frame and talked to me through the gap. I could barely make out her face. Through that gap, she told me to leave you alone. She said I'd only make life more difficult for you if I continue to see you."

"What about my father?"

"Your father never came to the door. I don't know if he was even at home."

"He was home all right. He never misses dinner. He probably refused to see you and let my mother handle it. She is the determined one."

Wordless, we both stared into the distance, trying to digest the images.

"Would you believe, my parents never said a word to me about your visit?" I returned to the subject. "I started to think you chickened out."

"Me chicken out? Why would I chicken out? I haven't done anything. Your parents are the ridiculous ones. I didn't believe you at first. Now I see you were right. They're nuts." Günter was hurt and angry. At a minimum, he had expected to be treated with common courtesy. He had been unprepared for my parents.

We talked all through lunch. I felt terrible. I felt I should have stopped him from putting his plan into action, I who knew my parents' quirks. Günter had had such good intentions and such high hopes. He had been so sure that proper etiquette would ease my parents' misgivings. Now I had placed him in a ridiculous position. My heart went out to him for having tried to go to bat for me. I hated my parents. And I hated myself for having let it happen. Now, I would lose him for sure.

The weekend came, and my parents stayed true to their word. They kept me cut off from my two best friends. It felt like a prison, only worse. At least, one doesn't go to prison without having done something wrong. I had done nothing. I sat in my closet-sized room and stared out the window. From our fifth-floor flat, my view was limited to the upper floors of the cream-colored apartment building across the street, the leafy treetops between the two structures, and a tiny speck of sky. That visible patch of sky was so small, that I could not even hazard a guess at the weather.

All I was allowed to do that weekend was to walk Tapsi, our dachshund, around the block. Four times each day, I walked her, and four times each day I incorporated a brief visit to a public phone into the trip. Each time I tried to call Günter, and each time he was out. In my private hell I began to picture the good times Lorena, Günter, and Dieter were having while I was incarcerated. A new feeling took up residency inside of me: jealousy. It was an unaccustomed sensation, and I did not like it one bit. *What is happening to me? I am not even myself anymore.*

I began to question whether hanging on to Günter was worth it. For a moment, I entertained the notion of giving up the fight to regain my freedom. But an instant later, I vowed, *No. I won't give him up and if it kills me. It's high time that I stopped letting my parents direct my life. I like Günter, and I'm not going to let them ruin that for me.* I could not know then how much of me would die before it was all over.

More Trouble at Home

I BEGAN TO LOOK FOR WAYS around my parents' embargo, no matter how small. Every other week, I worked half a Saturday in the office and banked that time. Why not take some of it off right now? My parents would not know how much time I had accrued. I discussed the idea with Günter, and he was as excited at the prospect as I was. "Let's both take a day off and do something together!"

Only two days later, we played hooky together. Our secret rendez-vous instilled in me a wonderful sense of freedom. I got up as usual, dressed in office attire, wearing my bathing suit underneath, packed lunch, and threw a towel into my bag. I always carried a *Hebammen-koffer*—a doctor's bag. It was not only the fashion, but the bag was also big enough to carry personal items that required protection from my mother's prying eyes. The diaries I had started three years earlier were always in the bag. I left our flat at the usual early morning hour. Günter picked me up at a designated corner, and together we drove to Saatwinkel, a dreamy cove along a small lake with a tiny, sandy beach, all within city limits. The weather smiled upon us. The sky was blue, the sun brilliant, and the temperature perfect. The lake shimmered in front of us. We spread out our towels and enjoyed the glorious sun-shine. Few people frolicked on the beach during the week so that we had the whole area to ourselves. We spent the day basking in the sun, picnicking, talking, and swimming to the small island of Baumwerder in the middle of the lake. I almost forgot my trouble. This is what life would be like if I didn't have to look over my shoulder all the time, I thought. Neither Günter nor I wanted the day to end, relishing the peace, sunshine, and water.

It was after 5:00 p.m. when we changed, packed our things, and reluctantly began to drive back. Only then did I reenter reality. A healthy tan had developed during my "work day." How would I explain that to my parents? To counteract my glow, we stopped at a drugstore and picked up some whitish makeup. During our last carefree minutes together, we stuck a few coins into the machine at a photo booth. Back again in office attire and paled to perfection, we pulled out four strip portraits that captured our happiness. I wanted to hold on to that memory forever. At home, I played the role of the bored, overworked teen and managed to get away with my charade.

Three days later, Günter left for a three-week hiking trip with his parents. Our good-bye was bittersweet. Since he had accepted the position in Berlin, he had spent all holidays and vacations with his family. I loved hearing him talk about them. He spoke with such affection. They seemed to be the parents I never had. I knew with certainty that I would never choose to vacation with my parents, at least not since the trouble with Günter had developed. And I did not like to speak of them either. I dreaded the weeks without Günter and was surprised how dear he had become to me.

The day after he left, my father and I went swimming at the stadium. To my surprise, Pappi told me that he had intervened on my behalf with my mother. As a result, I was allowed to see Lorena again. I was delighted. But Günter would have to remain off limits despite my mother's snide remark, "*Häng ihn Dir doch um den Hals*—Why don't you drape him around your neck."

Since I still had two weeks of vacation time left on the books with Lufthansa, I was eyeing a trip to the Goldstrand of Bulgaria. The trip could be booked through the same youth agency I had used for my Greek vacation. This time, Lorena wanted to join me. Since my father seemed to be in an upbeat mood, I took the opportunity to put the idea before him. Without any fight on my part, he approved. That same afternoon, I went to see Lorena to share my news. It appeared that my life was returning to normal.

Less than two weeks after Günter left, I received a postcard from him. In a small act of defiance, it ended with:

P.S. My regards to your parents.

The Cold War resumed without delay. My mother immediately connected Günter with Bulgaria. "Who's going on that trip to Bulgaria? That no-account? Maybe you'd better come to Italy with us."

I proffered a myriad of excuses: "I put in for vacation, starting September 28; you're planning to leave on September 4; I have a total of two weeks off; you're planning a four-week trip." The list went on. In the end, my parents left for Italy as planned in early September. My own departure was scheduled shortly before my parents' return. That meant five weeks of liberty for me. Tante Michen was given detailed instructions; I was given multiple assignments and the strict warning: "No one is allowed in this flat during our absence."

Tante Michen and I nodded in agreement. Regrettably, Günter was still on vacation during the first eight days of my delicious freedom. Just as Sonja and I had done the year before, I went dancing every night. I wanted to take full advantage of my rare independence. Günter's image faded a little as days went by. *Maybe it was only infatuation after all.*

Then, a few days before his return, I received another postcard:

I will drive back on September 12 and stop by your house on my way home.
Lots of kisses.
Günter

He arrived at my parents' flat at eleven-thirty in the evening, bringing me a little glass rooster as a souvenir. We talked until four in the morning and reluctantly parted. During the few remaining days prior to my vacation, Günter and I went dancing, to the movies, to dinner, to the stadium, watched TV, and even went to church together. We made every minute count, and I no longer questioned whether or not I wanted to give up Günter to regain my coveted freedom. He was the first thought on my mind when I rose in the morning and the last when I went to sleep at night. Everything else seemed irrelevant. I could have held hands forever. I had come to adore him and was sure that nothing could ever come between us.

Bulgaria

EARLY ON A TUESDAY MORNING toward the end of September, I flew on standby to Munich. Günter had offered to drive me to the airport, but had also conceded quickly when I offered to take the bus instead. "Go ahead, sleep in a little longer," I said, "I can handle the suitcase by myself." Secretly, I had been certain he would leave his comfortable bed at any hour for a few extra minutes together. I knew I would have. But I had misjudged him and was disappointed.

Since I flew on a Lufthansa employee ticket, Lorena ended up taking a different plane and met me at Munich airport, waving a piccolo bottle of champagne. Before boarding the flight to Varna in Bulgaria, we toasted to my rare independence. I felt like I was on parole from prison.

The flight was followed by a thirty-minute bus ride to a small hotel on the Goldstrand on the Black Sea. In the sixties, this socialist nation was THE place where East met West. At a time when the Iron Curtain prevented people of opposing ideologies from seeing one another, friends and families reunited in Bulgaria. Although Westerners and Easterners could not stay at the same hotels, friends and families would at least be able to spend time together in the town or at the beach.

Lorena and I had chosen the Goldstrand for a different reason. We wanted to soak up the sun and stretch out on its fair beaches one more time before fall and winter chills blanketed our homeland. But there was one thing the vacationers from Eastern bloc countries and I had in common: guarded and restricted lives. All of us thoroughly enjoyed these rare moments of freedom, although for different reasons.

Our hotel catered to a Western clientele and was chartered by several collaborating youth agencies. As part of the package tour, which offered Plan A (breakfast, lunch, and dinner), Plan B (breakfast and dinner) and C (breakfast only), Lorena and I selected double occupancy with breakfast and dinner. Hotel guests were booked in two-week intervals, so that each fortnight the staff welcomed a new group of vacationers. Upon arrival, we were shown to our room and assigned a dining table that was to be shared with eight or ten other guests from various parts of Germany.

The next morning we met our tablemates over breakfast. Most of us were single. The ice broke quickly when someone proposed nicknames. We became Yogi, Bubu, Molli, Drolli, Hakim, and Mobuto; I was named Haki, after the sea king in Norse mythology.

During the next two weeks, the group became inseparable. Our pleasures were simple since there was little to do aside from enjoying sun and sea during the day and dancing at neighborhood tavernas at night, where we also dared one another to partake of the local red wine. It was so sour that rumor had it that one hefty gulp would pull together the holes in your socks.

We heard of a flyboat, a futuristic Russian contraption that operated between the Goldstrand and Nessebar, a sleepy fishing village. Of course, we all signed up for the jaunt. The destination was unimportant; the point was the boat ride itself. It quickly became apparent that the craft did not fly at all; it hovered above the water being supported by air cushions.

Once in Nessebar, we walked about the village for a while, but when we could not locate a single restaurant or historic sight, we returned to the dock for the ride home. To our dismay we were informed that the last boat of the day had already left. There were no tourist accommodations in Nessebar and no buses to take us back. We were stuck. One couple decided to hitchhike and caught a ride on a slow-moving farm vehicle. Their return trip to the hotel took over twelve hours and lasted through the night. The rest of us piled into a dilapidated taxi with bad shocks and slowly pitched and bounced up the mountain and down the hilly countryside terracing back to the sea. For more than five hours, we lurched and plunged inside the sweltering automobile, the girls riding on the laps of the guys, and finally made it back to our hotel just in time for dinner.

Our two weeks together passed quickly. Complete strangers upon arrival, we had meshed into a tight group of friends. There was no competition, no domination, and no rebuff. We thoroughly enjoyed each other's company. Toward the end of our stay, we felt the urge to memorialize these once-in-a-lifetime friendships by creating mementos that would take us back to this holiday in years to come. Toting our cameras to the beach, we took group pictures, but not the mundane photos in which everyone mouths "cheese." No, we wanted our photographs to reflect the fun we had had together. To the hoots and hollers of the rest of the group, each girl, in turn, was hoisted onto the shoulders of the various guys. We laughed until our abdominals hurt. The whole picture-taking process took less than fifteen minutes; the consequences were to last much longer.

They first became apparent when Lorena stopped by with her vacation photos at our flat in Berlin. My mother's shoulders tightened as her eyes fixated on the images. Scrutinizing the pictures, she muttered, "*Da sind ja nur Männer drauf*—There are only men in these pictures." Indeed, the core of our group had consisted of six men and three women. In each picture, Lorena sat on different shoulders.

I looked at Lorena; she looked at me. What had seemed like a good idea a week earlier had turned into a big mistake. The photos of Lorena were more than my mother could handle. Snapshots of me sitting on the shoulders of various men would undoubtedly push her over the edge.

Unfortunately, just the night before, I had given my film to my father to have it developed. Now, I was going to be in a huge pile of trouble. The following day, when I returned from work, I immediately spotted my parents in the kitchen, hovering over the photos. My mother still wore her duster. There was complete silence when I approached.

"The pictures are back? Can I see?" I asked.

More silence. My father handed me the prints without a word. I could feel the heat—smoldering embers everywhere. Pretending to be unaware of the sizzle, I reached for the photos. I could not know what went through my parents' minds, but I guessed that they had studied each innocent pose, turned their impressions into probabilities, and probabilities into presumed realities. Sensing that the slightest misstep on my part could ignite a fire, I became extra-cautious, hoping not to draw attention to myself. Maybe it will pass, I said to myself and sauntered to my room.

For the first few days following the trip I had not seen or talked to Günter. In the past, our clandestine meetings had been limited to occasional forty-five-minute lunch hours, Monday night movie forums, and the hit-or-miss Saturday night dates that I could finagle under the pretense of participating in a permitted activity. When I did not hear from him within a couple of days following my return from Bulgaria,

I suspected that our relationship had quietly fizzled. It would not have come as a surprise. Relationships rarely flourish under the constraints ours was subjected to.

As soon as we met for lunch at the airport on the third day after my return, however, one thing was clear: The spark had not gone from the relationship. There was passion in that embrace, and the long kiss tasted sweet.

A couple of weeks later, Mobuto, one of my new Bulgaria friends, attended a convention in Berlin. He called Lorena and me, and we all agreed to go dancing on Saturday night. Despite the ban on dating Günter, I was still allowed, even encouraged, to go out with other chaps because my parents hoped that they would redirect my focus. When I was unable to get word about our plans to Günter, he called my home. My father answered and realized immediately that I was still involved with the one man my mother and he vehemently objected to. "*Dieser Scheich*—this sheik. Is he still hanging around?" he asked angrily as soon as I arrived at home. The word *Scheich* was meant to offend and implied a romantically alluring man of questionable character. "Do you think you can simply ignore our orders? Who do you think you are?"

"*Das Ei will wieder klüger sein als die Henne*—the egg wants to be smarter than the hen again," My mother added. "You thought we wouldn't find out, didn't you?"

I did not answer. I ducked and took the blows—waiting.

Next morning, after breakfast, my mother said, "Tell Lorena, I want her mother to give us a call." Her tone ruled out questions.

What is this all about? Mutti and Papa don't like the Schneiders. I bet it has to do with the Bulgaria pictures. I relayed the message to Lorena, and she informed her mother.

A day later, Lorena came to our house, "My mother wants to know what it is you want to talk to her about," she said to Mutti.

My mother exploded. "I don't want to talk to you, Lorena. I want to talk to your mother. If I wanted to talk to you, I'd tell you."

Lorena was irked. She was not used to be spoken to in this manner. She and I exchanged brief glances, then she excused herself and went home.

A day later, I had an appointment with our family doctor after work to talk about a potential tonsillectomy because of recurring throat infections. During this visit, he casually inquired about my social life. I readily shared my dating dilemma.

"How old are you now?"

"Nineteen. Almost twenty."

"Have you had any relations with this guy?"

An intense heat wave flooded my body. Even my ears blushed. *My parents don't even whisper the word "menopause." Not to mention sex. And this stranger wants me to go into intimate details?*

"No, of course not."

"Would you know how to protect yourself?"

Perplexed, I stared at him. *What is he talking about? I don't think Günter would hit me.*

"They don't make young women like you anymore," he said in a fatherly tone. "Do you know about the pill? If you ever have any questions, come and see me."

Flustered, I avoided eye contact and focused on the scuff marks on the linoleum instead. I had heard of the pill. Wasn't it limited to married women with menstrual problems? But I said nothing and hurried out of his office. Shocked by the doctor's candor and confused by his question, I walked home. *Who cares about the pill? I'm not going to bed with anyone.*

As soon as I walked into our flat, I knew something was wrong. Even Tapsi, our dog, wagged with restraint when she greeted me. Television and radio were off. The silence foreshadowed a calamity. The air smoldered with unbearable tension.

Raging Inferno

WHEN HOT ENOUGH, WOOD IGNITES by itself. Until this evening, only a few embers had been smoldering in our home. But when I stuck my head into the living room and yelled, "I'm home," after returning from the doctor's, sudden combustion occurred.

"Sit down," my father barked. "Your mother and I want to talk to you."

By this time of day, my parents had usually finished their cold supper. When I did not see the customary beer and bump in front of my father, I suspected trouble. A veiled glance in his direction confirmed my suspicion. As usual, he sat in his armchair at the head of the table, but instead of leaning back comfortably, his spine was stiff and erect.

From her place on the couch, to my father's right, my mother scrutinized me with a challenging glare. When Pappi pointed to the armchair directly across from my mother, I did as directed and warily edged into the seat. My mother unpacked immediately. Her violent verbal blast of criticism and accusations singed everything in its path. "We're at the end of our rope. We've tried everything." My mother's fingers drummed nervously on the fake-marble tabletop. "We've tried to talk sense into you. We've tried to talk to Lorena's mother. She refuses to call. We've given it a lot of thought and come to the only conclusion left. Lorena is a very bad influence on you. And we have to separate you." There was a long silence. I knew that my parents did not like Lorena and wondered what was coming next.

"From now on, we forbid you to see her. This time, we won't change our minds. Lorena is not allowed in our home; you're not allowed in hers; and you're not going anywhere Lorena goes. Is that understood?" My mother sneered.

I threw my head back. This was the second time Lorena was axed from my list of friends. "It's not her fault that Frau Schneider hasn't called. I've told Lorena, and she's told her mom. Maybe Frau Schneider is busy. She works, you know. And they don't have a phone at home."

"That's neither here nor there. The point is we don't want you to keep company with that girl or her parents. And the same goes for that *Scheich* of yours."

I balled my fists behind my back at the renewed insult and wanted to protest, but the intensity of my mother's outburst kept me in check. *Better not fight back. In the end, it's easier to work around her restrictions.*

My mother continued. "We've asked you to stop seeing this dolt. You've ignored us and dated him anyway. You pretended going out with your girl-friends." My mother's fist hit the table. "You've lied to us—and repeatedly."

There was another pause. "All we want to do is keep you from messing up your life. We're trying to protect you. Don't you understand that?"

"Protect me from what?" I hesitantly interjected.

"What if something happens?"

I grimaced recalling the conversation with our family doctor less than thirty minutes earlier. *Maybe he needs to have that conversation with my parents. I haven't done anything. I just want to be with my friends. Mutti and Pappi want complete control. That's what this is all about: control.*

My mother's mouth twitched. She picked up a rubber band and stretched it to near failure. "Until now you've had every freedom."

"Every freedom?" I mocked. "You call this freedom? Lorena, Fee, and the others are allowed to stay out until ten o'clock during the week and until two in the morning on weekends. And they don't have to ask for permission every time they want to go to the store."

"Other daughters don't lie to their parents. I see other daughters walk arm in arm with their mothers in the park. Not you. No-o-o! You marvel at everything Frau Schneider does. Frau Schneider this, and Frau Schneider that. Frau Schneider must be a superwoman." My mother drew a breath.

Unprepared for this turn in the dialogue, I scooted further toward the edge of my chair. *My mother is jealous! She's jealous of Frau Schneider.* "I'm just being polite. Frau Schneider is Lorena's mom. Do you want me to be crabby to her?"

"Schneiders have such a wonderful garden, don't they? You were never interested in our *Schrebengarten* when we had one. Everything we have is rubbish to you. We never get any thanks for what we've done for you. We sacrificed ourselves for your sake. All we've ever wanted is what is best for you."

"You don't know what I gave up for you," my mother added after a brief reflection. "I could've had a career. I gave it all up for you."

I cowered under her attack. I knew she twisted reality somehow, but I could not put my finger on it. Lord, how I hated it when she worked my guilt feelings. *I can't give in! Not this time. I have to stand up for myself.* In sullen submission I resigned myself to her heaviest blows.

Like an out-of-control wildfire, the flames of my mother's attack changed direction again. "Your father and I have worked and slaved to help you make something of yourself," she said. "Now, you're throwing everything away because of that loser, that *Rotzjunge*, that snotty-nosed kid. He's got you hypnotized."

"We put you through school," my mother resumed the tirade. "We agreed to let you attend business school after high school. You had such big plans."

"Since when do you approve of my plans? I wanted to work for Lufthansa in Frankfurt. Not until you're twenty-one, you said. I wanted to work in the United States. Same answer."

"If we had known you'd throw your life away, we would've put you in a school for the retarded," my mother countered.

"The retarded! That's crazy! "

"Watch your mouth, young lady."

We stared at each other. My mother was trembling with rage; I with terror. She seemed to be waiting for me to drop my eyes. But I kept holding her gaze and clasped my hands in my lap. *This is going too far! I've always brought home good grades. I have a decent job. I pay for my room and board. I don't do anything outrageous. I don't deserve this.* I raised my eyes to the ceiling.

"Pay attention. Your mother is talking to you," my father blasted.

They're both crazy. I glared at my mother again.

"You don't know this, but Pappi wanted to give you a car, a Fiat, if you must know. So you wouldn't have to take the bus anymore. I told him, 'Peter, she isn't worth it. Don't spend any money on her until she dances to a different tune.'"

Dancing to a different tune? What am I? A monkey? Besides. What car? You're making this up. I don't want your car. A car comes with more strings. I was angry now, too angry to speak and stared at the wall in back of my mother, looking straight through her.

My mother would not let go. She julienned me with lacerating comments. "As far as your father and I are concerned, you can go ahead and marry this creep, but understand one thing: If you do, the doors to this house will be closed to you—forever." She paused, letting the thought sink in.

I just want to date him for Christ's sake. Now, that the guilt trip hasn't worked, we move on to threats? I tried to appear indifferent but was shaken to the core. I tried to look like a swan that glides gracefully through the water, but in reality I paddled ferociously beneath the surface. *The doors to this house will be closed if I marry Günter? Fine!*

"And another thing," my mother added, lobbing her strongest ammunition at me. "Just so you know—if you marry this dope, we'll cut you out of the will. You'll inherit nothing! Let that be a warning to you!"

That was it.

"I don't want your money. I'll make my own money. I won't ask you for one pfennig."

I got up from the chair and walked to my room. I felt like a fly that had been swatted repeatedly.

"And one more thing," my mother yelled after me. "We know that this creep was here, in our flat, while we were on vacation in Italy. Against our instructions. He was seen." My mother spat out the last three words as if she had inadvertently swallowed poison.

Something in me snapped. In this moment we were close to raw hatred for each other. My mother was determined to break me; I was just as determined that she would not. *She's got to be bluffing. She doesn't mix with the neighbors. She doesn't have friends. I'll bet no one has said a word.*

I turned on my heels and walked back into the living room. With contempt in my voice I said, "Who said Günter was here? Tell me their name because they're lying."

I was the liar. But I did not care any longer. I, too, could bluff.

"It doesn't matter," my mother backed down.

"To the contrary. It does matter," I said. "I want to set that person straight." *I got you. You were bluffing. If someone told you, you'd be happy to give me their name right now.*

"What I mean is, your father and I don't mind you dating someone from a good home, someone with a good upbringing. But not this *Scheich*."

Good home? Good upbringing? Günter's parents own a single-family home—we own a condo. Günter's father holds a management position in a large company—Pappi is a street photographer. Günter's parents drive a Mercedes . . . Want me to keep going?

But, "You don't know what you're saying," was all that came out of my mouth before I proceeded to my bedroom for the second time. Once inside, I leaned against the wall and covered eyes and forehead with the palms of my hands. Something inside of me had broken.

EIGHT

COLD WAR

Trapped

SEETHING WITH ANGER and resentment, I sank into the armchair next to my sofa bed and stared out the window. Soon the evening would give way to twilight. I dropped my chin onto my bunched fists and balanced my elbows on my knees. An overwhelming feeling of hopelessness swept over me. Unable to absorb what had just happened, I asked myself, "How did we get from there to here?" I took stock of my options. Did I even have any? It was clear that my parents were committed to an "I dictate—you cooperate" approach. They expected faithful adherence to their orders. Having been brought up to obedience, I always had complied in the past. But then, how could I not yield to their rules as long as I lived in their house? With more than a year left until the magic birthday that would set me free, the future looked bleak, indeed. Even adulthood was likely to keep me tied to my parents because of the severe housing shortage in West Berlin. I was trapped in my own home. This apartment was my prison.

With a flick of her wrist, my mother had taken away everything that mattered to me. I knew that she would never allow me to see Günter. She had even axed my girlfriend, Lorena, because Frau Schneider refused to gang up on me. It was unlikely that my father would intervene a second time. Incarcerated and separated from my two best friends, I would be alone in this struggle. Lorena might remain my friend in abstention. But Günter? Why should he hang around for a girl with ridiculous parents? *He'll walk away as soon as he hears of tonight's drama.* I loathed my cowardice. But I could not help myself.

Another wave of hopelessness rose up from the pit of my stomach. The feeling extended far beyond my small bedroom. I felt cut off from the world. Outside, I was surrounded by the Berlin Wall. Inside, I felt walled-in by barriers far higher and less penetrable than the political monstrosity. As I stood in front of my small window and watched the setting sun paint the roofs golden, I wished I were dead. My world was devoid of color; I saw only shades of gray and black. Although the busses ran on schedule, the pedestrians walked down the street as usual, and everything around me had an air of familiarity, I wondered whether I would ever be able to feel pleasure again. The fact that I was still breathing was nothing more than an automatic function.

Looking back that night, I realized that I had made a huge mistake when Günter and I first met. When my parents forbade me to see him again, I should have rebelled on the spot. Instead of trying to meet him in secret, I should have fought for my rights. My parents' restrictions now reminded me of the dandelions we used to battle in our garden plot in Boxfelde. When we saw the first one pop up in the lawn, we should have pulled it right away, but we turned our backs and planned to do it later. The next time we looked, there were hundreds of them, becoming almost impossible to eradicate. The same had happened here. I had ignored the first sanction. Now, the diktats were multiplying like weeds.

Despite my desire to remain unattached, I had fallen irreversibly in love with Günter and had been catapulted into an emotional orbit unlike anything I had ever experienced before. He was on my mind first thing in the morning and last thing before I went to sleep. With Prussian stubbornness, I had vowed not to give him up voluntarily, despite all difficulties. But it was easier said than done. I was not a fighter. I was a runner. With the lines of battle drawn and the time for possible conciliation behind us, the war was on to keep my private Iron Curtain from closing completely.

I cried through the night. My eyes were so swollen that my face had taken on alien features by morning. I decided to call Günter as soon as possible and to tell him what had happened. I wanted to put the inevitable behind me. When I called him from my office midmorning, my voice sounded monotone and tired.

"Something wrong?" he asked.

"Can you meet me for lunch?"

"Sure. What's wrong?"

"I'll tell you later."

When I saw his white Opel parked at the curb, I took a mental photo. I wanted to store that image somewhere in the folds of my mind because I would probably never see that car again. Resigned, I crossed the street. *We're only one day short of celebrating our fourth month together.* I straightened my spine to erase that thought. It'll all be history in less than forty-five minutes, I told myself, and decided to omit the most embarrassing details of the previous night's scene. There would be no need to talk about the consequences of staying with Günter. But in the car, when pressed for details, I spilled everything, right down to the awkward mention of being cut out of the will in case of matrimony. I could have punched myself in the head.

Throughout my narration, Günter listened quietly. Even afterwards, he made no comment. At first, his silence was a relief. Then it felt uncomfortable. *The mention of "marriage" got to him. I knew it would scare him off. How embarrassing!* I hoped he didn't think I was eager *"unter die Haube zu kommen*—to end up under the hood." That expression dated back to the Middle Ages when married women wore bonnets while unmarried girls were allowed to show their hair. It was way too early in our relationship to talk about things like that. *What on earth made me confide in him?* I felt like a pebble that had been thrown into a pond, causing my friends to ripple away from me. To protect the last vestiges of my battered ego, I changed tactics. I pretended to be indifferent to the restrictions imposed on me. With all the strength I could marshal I turned up my chin, shrugged, and said, "It doesn't really matter. I'm going to the United States for a year anyway—as soon as I turn twenty-one."

Günter remained silent. I immediately loathed myself. Why did I have to put on such an act? America was nothing more than a pipe dream. Why couldn't I admit that I was hurting?

Following a reserved good-bye, I returned to the office. The deed was done. My mother had succeeded. Günter was out of my life for good although I would never admit to her that he had dropped me. I did not want her to have that satisfaction. No, I would continue to fight for my rights as if Günter were still in the picture. Only in the future, I would fight for no reason at all.

Several days later, the office phone rang. Günter acted as if nothing had happened and asked about my weekend plans. My heart sang. *He still cares! He must love me!* But because my domestic situation had remained unchanged, I said, "I wish we could do something together, Günter, but I'm stuck at home. My parents don't even let me out of the house to buy a newspaper. There's nothing I can do."

After I hung up, I wrung my hands. Why didn't I tell him that I missed him, that I cared for him, that I loved him? The truth was, I didn't know how to tell him. There was so much I hadn't learned in my nineteen years. There were a lot of social skills I had not been able to develop. Where did that leave me now? Reasoning with my parents was fruitless; asking for permission futile; active combat out of the question. I was incapable of jumping beyond my own shadow. Maybe time would be my teacher. Until then, secrecy and lies would have to do. Lies had become a necessity, and I had become proficient in lying.

I jumped into action the same afternoon. "Can you do me a huge favor?" I called my longtime friend, Fee. After explaining the situation, I asked, "Can you stop by my house on Saturdays and pick me up before you go out with Peter? You know what my parents are like. I want them to believe that you and I are going to the dance club together. Then, as soon as we're out of the house, you can go your way, and I'll go mine. I need to find ways to meet up with Günter. I know it's a lot to ask, but I can't think of anything else right now. My parents have known you since we were two years old and played in the sandbox. They won't suspect anything."

"*Kein Thema*—Not a question. I know you'd do the same thing for me," Fee replied. I could always count on her. I owed Fee big-time.

Next, I called Tante Michen. "You know that Mutti and Pappi never join family gatherings. If I make only brief appearances at upcoming family events and go out with Günter instead, do you think you and the rest of the family could keep it a secret?" My aunt understood my dilemma and assured me that nothing would slip.

During lunch at the airport the following week, I shared my plan with Günter. "It's a start. Maybe with time, we'll find other ways." He nodded and we held each other without further explanations. With an increased sense of self-determination, I looked forward to the prospect of duping my parents.

In short order, Günter and I worked out a new routine. He squeezed in as many lunch-hour visits as he could. On Saturdays, Fee, my steadfast friend, rode five stations on the bus to pick me up to go to the Riverboat. In reality, I linked up with Günter at the next corner, and she went her way with her boyfriend.

With Christine, another girlfriend whom my mother trusted because she was a stylish dresser, I arranged to go ice-skating on Tuesday evenings after work. Günter joined us, of course. He also joined my Spanish class, and on his suggestion, we both signed up for an enameling class. On Monday nights, we attended the movie forum together at the Rathaus.

Although all of our get-togethers remained clandestine, we now saw quite a bit of each other. We were rarely alone, but it was a start.

But our time together remained filled with anxiety for me. I fretted over the possibility of being found out because it would expose our carefully crafted scheme. Worried that my mother might appear around the next bend, I constantly looked over my shoulder. Still, it felt wonderful to be with Günter. It was so easy to enjoy his company, and it felt so right.

Weekends continued to pose acute problems. He could not reach me, and I could call only from a public phone. Within days, I knew the location of every booth in the neighborhood. The most convenient one, the one next to our apartment building, was out of the question because it was within easy view from our balcony. All other stalls were considerably further away, and I had to combine phone calls with dog walks. Since my mother insisted on walking Tapsi on a fixed schedule which rarely coincided with Günter's availability, it was difficult for me to reach him. Besides, the trips required longer than standard absences from home so that Tapsi and I usually had to run both ways.

"Room 922, please!" How many times did I huff those words from a phone booth to the concierge at Günter's reception? How many times did I tug a shivering dachshund into my coat when the temperatures were freezing? How many times did I try to placate the people waiting outside the booth when the call took longer than expected? Frequently, I failed to reach Günter altogether. Sometimes, our dates got so muddled that we did not connect at all. The consequence of those miscommunications was worst in the winter and on rainy days. One time, I ended up seeking shelter in a cold, unheated church for the duration of an entire evening. Another time, I sat for hours in the freezing stairway of our apartment building, unable to return home because Fee and I were officially dancing the night away at the Riverboat.

Opportunity Knocks

A FEW WEEKS AFTER THE START of our new dating routine, I received a tape recording from San Diego along with a short note. "My mother's employer has a job for you," my girlfriend, Sonja, wrote. "You can live at their place. It's all worked out. Get your visa right away."

I could not believe it. The United States? My way out? *If I can spend the next year in the US, I'll be twenty-one when I get back. Then my parents won't be able to lock me up anymore.*

Sonja's mother, whom I had never met, had even added a few words for the benefit of my parents. "Don't worry. We'll take good care of Jutta. Sonja is looking forward to seeing her best friend again."

I was delirious with happiness. *Saved!* Now, that Sonja's mom had encouraged and welcomed me, my parents had to let me go. They just had to! *One day soon, I'll be in San Diego!*

It was not quite the way my parents saw it, however. My mother stood in the doorway to my bedroom as she listened to the tape. Her only comment was, "Sonja's mother doesn't have any idea how difficult it is to manage you."

My father did not even take note of the recording.

After the initial flurry of excitement, I considered the downside to a USA venture. I wouldn't see Günter for a whole year. Would he wait for my return? What did I want more? Freedom from my parents or to be with the man I loved? The answer was I wanted both.

Next day, I told Günter about my news. He remained silent throughout my eager narration and did not share my enthusiasm.

A few days later, a thick white envelope arrived in the mail. Its odd size and colorful foreign stamps looked intriguing to me. The return address read:

HARRY AND HAPPY HALL

I had never heard of Mr. and Mrs. Hall. *Happy Hall? Is that an actual name?* The Halls turned out to be my prospective San Diego employers who were offering me a job in their franchised "juicerator" business. I had no idea what a juicerator was or what industry it represented, but with the help of my dictionary I deciphered that I was promised one hundred fifty dollars per month, free room and board, and a small commission on the juicers I sold. I was beside myself. One hundred fifty dollars equaled six hundred marks, close to what I earned at Lufthansa. In addition, I would get free room and board, plus a commission. *Surely, I can make a good living on that!* My dream of spending a year in San Diego seemed to move within reach.

The following week I paid a visit to the US Consulate and picked up an immigration application. If a visitor's visa did not allow me to work, I would immigrate, even though I had no intention of staying in the United States for more than one year. The consulate staff informed me that the US subscribed to rigid immigration quotas and categories within each quota. I nodded without comprehending the significance of that statement and departed cheerfully with the necessary forms in my bag.

I turned twenty that November. Birthdays were not a big deal at my home, but my parents gave me permission to celebrate with my friends at a local dance club the day before. At this pre-birthday party, Günter gave me a beautiful silver ring with a long, narrow amber stone. The ring was striking. When he slipped it on my finger, I was speechless. It spoke volumes for his desire to be friends. How much time must he have spent before he tracked down this stunning piece? When I threw my arms around him to show my thanks, I hugged him so tight that he had trouble breathing. I did not want to let go. Günter was the kind of guy a girl dreamed of. He was a diamond among rhinestones. And he was mine.

But for now, the ring would have to remain our secret. I would only be able to wear it away from home, never in my parents' presence.

My actual birthday was a letdown. Only my two first cousins, a second cousin, and my parents made up the guest list. I had to bake my own cake, and by seven in the evening, everyone had gone home.

Discerning Nose

THE MONDAY FOLLOWING MY BIRTHDAY, Günter and I skipped the movie forum and went to a drive-in theater instead. The film finished a good hour and a half before the forum let out. By then, a blustery November wind whipped through the deserted streets. We decided to drive to my house and cuddle in the car until it was time for me to go home. Knotted in a passionate embrace at the curb in front of our building, I froze in the middle of a long kiss. Out of the corner of my eye, I saw Tapsi hobbling down the eight steps leading from our apartment building into the courtyard. Behind her, my mother was slowly descending the stairs. The sight made my heart stop. *Oh my God! Why is Mutti walking Tapsi at this hour?*

Günter had parked next to a tall basswood tree, Tapsi's favorite business directory. I watched in disbelief as our little wiener dog headed straight for her much-loved potty tree, my mother trailing not far behind. Terrified of the consequence of being discovered, I eased out of my seat.

"What are you doing?" Günter asked, still unaware of the catastrophe in the making.

"MY MOTHER!" I squealed, pointing in the direction of our apartment building. And with one hasty swoop, I slid under the glove compartment, bulky winter peacoat and all.

"Go—quick—drive away!" I whispered from beneath the dashboard.

Bewildered, Günter turned toward the building and immediately grasped the situation. "Your mother won't know the car—or recognize me in the dark for that matter. Let's just wait it out."

Twisted into a pretzel and frightened out of my wits, I pleaded, "Go—please—go! This may be the end of the world as we know it!"

Suddenly, we heard Tapsi let out a couple of enthusiastic woofs. Her deep bark had that joyful, anticipatory ring. I guessed it instantly: Tapsi had sniffed out her master's presence. It spooked even Günter. He turned on the ignition. The engine kicked in while Taps whined and snorted outside and tried to climb up the side of the car.

My mother called her back and eyed the white Opel Kadett with suspicion as Günter slowly edged it out of its parking spot and into the traffic. Although, to my knowledge, she had never seen his car before, I was overcome by panic that she might have spotted me.

"Is it safe yet?" I asked a couple of minutes later from my hiding place under the glove compartment.

"Yes, yes, we're at the corner of Kantstraße."

Unfolding my limbs, I crawled back into the bucket seat. My heart pounded with such force that I feared my chest might explode. "What are we going to do now?" I asked. "Do you think my mother saw us? I'm afraid to go home."

We still had most of an hour to kill before I was expected to return from the forum.

"Let's drive to the bowling alley on Kurfürstendamm," Günter suggested. "You're all shook up. Relax. I really don't think your mother saw us."

"I'm not so sure."

While we milled around the bowling alley for what felt like an eternity, I could not stop trembling. Still rattled from seeing my mother, I was close to tears and not in the mood for anything. At the proper time, I emerged from Günter's car, almost two blocks short of our apartment building, and walked the rest of the way.

Before I inserted my key into the first of our double front doors, one behind the other, I took off my boots and wedged them tightly under my arms. Holding the doorknob with my left, I slowly unbolted the lock with my right, careful not to drop the shoes. Bit by bit, I pulled open the door. Then I eased the key into the lock of the second door. *Easy—easy!* There was a click. *Please, God, don't make that door creak!* Little by little, I inched it open and entered the apartment. Then I quietly pressed the handle of the hallway door. *Why do we have so many doors?*

All lights were off. No sound. *Good!*

In the darkness, I sensed a small shadow flitting around the corner and down the corridor. Tapsi! "Shhh!" In a hushed tone I shushed her, grabbed her tail the moment it got ready to thump the floor, and took her into my arms. Trying not to drop the boots, I tiptoed on my nylons down the hall to my bedroom on the left. My pulse raced. Despite the chilly outside temperatures, my forehead was covered with pearls of sweat.

My desire to get into bed as fast as possible without waking my parents was so strong that I slipped under the eiderdown covers even before I took off the peacoat or the fur hat. It was not until I felt the mattress under my spine, the comforter covering the tip of my nose, and Tapsi by my side, that I breathed a sigh of relief.

All was quiet. *What luck! Mutti must not have put two and two together after all.*

A few minutes passed. I was beginning to relax when, suddenly, the door to my room popped open. The ceiling light came on, and in its glare, I saw my mother fill the door frame. "*Pech, daß Deine Mutter ranter kam, nicht?*—Too bad that your mother had to come down, wasn't it?" she hissed. Then she turned off the light, closed the door, and returned to my parents' bedroom.

Paralyzed with fear, I did not sleep a wink. I watched the alarm clock's luminous hands jerk ahead at a snail's pace. *What is going to happen tomorrow?*

Quandary

THE FOLLOWING DAY, I RECEIVED the silent treatment, one of my mother's favorite whips. It always unnerved me, especially when the silence lasted a week or more. This time, however, I was glad we did not speak. Until communication resumed, the subject of Tapsi sniffing out her master "in flagrante delicto" would have to remain a moot point.

During that first week of December 1965, I worked on my application to immigrate to the United States. Despite the growing sense of urgency on account of my troubles at home, I was torn. I had always counted on spending time in America *before* turning twenty-one. Aside from the adventure, another reason for the journey had been to free myself from my parents' choke hold. Now, I suspected that they might stay true to their word and keep me home until I reached legal age which would, of course, nullify my need for a getaway. Besides, what would happen to my relationship with Günter, I asked myself again. Would it survive a separation? Each day, I liked him more, but my mother's unreasonableness in all matters concerning him, my resulting need for secrecy, my fear of being discovered, and the stress of keeping my lies straight had left their marks. I had become anxious and nervous and desperately wanted to return to my old cheerful self again.

While pondering these problems, I filled out my application. The forms contained lengthy biographical questions and asked my employment history. I testified that I had never been confined to a prison or a mental institution and that I was neither destitute nor a prostitute. I swore that I did not, and never had, suffered from epilepsy, alcoholism, or tuberculosis. But many questions required me to turn to a dictionary. In doing so, I discovered that I was considered an alien. Until now, I had believed aliens to be creatures from outer space.

The response from the consulate arrived soon thereafter: "We regret to inform you that your application has been denied. As of December 1, 1965, the US immigration quota for persons unrelated to US citizens is restricted to academics and skilled tradesmen." I was devastated. I had missed the chance to immigrate to the United States by a mere handful of days.

Disillusioned, I shared the news with Günter at our next secret get-together. "I can think of at least one positive aspect of that denial. Can't you?" He winked.

I smiled. He was happy with the latest turn of events. *He's right! I don't even want to go to America anymore.* If it hadn't been for my parents, I would've long given up on the idea.

A few days later, before saying good-bye one night, he looked deep into my eyes and asked, "Do you think you could be happy with me?"

My heart jumped. Because of the many roadblocks and the few opportunities for being alone together, I had not even given marriage a thought. But considering it now, I was positive that we would make a great team. We had so much in common: We both liked the outdoors, we both had artistic interests, we liked pretty things, and we had similar goals and ambitions. Not to mention that I had fallen deeply in love with him.

I nodded bashfully, unable to come up with words that expressed my sentiments.

"I hope I won't disappoint you," Günter said.

Disappoint me? How could he even think that? Being married to him and tackling the world side by side some day was at the pinnacle of my dreams. I wanted to support him in his pursuits and wanted him to support me in mine. I wanted us to be partners, friends, and soul mates. How could he ever disappoint me? I could not think of a single reason. But I said nothing. As so many times before, my emotions had only succeeded in choking me. I had no words to express my thoughts.

A few days later, another envelope from America arrived in the mail. I inspected it with curiosity. The sender was a man whose name I had never heard. The tiny white sticker in the upper left-hand corner read:

ROBERT P. MILLER

In the letter, Mr. and Mrs. Miller, two San Diego schoolteachers with small children, offered to hire me as their nanny and housekeeper. Pay and benefits would be identical to those offered by the Halls. Perplexed, I examined the two offers. Sonja had arranged the offer from the Halls. But who were the Millers? Despite my bewilderment, I was excited. At least something was happening.

The following day, the mailman brought a letter from Sonja. She wrote:

I heard it is easier to immigrate as a nanny than a secretary. That's why I talked with Happy and Harry Hall's son-in-law, Robert Miller. He and his wife said they would be willing to hire you as their nanny and housekeeper. They will contact you. Let me know what they said.

Sonja's letter clarified the reason for the two offers, but I still could not figure out how a nanny would better fit the "academics and trades-men" categories. Regardless, I threw myself into the preparation of another immigration application and mailed it to the US Consulate the following day.

When I shared this newest immigration opportunity with Günter, I sensed a change in attitude. As long as we had known each other, I had carried on about my plan of spending a year in the United States, and he had always put up with it. Now, I detected a trace of annoyance. Bit by bit, he seemed to disengage. He still came to the airport during some lunch hours, and we still saw each other as often as my confinement allowed, but his interest in me seemed to have dwindled. Unspoken tension arose between us.

I felt hurt but could not blame him. Because of my parents, I was rarely available and now planned to disappear for an extended period. *Günter must think I don't care about him. Not true. I'm just not myself anymore.* More and more I felt that my ability to live a normal life depended on my getting away for a while. If we were right for each other, I reasoned, we would still be good together after I had grown more comfortable in my new skin, the one I was determined to grow.

Aside from dealing with my parents, I now also had to come to terms with Günter's new mind-set. *What shall I do? Shall I go away for a year? Or shall I stay in Berlin?* If I stayed, could we be happy together despite my parents? I suspected that my mother would continue to try to control our lives if I didn't make a break for it. She tended to barrel through life insisting on having everything her way. For the past twenty years, more or less, I had taken my orders. Now I wanted to learn to stand up to her and hoped that going away for a few months would help me do that.

Caught in a quandary and unwilling to tell Günter about my anguish, I reacted by also withdrawing and pursuing other dating opportunities. I did not want to give him the impression that I was without alternatives should he back away. Dating other men was easy for me because my mother practically pushed me into the arms of any man who could drag me away from the one she hated most. Sometimes I accepted a date, just to get out of the house. Other times, I passed the evening by withdrawing to my closet-sized bedroom. On weekends, I often slept in excess of twelve hours each day and daydreamed the rest of the time. Curled up on the sofa bed with Tapsi, I stared at the small patch of sky while seconds, minutes, and hours went by. In my fantasy, I bowled with Günter—skated with Günter—danced with Günter—went to the movies with Günter. After ample visualization, a warm feeling would wash over me and transport me to more enjoyable places.

Christmas

THE DAY BEFORE GÜNTER planned to leave Berlin to celebrate Christmas with his parents in Bavaria, he picked me up from work. I was surprised and delighted. "And what may I attribute this unexpected pleasure to?" I joked.

"You'll see," he said with a mischievous twinkle in his eyes as he drove me home, cutting twenty minutes off my bus travel. He parked a couple of blocks short of my apartment building and pulled a bright red package from the backseat.

"It's your Christmas present. It would have been nicer if the occasion could have been a little more festive, but . . ."

"Oh no, I don't have your present with me." I covered my mouth. I felt foolish sitting there empty-handed.

"Don't worry. There'll be plenty of time later. I wanted you to have this in time for Christmas."

As I carefully unwrapped the box, a beautiful photo album emerged. It was covered in bright red jute.

"For your Bulgaria pictures."

"Oh, Günter, it's beautiful. Thank you so very much. And it's red. My favorite color. Your Christmas present will be waiting for you when you get back. I'm so sorry." During the time we had left before I had to go home, Günter told me how he and his father fastened a bright star to the roof of their home every year during the Christmas season. This year, the two men had planned to surprise his mother with an emerald ring to go with her favorite outfit. To achieve the perfect match, they had secretly absconded with her suit jacket and taken it to the jeweler. The thoughtfulness of father and son touched me deeply. The Bayers sounded like a dream family. How I wished my parents would exhibit similar holiday spirit. For a few moments, my thoughts transported me to the Christmas traditions in my home where the holidays were more of an inconvenience than a reason to celebrate.

According to German custom, Christmas Eve was celebrated with the immediate family, the first day of Christmas with relatives, and the following day with friends. My family skipped family and friends. We celebrated alone. We ate the holiday meal at noon on the twenty-fifth of

December and the leftovers the following day. Like Ebenezer Scrooge, my father bemoaned lost work opportunities while my mother lamented the preparation of goose or turkey.

My favorite time was the late afternoon on Christmas Eve when the three of us sat down for coffee and *Stollen*. By then, the tree would be lit, and the aroma of strong coffee would drift through the house along with the scent of candle wax. To the clanking of dainty porcelain cups on saucers we would smile and wish each other *Frohe Weihnachten*— Merry Christmas. Following coffee, I would listen to "Onkel Tobias" on the radio while my mother would place a few useful, unwrapped gifts beneath the small tree that I had decorated earlier in the day. Typically, there were new shoes, underwear, some garments from my wish list, and possibly a book. Rarely were there any surprises. By the time Yuletide songs piped from the radio, my parents had exhausted their holiday cheer. Because he hated carols almost as much as the Beatles, my father would roll his eyes and both parents would reach for newspapers or magazines. It was my signal to return to my room, and Christmas was over.

When Günter hugged and kissed me good-bye, my mind returned to the present. I carefully placed the photo album in my blue-checkered commodious purse. At home I hid it among bulky wool sweaters until sometime after my parents had gone to bed. Then I pulled it out again and lovingly stroked its cover. *This is no life. I can't even celebrate Christmas with Günter. I have to get away from here. Or I'm going to go crazy.*

Jealousies

BY EARLY 1966, THE LACK OF QUALITY time together, coupled with the mandatory secrecy, sparked sporadic crises. There had been little opportunity for Günter and me to get to know each other in-depth. We were rarely alone and struggled to maintain our identities while trying to adjust to the other's expectations. This caused tension and disappointment, although we had always made up.

The chief source of friction was my desire to spend time in the United States. The first serious discord I recall occurred on a Sunday morning in late January. All of Berlin was blanketed in soft, new snow. The usual urban hum was muffled by the white coverlet, and the winter sun had transformed plain snow crystals into shimmering rhinestones. The city looked magical.

Prohibited from phoning me at home, Günter contacted my girlfriend, Christine, and suggested that the four of us—his roommate, Dieter, Christine, he, and I—drive to the Grunewald. Literally called Greenwood, this part of the city is West Berlin's largest forested area, rich with conifers, deciduous nut-bearing trees, lakes, and ponds. Christine called me to discuss the odds of my getting away. As usual, my mother put up roadblocks.

"You two won't need to drive to the Grunewald. The Lietzensee is covered with snow, too. And it's only across the street. You can stay right here and enjoy the snow."

I was forced to admit that we intended to join Günter and Dieter. To my surprise, my mother neither allowed nor disallowed the outing. Uncharacteristically, she left the matter on the table. I did not know what to make of it and told Christine. She passed on the word, and the three of them drove to my house to, hopefully, pick me up.

While the guys remained in the car, Christine ascended the five flights to our apartment. As always, she looked like she had just stepped out of a fashion magazine. Dressed in matching off-white ski pants, jacket, gloves, and boots, she looked as pristine as the snow. But the coup de grace was her dazzling headdress. An off-white woolen scarf, trimmed with a white boa, framed her huge brown eyes peering from flawless olive skin. Wispy marabou feathers encircling her perfect features, she looked absolutely stunning.

Next to Christine, I was a picture of her country cousin. My ensemble clashed in every respect. Dark-grey ski pants, white boots, black furry hat, and several layers of mix-and-match sweaters did not come close to my girlfriend's splendor. My self-esteem plummeted the minute I saw her standing in the doorway.

After Christine had finished pleading with my mother for my temporary release from prison, Mutti launched into a lecture.

"Christine, I'm surprised you allow Jutta to use you like this. Can't you see she's hell-bent on seeing this guy and manipulates you into getting what she wants? You're a nice girl, Christine. This *Scheich* is no good and has all but destroyed our family. Don't let her take advantage of you."

It was degrading. Christine knew my story. She was my friend. Still. If I wanted to join Günter and the others, I had to stand there like a little kid, let the insults roll over me, and pray that my girlfriend possessed the necessary negotiating skills. To my amazement, after much discussion, my mother relented and allowed me to join the group. But by the time Christine and I finally emerged from the building, I was worn to a frazzle. In drab attire and with red eyes, I felt miserable.

"Christine, you go ahead and sit up front. I'll sit in back with Dieter," was all I was able to verbalize without bursting into tears. Then I slid into the backseat next to Dieter without saying so much as "hullo" to Günter. During the short ride, I stared wordlessly through the side window, unable to derive any pleasure from the spectacular scenery. All I could do was to try to squelch my tears. Meanwhile, Christine's appearance had not gone unnoticed. The silence in the car was broken only by the lively conversation coming from the front seats.

Upon arrival in winter wonderland, everything was coated with a glistening lace of ice crystals. The woods took on an ethereal look, like something from a fable. I heaved myself out of the car, devoid of any desire to frolic in the untouched splendor. Günter, on the other hand, had a fabulous time. He alternately pulled and pushed Christine on a sled while completely ignoring me. At considerable distance behind them, Dieter and I traipsed through the ankle-deep snow. It was humiliating. When Christine fell off and slightly bruised her knee, Günter was on the spot to kiss it and make it well.

I wanted to go home. But I could not let my parents witness my heartbreak. So I stayed and subjected myself to further agony. After half an hour or more, Günter proposed that we abandon the Grunewald on account of Christine's bad knee and go to his and Dieter's abode for hot coffee. There, he continued the banter while completely ignoring me.

When Christine poked fun at his sizable stockpile of chocolate bars, stacked high on a shelf in his closet, he immediately pulled one from the top, handed it to her, and said, "Here. My folks give me a couple of bars every time I visit. Enjoy." He might as well have strangled me with his bare hands. As long as I had known him, Günter had never offered me even one square from his supply, even though chocolate happened to be my all-time favorite treat. Of course, one of the problems was that I had never mentioned my fondness. Instead of coming straight out with it, I had always gazed longingly at his stash in the way I had been taught to ask for things. Now, watching Christine slip the bar into her purse nearly killed me.

A couple of days later, my wounds still raw, Günter and I had a long talk. He regretted his actions and explained that my constant talk about leaving for America, coupled with my refusal to sit next to him in the car, had provoked him to lash out. "You aggravated me. You brought out the worst in me."

We made up, but the sour taste remained, and I was not going to be outdone. Despite my limited opportunities to meet other men, I pursued dates outside our relationship. Some of them turned out to be so mismatched that I prayed for the evening to end. Others proved semi-enjoyable. None were as much fun as being with Günter.

Another surprise came when I stopped by briefly at his home one day. The bathroom door was ajar, and I noticed several pair of black lace panties prominently displayed over the shower rod.

"What's that?" I asked.

"That? Oh, nothing." With a silly grin, Günter flicked his wrist in the direction of the panty parade. "One of the girls here in the building is expecting company, and she didn't know what to do with her stuff."

I was taken aback but pretended indifference. He had never mentioned having female friends in the building. Wouldn't they have to be awfully close before they would feel comfortable enough to want to dry their intimate apparel in his place? Without going into it, I left a few minutes later, calling off our date. I had to think. Did I overreact or was I afraid to press for an explanation because I didn't want to lose Günter? Did I react differently than other girls would because my parents were so strange? *How do girls with "normal" parents handle situations like this?*

On our Tuesday night skate-ins, Christine continued to show off her eye-catching wardrobe. Although Günter no longer ignored me, he obviously took pleasure in being seen with her on the ice. The two of them would lurch about the rink supporting one another while I breezed by, having had many skating lessons in years past. But it pained me to watch him court my girlfriend. Sometimes, I felt so close to Günter that I thought we were one person. Other times, I did not seem to know him at all. To fight back, I, too, flirted with strangers.

"Everything moves in a circle," he said one day. "Don't you think this is a little strange?"

"You've noticed, too?" I retorted.

Nothing else was said. The intermittent tension between us remained.

I began to wonder if he was truly the one for me. And I could always count on my mother's help with such decision. She used every trick at her disposal to rid me of Günter. After flirting for some time with a pair of gorgeous azalea-colored slippers in the showcase of *Leiser*, Berlin's best-known shoe salon, I finally conceded because they were out of my price range. But my mother instilled new hope one Saturday morning when she said, "I tell you what. I bet you'd like to go out with that no-account of yours tonight, right?"

My ears perked up. *What does she have up her sleeve now?*

"I'll make you a deal. You can either go out with him or I pay for the shoes. Which is it going to be?"

My heartbeat accelerated. That was a tough decision. I coveted the azalea beauties. But how could I pass up an opportunity to officially go out with Günter?

"I'll go out with Günter," I said.

"I just wanted to see how far you'd go," my mother said with a perverse sort of pleasure. "You're not going anywhere, young lady, and forget those shoes, too. They could have been yours, you know."

With that pronouncement, my mother's attempts at driving Günter and me apart brought us, in fact, closer again.

The Ring

SINCE MY TWENTIETH BIRTHDAY in November 1965, I had worn Günter's silver ring only away from home. For two full months, this revered piece of jewelry had adorned my finger the minute I had left the house and had gone back into my pocket upon return. One evening, I realized too late that it was still on my finger during dinner. Becoming aware of my recklessness, I delicately inched my left hand into my lap. My parents did not react. *I hope Mutti hasn't noticed.* But when I returned from Spanish class a few nights later, she thundered, "Didn't I tell you to stop hanging out with that *Penner*—that loser? Or do you think I haven't noticed your ring? I'm not stupid."

Oh God. Instinctively, I ducked and prepared to take whatever verbal diatribe I had coming. To my amazement, my mother did not launch into her usual lecture but instead, with a sudden swoop, whipped her left hand right under my nose. Startled, I stared at her large ruby faceted into a fourteen-karat gold setting. She had worn this striking ring for as long as I could remember. "*Bald so schön wie Deiner, nicht?*—almost as pretty as yours, isn't it?" she sneered.

I recoiled. *This is surreal. Mutti is comparing rings.* I had always assumed my mother's primary motive during our altercations had been to protect me from getting hurt. Now I questioned her mental stability. *She doesn't know when to stop!*

Confused, I searched for past patterns of instability. I remembered a well-meaning neighbor once saying, "Jutta, your mother is sick to her soul." Believe me, I'm sick to my soul, too, I had thought at the time. But now I wondered, did she mean mentally ill? I rejected the idea at once. During my childhood, Mutti had watched over me like a mother duck. She had walked me to school, checked my homework, dressed me in the cutest little outfits, and was delighted when strangers praised me. I had been given roller-skating and ice-skating lessons, music and dance lessons, and attended summer camps. We had taken family trips to the North Sea and Italy. My life had been good as long as I had fallen in line. My mother had been overprotective, but there had been no indication of a mean streak, not until Günter had entered the picture.

I wanted to retort, "My ring is a present from Günter, and that alone makes it beautiful." But I did not speak.

Tonsillectomy

TOWARD THE END OF FEBRUARY, I checked into the hospital for a tonsillectomy to end recurring throat infections. As a matter of course, this type of surgery required one full week of hospital care plus three weeks of home recuperation. Under normal circumstances, I would have turned cartwheels for a month away from my boring job at the office, but the thought of being out of touch with Günter for such a long period was depressing.

The St. Elisabeth Stift was a rehabilitation unit, not a full-service hospital. Numerous physicians performed minor surgeries on site, while nurses managed patient aftercare. When I checked in the day prior to my procedure, I was assigned to a four-bed room. Two of my roommates were mending already while another young woman and I were scheduled for next-day surgeries.

On this first afternoon in the hospital, I explored my new surroundings. Patients awaiting procedures and those already recuperating milled about the dayroom across the hall which was furnished with two well-used, but comfortable couches, a scratched-up coffee table, and a shelf full of donated books. Those of us scheduled for operations the following morning paid close attention to the gossip circulating among convalescing patients. Doctors, nurses, procedures, food—all were discussed in great detail.

Before nightfall, each of us seven tonsillectomy patients, scheduled to go under the knife the following day, threw a couple of marks into a pot, intended to reward the hardy soul first to return to the dayroom after surgery. I had never been a hospital patient before and bet on a quick recovery.

When the nurse walked me into the operating room the next morning, Dr. Lorenz already throned on his small, round stool. He asked me to slide onto a similar implement in front of him, his standing slightly taller than mine. When the nurse handed him a syringe, the size of a turkey baster, I deflated like a balloon because I saw a giant needle protruding from the shaft. Upon the nurse's prodding, I opened my lips, but my teeth remained tightly clenched. No urging from the doctor or his nurse enticed me to do otherwise.

I don't remember how Dr. Lorenz managed to get the syringe into my mouth, but once he did, he injected an anesthetic directly into my right tonsil. As the needle stabbed at the raw tissue, I let out a blood-curdling scream. Tears streamed down my face. I gagged.

"Breathe," the nurse yelled. "Take a deep breath. Breathe!"

I tried to wiggle off the stool, but the nurse held my arms and shoulders in a lock. There was blood. I retched. The doctor reached for a huge cotton swab on a long stick and mopped my throat. I gagged again. I hyperventilated. More shrieks. I gladly would have agreed to live with diseased tonsils for the rest of my life. But Dr. Lorenz ignored my screams. Just when the pain became tolerable, he repeated the procedure on the clump of issue on the left side of my throat. I must have gone into a better place because I do not remember my tonsils actually being removed.

When the doctor was satisfied with his work, the nurse led me back to my room where I slept, exhausted, for the next twelve hours. No one prompted me to eat, drink, or go to the bathroom. When I finally woke up, I was barely able to swallow on account of my dry and swollen throat. Aside from an anticoagulant, I had received no medication.

I dimly recalled the pledge to return to the dayroom after surgery. *Did the others make it?* I reached for robe and slippers and shuffled across the hall, spittoon pressed to my chest. When I entered, still dazed and unsteady, everyone applauded. I was the last of our group to show up.

We were a pathetic-looking lot and talked as if hot dumplings had been permanently implanted. One young man, about my age, quickly distinguished himself as the leader. His name was Volker Bach. He had a great sense of humor, told one joke after another, and forced us to cringe and snort because all-out laughter was too painful. With glee, he raised a bottle of *Liebfraumilch* over his head, daring us to guzzle an entire glass of the pale libation. The mild white wine certainly was sure to bring tears to our eyes while acid washing the delicate tissues. Courtesy of Volker Bach, each self-styled masochist was given the opportunity to dine with him at a swanky restaurant following release from the hospital. I did not win the meal, but I was taken with Volker.

Günter had promised to see me at the hospital, but had to skirt visiting hours to avoid my parents. He came only twice during that week, and then only for short periods. I was disappointed but pretended not to have noticed. Considering that I did not look too attractive either, I was not surprised. To overcome my letdown, I flirted with Herr Bach who willingly reciprocated.

After I left the hospital, Herr Bach stayed in touch. He called often and visited me at home. Mutti was delighted. This young man worked in the assessor's office. That meant he had a job with a pension and a secure future. Volker Bach quickly became my mother's most promising prospect for breaking my bond with Günter.

While I was locked up at home, Günter was free. His unfettered ability to socialize pained me. Unwilling to admit to pangs of jealousy pummeling my heart, I struck back by dating Volker Bach more often than I would have cared to. As much as I had enjoyed his humor in the hospital, he now got on my nerves because he blatantly played up to my mother.

Günter said nothing to the arrangement, but pursued new adventures himself. After Spanish class a couple of weeks later, he simply said, "I wonder how this is going to end. Both of us are making new friends and are creating new bonds. In marriage, this is called growing apart." I was floored. Günter had noticed. He just hadn't said anything. I had wanted to make him jealous, but he had not taken the bait. In truth, I could not imagine losing Günter. But I did not want him to think I was dependent on him either.

One day, toward the end of my home recuperation period, when Günter and I were to meet while I was, as far as my parents were concerned, on an errand, he waited for me in his car, just a few meters down from our building. A few minutes before the agreed upon time, someone rang our doorbell but did not answer the speakerphone. With lightning speed, my mother grabbed her shopping bag and descended the five flights of stairs. She didn't even wait for the elevator. Of course, she discovered Günter parked at the curb and returned momentarily.

"You're staying home, young lady. I'm tired of your tricks."

When my father returned from work that evening, another round of shells exploded.

"Let's get a few things straight," he said. "You're not going to America. You're not dating anyone. You're not taking any more English, French, or ceramics courses. You're not going ice-skating, and you're no longer going to the movie forum. Until you turn twenty-one, you'll leave this house for one reason only—to go to work. One way or another, we'll knock this *Knilch*—twit—out of your head."

My mother chimed in, "This scumbag has destroyed our family. Who is he anyway? A little salesman who doesn't know what to do with himself in his own four walls?"

My parents were determined to separate me from Günter at all costs. I wouldn't be grounded. I would be imprisoned. With nine months to go until I turned twenty-one, it wasn't a game anymore.

My mother continued, "I don't hate anyone in the whole world as much as I hate this . . . this . . . *Klinkerputzer*—this doorknob polisher. As we told you before—we'll disinherit you. We'll sell this condo and move away. And we'll squander your inheritance—to the last pfennig."

While I pondered how I could manage seeing Günter in the future, my parents' words only dripped into my consciousness, one word at a time.

A lost inheritance? Big deal.

Moving away? Please, don't let me stop you.

"Look at you! You look pathetic," my mother started again. "Go ahead and become a prostitute. No doubt, that *Scheich* of yours would love that."

I heard her words, but they no longer penetrated. I had to make a conscious effort to commit them to memory so that I could mull them over later.

Prostitute? Did she say prostitute?

After the last shell was fired, I returned to my bedroom and closed the door. I felt completely drained. Sitting on the edge of the sofa bed, I stared into the room without seeing. All emotional ties to my parents lay trampled on the ground. I felt so alone. There was only one ally on my side of the camp. That was Günter. He had stuck by me throughout this ordeal.

I swear. The minute I turn twenty-one, I'm out of here. But what will my life look like between now and then?

The next day marked the beginning of my last week of recuperation at home, now under complete confinement. I desperately needed to cancel a previously arranged clandestine date with Günter, but had a difficult time getting to a phone booth. He was still unaware of the latest developments. My nerves frazzled. When I finally got the chance to make a brief call from home during the five minutes it took for my mother to take out the garbage, I reached only his roommate.

"Dieter, I have only a few seconds. Please tell Günter I won't be able to leave the house until I get back to work next week. My parents are watching me like hawks. Tell him I'm sorry."

In the meantime, Volker Bach had not given up. He fancied himself my knight on the proverbial white horse, who would provide damage control and end up with the girl. He knew how to work the angles. By arriving with armfuls of flowers, not for me, but for my mother, he quickly wormed himself into her good graces. While she lapped up his attention, he lost my respect.

I could hardly wait to walk to the post-operative appointment at the doctor's office during my last days of recuperation. On the way, I called Günter from a phone booth.

"What's the doctor's address? I'll meet you there," Günter said.

Was I glad to hear his voice! There would be so much to talk about. The thought that Günter would drop everything to meet me at the doctor's almost made me choke.

We sat in the waiting room, held hands, and whispered in hushed tones. I tripped all over myself, trying to catch him up on recent events. But I also remained edgy, fearing that my mother might walk through the door at any moment.

"You know what?" Günter said after a while, "It looks like it might be a while before the doctor will see you. I saw a pair of red shoes at *Bilka*. They had your name written all over them. Shall we try to get them now? I bet it'll make you feel better." Günter was so sweet. Who else would be on the lookout for a pair of shoes for me? The red slippers with navy-blue trim were perfect. He knew exactly what looked good and what I liked. *Günter is a diamond among rhinestones*, I thought again with affection.

As expected, the doctor cleared me for work, and Günter drove me home. For the first time in my life, I couldn't wait to get back to the office. Boring work was nothing compared to imprisonment. "We'll be able to talk on the phone again every day, and maybe we can meet at the airport for lunch, whenever you can get away?" I suggested, filled with hope.

After a long hug and kiss Günter said, "And all because of me. You're locked up, and I have my freedom. I don't even know what to do with it. I stayed home all weekend because I felt bad for you."

At this moment, I could not have felt closer to him. All other men were history.

The Jugendamt

PRIOR TO HOSPITALIZATION in February, I had accomplished two things: I had sent off my second immigration application, proffering my domestic aptitude rather than my secretarial proficiency, and I had terminated my employment with Lufthansa, effective May 1. After two years of uninspiring work, I was ready for change. High on my priority list were positions requiring English language skills. To locate a potential employer, I perused *Stellenangebote*—help-wanted ads—in the newspaper.

The day before I was scheduled to return to Lufthansa for my remaining few weeks with the company, Mutti broke her silence by asking, "And where do you see things going from here?"

I sensed her struggle for self-control. Assuming she was referring to my unyielding stance regarding Günter rather than the status of my employment, I replied, "How am I supposed to know? I'm locked up," making sure my tone of voice reflected adequate disgust.

"You're going to be locked up until you come to your senses and quit lying," my mother retorted, quickening her speech, her restraint quickly succumbing to her narrowly concealed infuriation.

I threw back my head. *I wouldn't have to lie if you were reasonable.* But I did not reply.

"If you had your way, you'd go out with that jerk every night, I suppose," my mother said. "Your father and I know you're lying. You tell us you're skating with Christine. In reality, that *Scheich* of yours is there, too." My mother shot a sideways glance, hoping for a reaction, but I remained stoic and continued to stare straight past her, without so much as a blink.

"We know he is, because we've followed you," my mother disclosed triumphantly.

So, they spied on me. No surprise. When Fee and I walked around the lake a few weeks ago, we saw you crouched behind a maple tree. As if that didn't look ridiculous!

My mother continued her sermon, "No one has had as much freedom as you. At nineteen, you traveled alone to Greece and Bulgaria," she said for the second time. People were shocked when they heard that."

"Who was shocked?" I probed.

No response.

"And don't think we don't know that Herr Bach is only a front man. He picks you up, and then you meet your no-account at the next corner."

Mutti doesn't have a clue. Fee is the front man. Volker still has his sights set on becoming more than a friend.

"Your father and I just want to keep you from making a big mistake," my mother changed the course of conversation. Young girls, like you, don't have enough sense to see that yet." Her patronizing comment made the roots of my hair stand straight up.

"Reason comes with maturity. It can't be expected at your age."

I was livid. *Isn't that just grand? Mutti. The authority on intelligent decisions!* I puffed up my cheeks and forcefully exhaled through my lips, making a small whistling sound. My mother ignored my display of defiance and, instead, hinted at something that made my ears perk up.

"I've made a mistake once and regretted it all my life," she said in a confidential tone. "If someone had pointed it out to me, it could have been prevented."

What is she talking about? "I think everyone is responsible for their own actions," I snapped. "Others can make suggestions, but we all have to live with our own decisions and mistakes."

A veil of incomprehension crossed my mother's face. Apparently, we were on parallel tracks, paths that would never meet. What grave mistake did she make, I wondered. Was she referring to her marriage? Having had me? An abortion? An affair? As if my thoughts were printed across my forehead, my mother added, "I'm not talking about your father."

Despite this supposed clue, I could not fathom the gist of her message.

I was never happier to be on my job than the day I returned to Lufthansa following my four-week absence. At last, I was again among people who talked! There was laughter. And there was life!

Günter and I met at the airport for lunch that day. I mentioned the odd exchange with my mother the day before and the questions it had raised. But he was more concerned with the upcoming Easter holiday which was only three weeks away. He wanted me to accompany him on a car trip to his family home in Bavaria for the holidays. He wanted me to meet his parents.

"You know I'd love to. But honestly, Günter, I don't see how I can. These days, I'm not even allowed to go to the mailbox by myself. My parents are dead-set against you, and to get them to okay a trip like this is out of the question. I have to wait until I am twenty-one." The outlook for a summer holiday together was just as bleak. Günter became so discouraged about our future together that he mulled over a visit to the *Jugendamt*—Child Protective Services.

"Your parents can't lock you up like this. That can't be legal. There must be something we can do. I'm going to call the *Jugendamt* and see what I can find out."

"Sure, why not."

When we parted, our moods were as grey as the wintry day.

During the following week, I received another letter from Harry and Happy Hall. This time, it included a questionnaire and an official-looking slip of paper embossed with a large seal. "Please complete these forms as soon as possible and submit them to the consulate," the letter read.

I was baffled. *Has my immigration application been approved?* As instructed, I immediately worked on the questionnaire and posted the completed package.

The next time I met Günter at the airport, we discussed the results of his phone conversation with the *Jugendamt*. Based on the information he was able to provide to the authorities, they suggested I schedule a personal visit. Thus, I arranged an after-work meeting with a Fräulein Schmidt to take place a few weeks later.

My footsteps echoed as I walked down the long, bare hall on the second floor of the government building. The harshness of its institutional white was relieved only by the doors on either side of the corridor, leading into small offices. Plaques next to each entrance indicated room numbers. There—room 246. I knocked softly.

"Come in," a female voice answered.

Ill at ease, I opened the door. Over dark-rimmed glasses, a middle-aged woman peered at me with kind eyes. "Fräulein Schmidt" read the narrow brown nameplate. She beckoned me to take a seat on the chair next to her desk.

Clutching my black leather purse, I followed her instruction.

"You are Fräulein Umbach?"

"Yes."

She glanced at a small piece of paper in front of her. "Herr Bayer called on your behalf. What is your relationship to him?"

"He's my boyfriend."

"How old are you, Miss Umbach?"

"Twenty. I'll be twenty-one in November."

Fräulein Schmidt looked at me quizzically. "According to Herr Bayer, your parents are unreasonably strict and don't allow you to see him. Is that the issue?"

Slowly, I warmed to my inquisitor and related the circumstances that had led to the problems with my parents. Fräulein Schmidt listened attentively, interrupted occasionally with questions, and finally spoke. "You're still under twenty-one. Your parents are legally responsible for you. However, from what you're telling me, they may be overstepping their authority. At your age, you should be allowed some basic freedoms. And, of course, you should not abuse those privileges."

For the next twenty minutes, we talked about reasonableness, consideration, moderation, and restraint. I felt validated.

"Okay. I understand. I have the right to go out with Günter. But how can I make my parents understand that?"

"Would you like me to talk to them?" Fräulein Schmidt asked.

"No—oh no, I don't think so," I was quick to stall any attempts of intervention on her part. *I'll have hell to pay if Mutti and Pappi find out that I've spoken to Child Protective Services.* "No, please don't call them yet," I added. Then I told her about the status of my efforts relative to the year in the United States. We agreed that I should first await word from the US Consulate. If it was negative, I would contact Fräulein Schmidt again. She would then get in touch with my parents, and if necessary, intercede through the court system.

Job Search

FOR THE EASTER HOLIDAYS, Günter went to his family home without me. On the day before he left, he invited me to his apartment after work for something I had not done since I was a little girl: an Easter egg hunt. We were limited to half an hour because that was all the time I was able to shave off my commute. Günter had hidden a variety of cosmetic creams around his flat, and I unearthed each one with squeals of delight. He certainly knew how to make a holiday special.

"Come home with me," he said as he held me by the shoulders, searching my eyes. "If only it were that simple. You know I'd love to." Glum and unhappy, I averted his gaze and stared at the coffee table. During the upcoming weekend, now lengthened by Easter Monday, I would face the usual oppressive silence at home when I could have fun with Günter and his family instead.

"I just won't let you go," Günter said as he put his arms around me.

I leaned my head against his shoulder and prayed, as I had so many times before, that the seven months until my twenty-first birthday would pass quickly.

Upon returning to my parents' apartment that evening, I discovered new mail from the US Consulate. My sullen mood turned hopeful again. *Is this going to be my long-awaited approval to immigrate?*

But the short letter only said, "The documents have been forwarded to the local employment office in San Diego." My hands dropped into my lap. The gloom returned. *I bet I won't get approval until after I've turned twenty-one. If then. I might as well forget the whole thing.*

The dreaded Easter weekend still before us, Volker Bach called to invite me to a movie. My mother fielded his call. "Herr Bach, can you stop by a few minutes early? I'd like to talk to you about something."

I rolled my eyes. *Does Mutti want to tell me something by talking to Volker?* She often used this technique. She talked about me to someone in my presence and acted as if I wasn't in the room.

Volker arrived ahead of time, as promised, and my mother went into great detail about my stubborn refusal to give up Günter. "Herr Bach, I have to ask you something. Have you ever aided my daughter in meeting this man?" she asked. "Because if that's the case, we won't let you take Jutta out anymore. We have forbidden her to see this man, and we're not going to be hoodwinked."

Volker denied any wrongdoings.

My eyes darted from one corner of the room to the other. I avoided looking at either one of them. *I'm not crazy about Volker. But I hate having him witness my humiliation.*

"Unfortunately, my husband and I have not been able to put a stop to our daughter's shenanigans," my mother continued. Then she described in detail how our family troubles were the result of the doings of a loser. She even declared that I wanted to become a pharmaceutical representative, like Günter, so that we could ride around the city together. She was so off base.

"*Aber den Zahn kann sie sich ziehen lassen*—she might as well have that tooth pulled," my mother continued. "That guy is nothing more than a *Bundeswehrdrücker*—a draft dodger—Herr Bach. I'm afraid Jutta will have to stay home until she's twenty-one, unless we can talk some sense into her. Or maybe you can," she added after a moment's reflection.

There it is again. My parents won't let me go to America until I am twenty-one. I'll be stuck in the house for another seven months. And now I might even get lectured by Volker!

Following my mother's speech, Volker and I were allowed to go to a late movie. He was surprised but also flattered by her dragooning attempts and saw himself moving closer to his goal of supplanting Günter. His high opinion of himself annoyed me to no end. I did not enjoy the film or the drink afterwards, but I appreciated the opportunity to get out of the house. I pushed for a confrontation at home by staying out until 2:00 a.m., but my parents did not react. I knew they would have called the police had I returned after midnight after being in Günter's company.

Following his brief Easter holiday, Günter and I met at the airport again. I told him about my conversation with Fräulein Schmidt of Child Protective Services, my mother's strong-arm tactics with Volker, and the status of my USA visit. "Most likely, I won't be able to leave until I turn twenty-one," I reported with disgust.

"Your parents certainly worked that out nicely, haven't they?" He spat out the words.

After a long pause, I said, "Will you come and visit me in America?"

"You won't go." Günter replied.

"I won't? Sure, I will." My resolve always strengthened when someone suggested I could not do something.

"Just wait," he said.

By now it was the middle of April 1966. Two more weeks, and I would be out of a job. Half-heartedly, I responded to want ads for various clerk/typist positions. Nothing interested me. Finally, I applied to a marzipan factory but did not follow up until after the job was already awarded.

Full of despair, I spoke to Günter about my slow-moving efforts to get away to America. "I need to get out of here, Günter, or I'm going crazy." This time, he understood. He even understood that I contemplated going to the movies with Volker again, just to get away from my parents.

To cheer each other up, Günter and I took another Friday off from work without my parents' knowledge. We spent the day visiting Schildhorn, a spit of land along the eastern bank of the Havel River. It was a beautiful, sunny spring day. We walked and talked and walked and talked. Following an unhurried lunch at one of the many restaurants, we sat near the thick reed belt that surrounded the river shore and listened to the twitters of warblers and the distant quacks of ducks. It felt wonderful to be together for an extended period of time without having to watch the clock.

The end of April brought my last day at Lufthansa. I was still without prospects for a new position. *Why in the world did I quit?* I asked myself. Aside from mindless tasks, Lufthansa had allowed me to work a full hour's drive away from home, making spy visits from my mother unlikely. I had been able to see Günter during many lunches and to talk to him daily on the phone. *When will we be able to see and talk to each other again like that?*

"There are plenty of offices in the buildings around the corner, in the Kantstraße," my mother said. "If you work there, you can come home for lunch every day."

Yeah, right, I thought.

On our last lunch hour together before I was jobless and stuck at home again, I gave Günter a small bouquet of forget-me-not flowers.

"Do you really think they're necessary?" he asked, stroking my cheek.

We said good-bye and held each other as if we were never going to see one another again. I could not hold back my tears. "If I hadn't been so stupid and quit, this would not have happened. What was I thinking?"

"Be strong," Günter said and stroked my cheek again. Then he gazed at me tenderly. "This, too, shall pass."

The following morning, I woke up jobless but with an interview scheduled at Demuth & Co., a small accounting firm, located in a beautiful old villa in West Berlin's fashionable district of Dahlem. At least it was a long distance from home. The villa and its location were superb, but the job made me cringe. Greeting me at the door were my prospective supervisors, three old ladies in their fifties, with giant round posteriors molded by years of chair sitting. Lufthansa looked terrific by comparison. Disheartened, I declined the offer.

Next morning, I rode the bus to the British military barracks near the Olympic Stadium and scrutinized job announcements posted on the wall of the employment office. Although I would be able to apply my knowledge of the English language, the pay was two hundred marks less than I had earned at Lufthansa, and there was no opportunity for advancement, I was told. Subdued, I rode home. Sitting in the bus I wondered: Should I look for a job near Günter's home or office so that we could see each other more often? Or should I hold out for a job with good pay and promotional opportunities? If America were to come through, neither would matter. *Today is Wednesday. I need to have a job by Monday, or I'm going to go nuts.* Depressed, I decided to continue my search in the afternoon.

"You're not planning to introduce yourself anywhere in the afternoon, are you?" my mother inquired.

"Hmm, yeah. I want to check out other airlines."

"One doesn't apply for a job in the afternoon. One applies in the morning. You're staying home this afternoon. You can look again tomorrow morning." I didn't have it in me to fight anymore. Battle fatigue had set in. Reluctantly, I retired to my room.

The next day, I visited Pan American Airlines. Although they had no openings, I took a typing test and placed my name on the waiting list for future openings.

Friday arrived. The outlook was bleak with another depressing weekend ahead. I rode the bus to the US Air Force at Tempelhof Airport and took tests in English and typing. The examinations were scored immediately, and I passed with an "A" in English and a "B" in typing. To my amazement, I was offered a job in the procurement office with a starting pay of 540 marks to be increased to 738 marks following probation, more than I had earned at Lufthansa. And the best part, I was to start three days later, on Monday. Yessss! Only one more weekend, and I would be out of the house again. My whole body relaxed.

That afternoon, I informed my mother of my new job, and the same evening, she asked out of the blue again, "And how do you envision the future? Are you going to go to HIM when you turn twenty-one?"

Caught by surprise, I answered, "Maybe," and made sure my face remained expressionless. I had not thought at all about what I would do if America did not materialize.

"I hope you won't regret your decision," my mother said. "Your twenty-first birthday will be a turning point anyway."

I certainly hope so!

The New Job

ON SATURDAY MORNING PRIOR to the start of my new position with the United States Air Force, I had to shop for a few items. I was about to leave the house, when my mother said, "In case you plan to meet HIM somewhere along the way, tell him I want to talk to him. I want to hear how he envisions the future because it can't go on like this. A solution must be found."

My eyes must have been as big as saucers. To begin with, this was the first time that my mother hadn't called Günter an expletive. Even though she could not bring herself to allow his name to cross her lips, it was a start. For the first time, a crack in the impenetrable parental wall seemed achievable. I looked at my mother in amazement but did not comment. Not wanting to parade my sudden burst of optimism, I proceeded with the shopping task at hand and slowly wandered out into the fragrance-laden spring air. Several times during the morning, I tried to call Günter from a pay phone. No answer. Leaving messages with the concierge was pointless, because the situation was far too complicated to explain. We needed to talk in person. By the following morning, my optimism had turned into doubt. What if he won't agree to meet with my parents? What if he'd rather marry a girl from a normal home? My heart dropped to my ankles at the thought. *If I lose him, I've lost the one thing that matters.*

On Monday, May 2, 1966, I started as a clerk-typist with the US Air Force at Tempelhof Airport. The base was located in the same crescent-shaped set of buildings as Lufthansa's offices, but at the opposite end. The procurement office consisted of a series of ten or twelve interconnecting rooms off a nondescript hallway. The chief, Mr. Mack, a German-American, occupied the space at the very head of the chain. He had held a government position in the United States and had been transferred to occupied Germany because of his knowledge of the language. Judging by his shuffling gait, he was near retirement.

I was to share the office immediately adjoining his with Birgit Fischer, a young woman my age. We typed purchase orders, in quintuplicate. Mistakes were corrected with a special eraser, one copy at a time. If not careful, erasures caused holes in the parchment, and the entire document had to be retyped. Whenever Mr. Mack did not hear the clanging of typewriters, he rose from his chair and shuffled out of his office on soft-soled shoes. He wanted to make sure we did not goof off. Therefore, Birgit and I typed nonstop from morning to night, stopping only for our thirty-minute lunch and two fifteen-minute coffee breaks.

My new work schedule was far more rigorous than the one I had been accustomed to at Lufthansa. There were no phones in our office either so that personal calls during work hours were out of the question. Since the lunch break was limited to half an hour and the gated compound necessitated check-in and check-out procedures, noontime get-togethers with Günter were impossible. I barely managed to leave word for him with the details of my new employment by running to a public phone during lunch on my first day.

But at the end of that first workday, Günter waited for me outside the base. When I saw his sleek, new red Kadett parked alongside the curb, my steps quickened. I was surprised and elated. Although I felt exhausted from nonstop typing, we both delighted in the fact that my new workdays ended half an hour earlier. I had not mentioned this change to my parents, of course, creating an extra thirty minutes of unencumbered time each day.

To celebrate my additional half hour of unsupervised existence, we drove to the Tiergarten, West Berlin's largest urban park and the city's equivalent to New York's Central Park. The name means "animal garden" because it had once served as a royal hunting preserve. The river Spree runs along its northern boundary; the city's famous zoo adjoins at the southwest corner. In between, the square mile consists of well-maintained lawns, ponds, riding paths, trees, shrubs, statuaries, and immaculate flower beds. Benches are tucked here and there for quiet contemplation. We chose an idyllic location, made ourselves comfortable on one of the many green wooden benches, and caught up on the news. We had not spoken since my mother's latest directive, insisting on a talk with Günter.

When he did not immediately comment on my mother's demand, I suspected again that my worst fears had materialized. Günter was not going to sing from my mother's song sheet. Avoiding the potential bad news a little longer, I changed the subject and related the earlier exchange with my mother, in which she had asked if I might go to him after I turned twenty-one.

"What did you tell her?" Günter asked.

"I said I might."

"Not a bad answer," he replied.

I grinned sheepishly and blushed when I met his glance. "I have no idea what I'm going to do if America doesn't work out," I said out loud.

"*Du hast doch mich*—but you have me," Günter said, wrapping his arm around my shoulder as he drew me closer. Then he assured me that he had no qualms entering the lions' den for a talk about our future together.

A couple of days went by. Günter called my house to schedule the requested meeting. I answered the phone and tried to hand the receiver first to my mother, then to my father. But both waved me off as if swatting away a troublesome gnat.

"Tell him your father is not feeling well," my mother said. "The meeting will have to be postponed."

Distraught, I relayed the message to Günter. Since there was no opportunity to talk freely, our conversation ended shortly thereafter.

The following evening, Günter and I were only able to sneak in fifteen minutes together after work. "Is it always going to be like this?" he asked. "*Alle Jubeljahre mal ein viertel Stündchen*—once in a blue moon a quarter of an hour?" He sounded disappointed and annoyed, and I was unable to offer hope for improved prospects. Our dreams had been crushed once more. *Six more months before I turn twenty-one.* It seemed like an eternity.

During the first week in May, Günter turned twenty-two. His birthday was on a Monday, a weeknight, and he suggested celebrating the Sunday before. Aside from work, I was still incarcerated at home. In order to get away for more than a few stolen minutes, I had to beg for permission. Over time, my fears regarding the outcome had become so intense that I had turned more and more reluctant to even bring up the subject. The endless confrontations had turned my once plucky self into a quivering bundle that was content with a fragile status quo. But I owed it to Günter to try. When I finally summoned enough courage to approach my mother with the question, ready for arguments and refusal, she gave me the green light without resistance. For the first time since the parental edicts that kept me home until age twenty-one did she allow me to visit Günter. I was flabbergasted. I did not know what to say or think. Blindsided by hope, I felt as light as a feather. Günter and I spent a lovely evening together. It felt so good.

When he picked me up from work a couple of days later, he brought up the subject of my America plans again. "Are you really serious about going?" he asked. "Because if you go, chances are, you'll find someone else."

"No way, Günter. I don't want anyone else. I just have to get away for a little while to become myself again. I'll be back in a year's time, I promise." I loved Günter more than anything in the world, and I knew that nothing would keep me in the USA.

He nodded faintly. He did not like it, but he understood. And I loved him for that.

The Big Talk

A MONTH LATER, IN EARLY JUNE, the US Consulate informed me that my immigration to the United States had been approved, subject to some final paperwork. I had been given permission to immigrate as domestic help, based on my employment contract with Harry and Happy Hall in San Diego. My longtime wish, the year in America I had fought for so hard, had come true. But was I happy? I didn't feel anything one way or the other. I felt beaten to a pulp. It had all come to pass so much later than I had hoped. Since I would not turn twenty-one until the end of November, the earliest departure date could be set for some time in December. Or should I wait till spring or summer?

My parents took the news with calm. "I see," my father said. My mother did not comment at all. When I told Günter, he only murmured, "So, I guess you're going after all." I nodded uneasily. I was uncertain whether the main cause of my discomfort was my attachment to Günter or my fear of the unknown. If I could have, I would have cancelled my escapade. Wouldn't it be nice to stay in Berlin and really get to know the city together with the man I love? And without suspecting my mother behind the next tree? But I had worked too hard and enlisted the help of too many people to back out now. Besides, the Cold War with my parents had used up my reserves. I was tired to the bone. Unsure of the myriad of my own feelings and aware that neither Günter nor my parents were happy with my plans,

I avoided the subject of immigration altogether. The only person truly excited about my America plans was my girlfriend Sonja.

By coincidence she arrived a few days later for a six-week holiday. I had so many questions. Are Happy and Harry Hall nice people? Where do they live? What will my job be like? Do I need to bring winter clothes? Will we see each other often?

Despite my continuing prison sentence, I became more optimistic and energetic again, and my attitude improved.

In the middle of July, close to three months after their initial request, my parents finally created time to meet with Günter for the "Big Talk." I was keyed up for days in advance. My optimism surged. *Finally, everything is going to be okay.*

My parents agreed to meet him at our home on Wednesday, July 13, at eight o'clock in the evening. The weekend before, I had vacuumed, dusted, cleaned, and spiffed up the entire apartment. Everything was in its place. Everything looked perfect.

Returning from work on the long-awaited day, I briefly dropped by Günter's apartment for one last-minute strategy planning session, but he was out. I hurried home to make final preparations. I checked the bathroom and wiped the sink. I squared the tablecloth. I even mixed drinks and placed them in the refrigerator, hoping they would break the ice.

Shortly before the appointed time, my mother took down the garbage. *What timing!* Five minutes later, she wasn't back yet. *I can't believe it. She must be talking to a neighbor. At a time like this!* Ten minutes passed, then fifteen. Still no sign of my mother. I peeked into the living room. My father lounged unperturbed in his favorite chair with the newspaper. *Something is amiss. Günter wouldn't be late.* Slowly, I walked down the hall. My glance fell onto the intercom on the wall. The white plastic receiver hung in its cradle. On a hunch, I picked it up and listened. It was a strain, but I could make out a muffled voice. *My mother's? Is Mutti still talking to a neighbor?* I continued to eavesdrop. Then I heard another faint voice. Unmistakably male. *Günter's? Is Mutti talking to Günter downstairs? And I'm sitting here with the drinks?*

I slammed the receiver in its cradle. Tapsi's ears perked up. Her tail wagged as she looked at me. "No, Taps, no walkies. Not now." *What the heck!* I picked up the dog, grabbed my keys, and rushed out the front door to the elevator. As usual, the lift was in use, and I flew down the five flights of stairs instead. *Tell me this is a bad dream!*

When I stepped out of the building, a blast of flower-scented air caressed my nostrils. With the dog under my left arm and the entrance door held open with my right, I halted on the terrazzo landing looking out. There, at the foot of the eight stairs leading into the courtyard, only a few feet ahead of me, who did I see leaning against the banister? My mother! No trash can in her hand. Several steps down the path I saw Günter, looking very respectable in a conservative tan suit, his black-and-tan striped tie adding a touch of sophistication.

Dumbfounded, I stared at the scene. I looked at my mother as if she had grown wings. *Mutti tricked me. She knew how hard I had worked to prepare for this one-on-one and how much I'd wanted the talk to go well. Instead, she snatched Günter alone.* I stood there, mouth agape, unable to speak. I was just about to ask, "What is this all about?" when my mother slowly turned to me. An obstinate look hardened her glance when she said in a clipped and condescending tone, "*Du kannst gleich wieder nach oben gehen*—You can go right back up. Herr Bayer and I are going to take a little walk."

I shot a questioning glance toward Günter. His face was unreadable. I remained rooted to the terrazzo.

My mother turned to him and motioned him to follow her down the path to the sidewalk. In disbelief I watched as they strode in a measured pace toward the street-side gate, Günter a few paces behind my mother. Mutti unlatched it, opened it, and they turned left onto the sidewalk.

I was speechless. Anger rose up and left me trembling. Blood rushed to my face, but my feet remained immovable. *She can't freeze me out like this! Shall I follow? Shall I make a scene in public?* Part of me wanted to run down the street and force the two of them to turn back. The other part just stood there defeated. Another illusion had collapsed. All hopes were smashed once again. Tears streamed down my face. Realizing that I had forgotten Tapsi's leash in my hurry, I slowly turned around, walked back to the elevator, rode up the five flights, and returned to our apartment to pick it up. Then I made the trip down again. Beaten, I dragged through the courtyard. The light, flower-ruffling breeze picked up the scent of the rosebushes along the path. A few birds bolted up. But I was oblivious to my surroundings. As if in a dense fog, I walked toward the sidewalk.

Günter and my mother were nowhere to be seen. Words had yet to be invented that could describe my letdown. Tapsi and I staggered to the little pocket park a couple of blocks away and collapsed onto a wooden bench. Absentmindedly, I caressed her soft fur and talked to her through my tears.

"Can you believe it, Taps? Mutti hijacked Günter! She knew how much we wanted to straighten out this mess. Still. Where did they go, Taps? Where is Günter? Let's hope he'll find us. I have to know what happened." We sat and waited until the twilight gave way to darkness, but neither Günter nor my mother reappeared.

When Tapsi and I returned home, I went straight to my room. I could hear my parents' hushed voices in the living room, but I no longer cared. Reclined on my sofa bed, I stared out the window into the darkness. The world on the other side of the glass was different from mine. It looked inviting, but it was closed to me.

The next morning, during my 9:00 a.m. coffee break, I ran to a phone booth to call Günter. Unavailable. I ran back. There was barely enough time to accomplish both trips during one fifteen minute break. I tried again during lunch break. Unavailable. I was quickly turning into a bundle of raw nerves.

Günter picked me up after work. He confirmed that the meeting had amounted to nothing more than the usual one-way sermon. "We talked for less than ten minutes," he recounted. "Your mother did almost all of the talking and wouldn't give me a chance to say much of anything. She pointed out once again that you're underage and that your parents are responsible for you. Until you turn twenty-one, she said, you won't be allowed to see me. After that, it'll be up to you, although your parents are against our friendship. And of course, she warned me not to get my hopes up. You won't get an inheritance if you stay with me. As if I cared."

Even though this last piece of information was no longer news to either of us, I turned crimson. I felt so ashamed. Günter's in-laws! How he must look forward to calling them that.

"Where did you go? I didn't see you anywhere," I asked.

"We just walked up the next street. Whenever I tried to speak, she'd cut me off right away. And when she was done talking, she abruptly said good-bye, turned around, and walked back. I went to my car and drove home. There was nothing more I could do. I wished I had known you were still out there somewhere. It was all so frustrating."

Günter and I sat in silence for a while. It was clear that my parents did not want any improvement in relations.

Günter's Family

SHORTLY AFTER THE "BIG TALK," Günter went on summer holiday with his parents. Three short weeks of hiking and fun for Günter and twenty-one long days of desolation for me. I could barely stand the idea of being out of touch. To avoid fanning the home flames with mail from him, we agreed that he would write to me *postlagernd*—general delivery—at the airport. Every day, I rushed to the post office to inquire about mail. And once each week, for the next three weeks, I received a postcard. I drank in every word, every line, every sentence. I heard his voice and I felt his love. At night, I lay in the dark and stared at the ceiling. I did not need light to read his messages. I knew the words by heart.

Then in the fall, my parents went on their annual trip to the Mediterranean. I was assigned my usual chores; Tante Michen was to keep an eye on me. But, on one of those weekends, Günter and I finally got to make good on our plan to visit his family in Bavaria. His parents lived in a beautiful two-story home in a quiet little town. The white stucco house and the front yard that was concealed behind a low wall looked lovingly cared for. A small veranda was tucked under a protective overhang and led into the backyard. His mother had decorated the breakfast nook with hand-painted crests of surrounding communities. Father and son had turned the basement into a party room with a wine-bottle-label covered table and drip candles. I was put up in the downstairs guest room while Günter moved back into his upstairs room that he had occupied as a teen. Everything in the house pointed to a happy family.

During dinner, we sat at the dining room table and enjoyed *Kalbsnierenbraten*, a sirloin roast, stuffed with kidneys. I had never tasted anything more delicious.

"What do you eat at home?" his mother asked. I was stumped. Eating was not much of an event at our house. I had never had sirloin roast before, and I did not think stew, pork chops, or potato salad, compared favorably. *She's checking me out. She wants to make sure I'm good enough for her son. Oh my God. I'll never pass with my family baggage.*

The next day, Günter's dad prepared the main meal. He liked to cook and did not think it unmanly. I liked him immediately.

In the afternoon, we walked to Günter's old high school, visited a friend, and then dropped in on both sets of grandparents. I barely knew my Oma and Opa on my mother's side. The ones on my father's side had passed away when I was less than six years old. Günter had close relationships with both sets of his grandparents. I found the ones on his father's side particularly loving. They warmly welcomed me into the family, and within less than an hour, had promised us their bedroom set following their demise. I was touched. How could it be that I felt far more at home with Günter's family than with my own?

NINE

CONNECTING
THE DOTS

The Day Everything Changed

THE ALARM GOES OFF WITH A RACKET: 6:00 a.m. I must have
dozed off. Letting go of Tapsi, I fumble in the dark for the small button
on top. Taps yawns, stretches, and quickly tunnels back under the covers.

As I swing my legs over the edge of the sofa bed, I feel a sharp pain at
the crown of my head. Mechanically, I reach back and pull out a curler pick.
That's right. My curls. My twenty-first birthday. I feel discombobulated, out
of sorts. Thought fragments race through my mind. Then I begin to recall
details. Gradually, everything falls back into place. In the jerky loops of a
bad home movie, I watch a rerun of what happened less than fifteen minutes
ago when my parents stepped into my room. Instead of congratulating me,
my mother had spoken six loaded words that colored everything:

"Your father is not your father."

In my internal movie, uninvited images continue to roll by, making
me relive the episode all over again.

"Pappi isn't my father? Who . . . ?"

"Your real father's name is Fritz Zywietz," Mutti says. "He's a busi-
nessman. He lives in Hamburg."

Fritz Zywietz? Who is Fritz Zywietz? I stare at my mother in disbelief.

"Your birth father and I met during the last year of World War II,"
she says. "We were both conscripted by the *Luftwaffe*—the German Air
Force—and stationed in Thüringen—Thuringia."

Thüringen. I vaguely recall hearing my mother talk about the place in the past, about getting drafted and being sent there. It's coming back to me. Didn't Mutti tell me she didn't make any friends there?

"We were both married to someone else already," my mother says as she stands next to my bed, supported by my father. *My father. He is not my father? Then who is he?*

"Fritz Zywietz was a good man, but the times were against us," my mother says.

I try to let her words sink in, and for what feels like an eternity, neither of us speaks.

"You can call him in Hamburg if you want," my mother goes on.

"You don't have to," Pappi cuts in.

I pucker my lips. "What?" a meaningless word to fill time.

"Pappi didn't want a divorce," my mother starts again, her voice trailing off.

"I knew it," I hear myself say. *Why did I say that? That isn't true. I was clueless.*

My mother looks at me in disbelief. Her knees buckle. She teeters back and collapses on the floor. Pappi fumbles, scoops up her limp body and half carries, half drags her out of my bedroom. In leaving, he flicks off the light and the room plunges into darkness once more.

That's what happened fifteen minutes ago. Now I am sitting on the edge of my bed and pinch my arm. *Was it a dream?* But the pain is real.

For a moment, I try to let these two fathers, my birth father and my stepfather, take shape in my mind. Hundreds of questions boomerang through my head. My mother had an affair? The same woman who did not allow me to have an ice cream with Günter had an affair? Unrelated, fleeting images chase one another in my skull.

As if in a trance, I head for the bathroom, take a sponge bath, brush my teeth, remove the curlers, and pull a comb through my hair. Without thinking, I put on my dark-grey ski pants, the warm sweater Sonja knitted for me, boots, a peacoat, and a fur hat. Only then do my eyes fall on the dressy navy-blue suit that is hanging on the closet door. Along with the matching pillbox hat I hung there last night. But this morning, attire and makeup have become irrelevant.

The fog in my head begins to clear. *My appointment at the US Mission.* I almost forgot. This afternoon, I am to swear under oath that the information I provided on my immigration application is true and correct. Today's action will finalize my two-year struggle of arranging a one-year stay in America. Today's action will result in a long separation from Günter. Günter. I feel terrible about leaving him, but I can't allow myself to think about that. Not now.

I step into the kitchen and spot a tray with a pot of tea, two slices of white bread, and a hard-boiled egg. My mother must have prepared breakfast for me and returned to bed. But the thought of food turns my stomach. Mind in utter turmoil and confusion, I leave the house without breakfast or saying good-bye.

Oblivious to my surroundings, I step into the elevator, pull the door closed, and press the ground-floor button. After the initial jerk, the lift descends with a hum. Downstairs, I push open the door, enter the vestibule, and exit into darkness. Cold wind whips soft rain into my face. On autopilot, I navigate the long block to the bus station. Along the way, the dampness releases my hard-won curls. When the bus arrives I step in, show my monthly pass, and plop onto a handicapped seat behind the driver. The usual commuters sit in their favorite places. But today, I take no notice. Eyes fixed, I stare straight through them.

At the corner of Kaiser-Friedrich-Straße and Kurfürstendamm, I transfer to the nearly full double-decker airport bus. I climb to the second level and, miraculously, find a seat next to the window. *Good. This trip will take forty-five minutes. Time to think.*

The bus lurches away from the stop. I lean against the window and allow my head to slump into my upturned coat collar. City lights pierce the darkness. There are red, green, and yellow traffic lights, pasty electric streetlights, bright white beams from oncoming traffic, ribbons of red taillights, and the dimly lit display boxes on the sidewalks of the Kurfürstendamm. Despite the early hour, the city is alive. Outside, the world pulsates. Inside, I feel unhinged from reality.

Pappi is not my father? He's my stepfather? Everyone says I resemble him. How can I?

Mutti had an extramarital affair? She doesn't even believe in a premarital kiss.

Slowly, everything begins to fall into place—the postwar turmoil, my severe upbringing, my mother's need to control every facet of my life, my father's noninvolvement, and my parents' fierce opposition to Günter.

Did Mutti lock me up because she was afraid I would get pregnant?

I knuckle away a tear. The woman on my left gives me a furtive glance. I turn away and stare out the window again. Seemingly unrelated thoughts dart through my mind:

I've been more or less grounded for the past fifteen months because I wouldn't give up Günter. If Mutti and Pappi had bothered to get to know him, they would've realized that he's a wonderful man.

I don't really want to go to California anymore. But I've enlisted the help of so many. I have no choice. I hope and pray that Günter will wait for me.

Who is this Zywietz guy? Has he ever tried to get in touch with me? Do we have anything in common?

Why was I told today? On my twenty-first birthday?

The bus ride terminates at Tempelhof Airport and the pneumatic doors open with a whoosh. Their distinct sound, along with the driver's insistent "*Endstation! Alles aussteigen!*" pull me back to the present.

Fellow passengers scramble down the narrow spiral stairwell. I take a deep breath, straighten out my coat, and follow. On the sidewalk, commuters fan out into all directions. A fine mist settles onto hair and face. I trail behind a group of several men and women who press toward the entrance of the US Air Force base. We flash our identification cards at the guards and funnel into the base. Once inside, I hurry along the sidewalk, climb up a wide set of stairs, pass down the long corridor, and enter the procurement office.

Inside, Birgit Bischof, my office mate, warms her hands on a mug of steaming Nescafé. I barely take notice, hang up my coat, drop my purse into the bottom drawer, and slump onto my three-legged typing stool.

"Are you okay?" Birgit asks.

"Yeah."

I glance at my in-basket. Overflowing. My thumb flicks through the pile of long purchase orders. They look daunting. *Aren't there any short ones?* I decide to postpone the start of my workday by taking a quick trip to the ladies' room.

Back down the long corridor I hurry and push open an unmarked door. Once inside, I lean against the tiled wall and rub my eyes. *How is it that I don't know anything about this Fritz Zywietz?* My hands drop. I gaze at my face in the mirror. A stranger stares back. *Do I look like him?*

I stagger back to my office. I'd better pull myself together. If he doesn't hear my typewriter drone, Mr. Mack is bound to shuffle around the corner to check on me. I reach for a set of purchase-order forms and place the appropriate number of carbons between the pages.

Today's papers will finalize my immigration. For two years I've impatiently waited for this day. Now, I don't care anymore. *Isn't that ironic?*

I want to ring Günter and tell him what happened. *Does Tante Michen know?* Since Fräulein Bischof and I do not have phones, my calls will have to wait until lunchtime.

The morning creeps along. We type one purchase order after the other. First drafted by a purchasing officer, each document must be typed in quintuplicate. I keep having to erase mistakes, one carbon at a time. Mr. Mack feels compelled to pass by my desk several times.

An eternity later, the lunch bell rings. I grab my purse, pick out two ten-pfennig coins, and run to the pay phone. As usual, the booth is occupied. I am first in line. Waiting, I shift from one foot to the other. *I have less than twenty-five minutes left. Why can't people hurry when they see someone's waiting?*

Finally, it is my turn. I step into the booth, remove the receiver, place the coins into the slot, and dial my boyfriend's office number.

"Herr Bayer is out of the office. Can I take a message?" the receptionist asks.

"Yes, please. This is Jutta Umbach. Would you please tell him that I'll try to reach him at home tonight. It's urgent."

"Glad to."

I hang up. *Why couldn't he be there?* Now, I won't be able to call him until after my appointment at the US Mission this afternoon. Maybe I should just stop by his apartment afterwards. A quick glance through the phone booth's glass door tells me that two people have queued up already. While I fumble through my purse for additional coins, the middle-aged lady at the head of the line tenses in anticipation. Her shoulders drop again when she sees me plunk more money into the slot. I dial Tante Michen.

"Firma Bielcke," she answers.

"Tante Michen, something's happened. I have to ask you something."

"Don't you even give your aunt a chance to wish you a happy birthday?" she asks. "This is the Big One, the one you've been waiting for!"

"I know. I know. Tante Michen, I'm sorry, but I don't have much time," I interrupt. "I'm on lunch break. Mutti told me this morning that Pappi is not my father. She said a guy by the name of Zywietz is. Is that true? Did you know that?"

Silence at the other end.

"You know then," she sighs. "Yes, it's true. We were all sworn to secrecy. I'm sorry. I wanted to tell you, but I couldn't."

I take a deep breath. Deep inside, I had hoped that my mother's announcement this morning was nothing more than a terrible nightmare.

"It happened during the war. Your father was missing in action. Fritz Zywietz was going to leave his wife and marry your mother. But when the war was over, your Pappi came back. Your Pappi didn't want a divorce and adopted you. Then he made the rest of us promise that we'd never tell."

My head is spinning. *So, that's what happened.*

"Thanks, Tante Michen. I don't know what to say right now. I have to think. But thanks for telling me."

"I'm so sorry you had to find out this way."

"It's okay. Bye." *I expected things to change today, but in a very different way.*

I place the receiver in its cradle and slowly open the door. The woman in the front of the line glares at me while she squeezes into the booth before I can fully exit. Her facial expression leaves no doubt that I have taken more than my share of time. Behind her, four more people have queued up.

I trudge back to the office. *Fritz Zywietz.* How could he exist all these years without my knowing?

Promptly at 2:00 p.m., I leave the base and board a bus to the US Immigration Services in the fashionable district of Dahlem. I feel exhausted. Pull yourself together, I remind myself again. If you act as confused as you feel, you may be denied immigration. I exit the bus at Clay Allee and walk toward the colorless building that houses the US Mission. The November-grey skies match my mood. So do the bare trees lining the street. The doorman directs me to a long corridor with offices along one side and points out a door. I walk to it and knock gently. When I ease it open, a puff of stale air escapes, but its warmth feels somehow reassuring. I announce myself to the young man behind the counter, but even though we both speak German, I have trouble understanding what he says. Not even his name stays with me. He motions for me to take a seat, and I do as instructed.

Another man, wearing spectacles, appears and leads me to a desk. He asks numerous questions; I answer mechanically. Finally, he prompts me to raise my right hand to swear that the information I have provided in my own hand months earlier is true and correct.

"I swear."

Done. He gathers the papers, writes something at the bottom, and assures me that I will receive my visa in the mail. "Probably within a month," he says. I thank him and hurry back to the bus station. I want to stop by Günter's apartment before going home.

Suddenly, something feels different about the world outside, a world which was barred to me for so long. *In two months time, I'll live on another continent. What will that be like?* Despite pacing back and forth, I feel tired.

When the bus pulls up, I climb to the upper level. Since all of my favorite seats in the front row are taken, I drop into an aisle seat. The bus bumps and grinds down the tree-lined street. Suddenly, my heart skips a beat. I just raised my right hand and swore that the information I provided is true and correct. I wrote "Karl Umbach" into the space that asked my father's name. *He isn't my father!* When I filled out the forms several months ago, I didn't know. *Did I just commit perjury?*

Heat floods my body. I unbutton my coat. Should I go back and tell them? What if they perform a background check? Can this be construed as grounds for denying me immigration? I contemplate getting off the bus at the next stop and returning to the US Mission when another thought pops into my head. Did my mother reveal the name of my birth father this morning because she realized that I had provided false information? *Was she afraid I might be sent to jail?*

By now, I am closer to Günter's apartment than to the consulate and decide to let it go. I feel worn out. I get off at Mommsenstraße, cross the street to his building and check in at the reception. A few minutes later the concierge smiles, "Go on up. Herr Bayer is expecting you."

I hurry to the elevator, get off on the ninth floor, and knock on Günter's door. He opens immediately. "Well?"

"It's done."

Nothing else is said. No glance. No kiss. Uneasiness hangs in the air like dew in a spiderweb.

"There is something else," I say, still standing in the door. I brush by Günter and barely have time to drop into a chair before my floodgates open. I burst into tears and cannot speak for several minutes.

"What happened?"

"My father is not my father. I found out this morning."

"What?" Günter looks confused. I tell him the whole story. My body shakes as I sob. He sits down beside me and puts his arm around my shoulder. His gentle touch strips me of my last vestige of self-control.

"My parents never mentioned Fritz Zywietz. Not once in twenty-one years. Our whole relationship was built on a lie."

"It'll all turn out," Günter says softly. "Remember, you have me."

An avalanche of warm sentiments runs through me. I could not feel closer to him.

"That's why we had to go through hell trying to see each other. Don't you see? My mother wanted to keep me from getting pregnant—like she did. That's why she locked me up. My father never intervened because he was my stepfather. He left everything to my mother. It's all falling into place."

Günter holds me and strokes my cheek.

"If I hadn't gone to the US Immigration Services today, my mother might never have told me."

"Does it really matter?" Günter asks. "You are twenty-one now. You don't depend on your parents anymore."

Günter is right. I'm twenty-one now. This is my birthday. Today is the day I have waited for.

"And you're still planning to go through with America?" he asks.

The air is charged with what is left unspoken. I'd rather not go. I'd rather stay right here, here with Günter. But because every aspect of my existence has been controlled until now I feel ignorant and unprepared for life. I want to be a full partner to Günter some day, but I don't think I'm ready. I don't think I know yet what other girls my age know. I don't even know myself. I must go away and become the person that lives inside of me. Then I'll come back.

My head barely moves when I nod, "I'm still going."

Café Schmidt

DURING THE FIRST WEEK of December, I receive final approval to immigrate to the United States. It makes me both happy and sad. Happy because I have fought hard for this moment; sad because Günter won't come with me. With a good job and strong family ties, he has no reason to go on a wild adventure. But I must. I must learn how to talk, how to listen, how to compromise, and how to stand up for myself, things that other people already know.

The following day, I tender my resignation to the US Air Force with an effective date in mid-January. Then I research flight options and set my departure date for Monday, January 30, 1967. Icelandic Airlines offer the best fares between Luxembourg and New York. I build my trip around that. I purchase the ticket and add New York to San Diego on American Airlines. Before I can book Berlin-Luxembourg, Günter says, "How would you like to spend your last weekend with me at my parents' house?"

A thousand-watt smile lights up my face. What could be a better send-off? I wouldn't have to tiptoe around our apartment, trying to avoid disaster. I could be myself those last two days in Germany. And Günter and I would be together! Then reality kicks in. "I'd love that, but . . . I doubt that my parents will go for it. They'll want me home until I step on that plane."

He looks at me askew. "You're twenty-one now, remember? You can do what you want."

"You're right. But how do I bring up the topic without starting World War III? I don't have any fight left in me. I'm exhausted."

"Just tell 'em!"

It is obvious that Günter is tired of my parents' interference and my inability to stand up for myself. He wants to see me exhibit a little spine. He is right. I am an adult now. I am entitled to make my own decisions. But I still haven't learned how. I do want to spend my last two days with Günter and I do want to spend those days without having to walk on eggshells. *Heck, I'll have to start somewhere.* I decide to jump into the fire.

"Okay, let's plan on it."

"Great," he says. "You'll be glad you did."

When I book a coach passage between Munich and Luxembourg, travel arrangements are complete. I just have to tell my parents.

Never before have I openly stood up to my parents. Chances are the encounter will be anything but pretty. I'll just have to hold my ground, I tell myself. And I resolve that I must tell them at the earliest opportunity so that they will have time to adjust to the news. Somehow that strategy flies out of the window right away because I fear an angry reaction.

No need to ruin Christmas and New Years over it, I decide. I'll tell them right after New Years. That'll still give them almost a month to get used to the idea. And it'll give me a couple of weeks to figure out how to approach them.

Günter plans to visit his parents for Christmas and invites me to come along. As before, I do not dare to spend the holidays away from home, and certainly not the last one prior to my year in America.

"I'll tell my parents that we moved up my Berlin departure, but I can't ask for Christmas away from home, too. Asking for too much might be counterproductive," I tell him.

"You've always told me that your family doesn't care about Christmas. Then what's the problem?"

"Believe me, I'd much prefer spending the holidays with you and your parents. I just don't have it in me to ask for Christmas away from home, too." Günter is unhappy with my cowardice, but I get a nervous stomach just thinking about how to bring up my early departure date without adding the additional request.

We spend Christmas apart, and Günter returns to Berlin just prior to year's end. For the first time, we ring in the New Year together. We toast with friends on New Year's Eve, and Günter takes me out to dinner on New Year's Day. We order *Spanferkel*—suckling pig—for good luck. He also introduces me to a drink I never heard of before: *Bommi mit Pflaume* in a shot glass. A small plum swims in vodka.

"How do you drink this?" I ask.

"Just put the plum on your tongue and pour the vodka over it," he advises.

"All at once?"

"Usually, yeah."

I must be the only adult in all of Berlin who has never had *Bommi mit Pflaume*. When you have lived a sheltered life, you have a lot of catching up to do. I do as instructed and feel the burn all the way to my stomach. Moments later, I am forced to visit the ladies' room. When I rejoin Günter, I have a broad grin on my face. Here we are: a man and a woman sharing one of life's experiences. Isn't that wonderful? I consider it a preview of our life together.

January has arrived, and I remind myself that the time has come to inform my parents of my updated departure plans. Since the atmosphere at home has been dicey ever since I received my immigration papers, I continue to put it off.

Mr. Mack helps me garner a large foil-lined cardboard box from the commissary, perfect for shipping. I plan to take my suitcase on the plane and ship the box. But for the remaining couple of weeks, the carton sits next to my desk in the office because I am afraid to bring it home. There is no official ban on the subject of my imminent departure, but it feels uncomfortable.

With each passing day, I promise myself to bring up the matter of my early departure without further delay, but I never quite summon enough courage. Each time, I feel like a schoolgirl before an English exam— anxious and uneasy, wishing it were already over.

With less than two weeks before leaving Berlin, I can no longer postpone telling my parents and invite them to coffee and cake at the Café Schmidt, an esteemed *Konditorei* in the Wilmersdorfer Straße. There, I will inform them of my going-away date. Receiving the news in a public place will force them to practice restraint.

On a Sunday afternoon, the three of us, and Tapsi, walk the six blocks to Café Schmidt. Pappi is in a splendid mood. On the short stroll, he clasps his hands behind his back like an elderly statesman. He bows and doffs his hat to oncoming neighbors, proud to be indulged by his daughter.

When we enter the café, my heart feels stuck in my throat. We locate a vacant table for three in the middle of the room. An ideal location, I note with satisfaction. Tapsi settles quietly under the table, and I play the part of a big spender. "Pick whatever you like," I encourage my parents. This is the first time I have ever taken them out. Each of us selects a pastry, and we order coffees. My increasing uneasiness is concealed behind a forced smile.

As soon as the delicacies arrive, I remind myself to promptly bring up the subject of my moved-up departure date. *Tell them!* But nothing comes out of my mouth. Just thinking the words makes me perspire.

"Would you like some?" I hold up sugar and cream and look from one parent to the other. My dad passes. My mother pours a little cream in her coffee and stirs it with the delicate silver spoon. I pick up my cup and force myself to keep a steady hand. *Say something.* Still, no words come out.

Nibbling from teeny silver forks, my parents savor each bite of their scrumptious pastry. I consume mine with paralytic slowness. I can't taste a thing. Forcing a smile, I rehearse my speech in my head for the umpteenth time. Then I sit there like a tin soldier waiting for a sign from heaven.

In no time, cake and coffee are gone.

"Well, this was real nice. Thank you," my father says. "I think we should consider heading home."

"*Zahlen bitte,*" I summon our bill from the waitress.

This is my last chance.

"There . . . there's something I wanted to tell you," I squeeze out the words. "You know I'll be leaving for America on Monday, the thirtieth, right?"

Both my parents nod solemnly. My mother gives me a suspicious look. Her back stiffens.

"Well, actually, I'm going to leave Berlin a couple days earlier."

My mother's torso grows longer.

"Günter and I plan to drive by car to Munich. We'll leave Berlin the Saturday before and stay with his parents for the weekend. Monday morning, Günter will take me to the bus heading for Luxembourg." *There, I said it.* I take a deep breath.

The silence that follows is even more uncomfortable than my awkward announcement. For a moment, my parents stare at me in disbelief. We sit at the little table like three people struck by lightning. On the walk over, I had contemplated different ways they might react. I thought they might subject me to the silent treatment; I wondered if my parents would beg me to change my mind and stay in Berlin until the thirtieth; I even considered that they might say, "We don't like it, but we understand." In the end, they do the one thing I hadn't expected.

My father is the first to jump up. His face twists up with fury. I watch as blood surges to his face. "*Das schlägt doch dem Faß den Boden aus—* that knocks the bottom right out of the barrel," he thunders, throwing his spoon into the saucer with a loud clang. The heads of the couple next to us jerk around in surprise. I sense the room is growing warmer. "Is this the reward we get for all we've done for you? Is this how you show your love and respect for our toils and sacrifices over the years? You're going to spend your last days with that *Schnösel*, that arrogant, brazen snob, instead of spending them with us, your parents?" His words tumble out in staccato spurts like angry machine-gun fire.

He grabs Tapsi's leash and storms in the direction of the front door, my mother on his heels. I quickly settle the bill at the cash register and follow. All eyes are turned on us.

My father, a tall man of over six feet, stomps out the café, down the Wilmersdorfer Straße, turns left into the Kantstraße, and takes the six blocks in huge strides. He looks like a tornado whirling down the street. He drags Tapsi with him, her short legs barely able to keep up. My mother, considerably shorter, sprints alongside my father. I follow at a safe distance. The dash home takes less than ten minutes, half the normal time. Since I did not bring keys, I try to catch up in time to join my parents at the front door.

All through the walk, my father's outburst keeps me thinking, and by the time we reach home, I have made a decision. If there was any doubt whether I have come to the right conclusion, I know now what I must do: I have to get out of Berlin. I have to break away from my parents.

We enter the building, squeeze into the small lift, and get out on the fifth floor. No one speaks. My father unlocks our apartment doors, and my parents proceed to the living room. I hang up my coat, pick up Tapsi, and quietly retreat to my domain. I hear my father lament what a terrible child he and my mother have raised. She concurs with each of his pronouncements and elevates them to even higher levels. The grievances become louder and louder. There is no letup.

After a while, I have to go to the bathroom. Glancing through the open living room door, I see my father slumped into his chair, head bowed, shoulders sagging, forearms resting lifeless on his thighs. Tears stream down his face. He sobs uncontrollably and makes no effort to brush them away. His pitiful cries turn into a wail. It is my father, not my mother, who seems unable to cope with my early departure. I don't know how to deal with that.

The air in the hall grows heavy and presses like iron armor on my chest. I cannot listen any longer, grab my dog, and tiptoe to the front door. My parents do not hear it close.

It is winter and freezing outside. I am barefoot. But I do not care. All I want is to escape. To avoid drawing attention, I do not call for the noisy elevator but rush down the five flights of terrazzo stairs, having no idea where I might go.

Tante Michen is out of the question. She'll be the first they'll contact. She'd have hell to pay if she shelters me. Lorena? Her parents don't want to get involved in our family's issues. Fee? She and her parents have only one bedroom. Günter? He already shares the tiniest of apartments with a roommate. The police? What can they do? I'm an adult now. They'll send me straight home.

When I arrive in the downstairs vestibule with Tapsi in my arms, my feet feel like ice, I am soaked in perspiration, and my hands shake uncontrollably. I can think of only one way out: Herr and Frau Starr, the nice elderly couple who occupies one of the downstairs units.

I ring their doorbell. Frau Starr answers. "Jutta? What's wrong?" She takes a second look at my disheveled appearance. "You look troubled. Can I help?"

"I . . . I . . ." Tears stream down my face as if the Rhein River had been rerouted. "I ran away from home," I cry. I realize how ridiculous this must sound. I am twenty-one years old.

The Starrs never had children, but Frau Starr is as warm and kind as anyone's favorite grandmother. "First of all, come inside. It's freezing out there. You're trembling. You don't want to catch a cold."

Pressing Tapsi to my chest, I hesitantly cross the threshold. *I can't stay with them.* The three of us crowd around their small living room table.

"What happened, Jutta? What made you so upset?"

Trembling and scarcely able to speak, I begin to explain about Günter, about America, about Café Schmidt, and about my early departure plans. Each sentence is followed by a renewed burst of tears. "I'm not going to go home—ever again," I keep repeating. "Don't make me. Please, don't make me." After sitting and talking for thirty minutes or more, I begin to calm down.

Then the doorbell rings. *That's got to be my mother! She heard us talk!*

"Don't open the door. Please don't open," I beg the Starrs. The doorbell rings again. We look at each other.

"We cannot hide you from your parents, Jutta."

"No . . . No . . . No . . ." I am shaking violently. Tears flow in rivulets.

Frau Starr gently pats my face. Then she walks to the front door and opens it. I hear my mother's muffled voice. Then Frau Starr's. Herr Starr sits by my side with his arm around my shoulder. I squeeze Tapsi to my chest. My mother steps into the living room.

"I'm not coming home. Ever." I cry out and quiver like gelatin. Through tear-filled eyes I notice that my mother looks uneasy, too. She has never cared to air family business in front of strangers.

My trembling intensifies. My jaws clatter. My mother glances at me and says, "It's all right. Let's go upstairs."

"No," I cry. "I'm not coming with you. You and Pappi just berate me."

"Nothing more will be said," my mother says. "You can come home now."

Final Days

I CAN'T STAY WITH THE STARRS, and I can't think of anywhere else to go. Reluctantly, I follow my mother upstairs to our apartment and immediately retreat to my bedroom. *Two more weeks. I can do it. I must!*

My parents talk in whispers in the living room but leave me alone. For that I am grateful and plunk down on my sofa bed. I see clear darkness stretch across the rooftops. Hugging my knees, I mutter, "I finally stood up to them. I did it. Günter and I will spend our last two days together." But my tank is empty. How could a marriage survive, unless I first learn to stand up for myself?

The next day, I call Günter from a pay phone. "Guess what I did yesterday? I told my parents that we'll spend the last two days with your folks."

"Excellent. How did it go?"

"Even worse than expected. They couldn't accept it." I tell him the rest of the story. "I'm exhausted, but I didn't give in."

"Good for you. I'm proud of you. I'll pick you up at your house the morning of the twenty-eighth. We'll talk about the time later. Dieter says he'll ride with us so that he can visit his family for a couple of days."

"Great. Thanks, Günter. I'll call when I can. It'll be hit-and-miss because I still don't feel comfortable calling unless I'm walking Tapsi or my parents are out of the house. The walls have ears, you know."

"Hang in there. This, too, shall pass."

We hang up. Tapsi and I continue on our walk. *I didn't tell him that I ran away from home last night.* I have always sugarcoated my parents' idiosyncrasies to make them appear more "normal." What will happen when Günter finds outs what they are like? I haven't been totally open with him. I feel bad.

On another walk I call Fee. "Remember how I vacillated between going to America and staying in Berlin?"

"Of course. Have you decided to stay after all?"

"No, just the opposite. You won't believe what happened." I tell her all about Café Schmidt and the aftermath. "I feel like a dehydrated sponge, Fee. I have to puff up again before I can do anything else."

Fee commiserates and asks, "Are you going to have a farewell party?"

"Are you kidding? I'll be lucky if I get to call everybody to say good-bye."

The last two weeks in Berlin are pure agony. The air is charged with resentment and hangs over our apartment like a dark cloud. Having terminated my employment with the US Air Force, I am stuck at home where the oppressive silence mirrors the crippled state of our relationship. My father ignores me; my mother and I exchange a bare minimum of words. My only objective is to get through the remaining days without confrontations. Keeping to my room most of the time, I alternate between feeling numb to feeling anxious and back to numb again. My concept of time ceases to exist. A day is like a week. Between two nights lies a gaping abyss. I sleep. I eat. I walk Tapsi.

On my last workday, I lug home the cardboard shipping carton. Important things are to go into the suitcase, miscellaneous items into the box. I pack the box in frantic spurts when my father is at work and my mother is food shopping or taking out the trash, because I do not want to draw unnecessary attention to my departure. During those brief periods, I glance about my room and throw things into the box that catch my eye. Most of the items will probably turn out to be useless, but their stock has gone up lately because these pieces will represent my connection to the past. I pack the linen couch pillow I stitched in home economics. It takes up a lot of room and is hardly worth the shipping costs. I don't smoke, but I add the bronze-colored ashtray from Lufthansa. The drip candle in the VAT bottle is my worst addition. No doubt, the wax will disintegrate during the journey, but it is something I made. I run my hands over the dresser, the wallpaper, even the doorknob. Then I press my face into the couch pillows as I have done so many times when I was without hope. This room and I share so much misery. It feels like a friend.

Meanwhile, my suitcase remains stored on the upper shelf in the hall closet. I am afraid of getting it down and causing an uproar. If I forget something—oh well. I'll be back in a year's time.

I dawdle the time away. I think of my birth father. *Does he ever think of me? Should I try calling him?* I picture myself sitting on our small fur-covered stool by the phone in the hallway, dialing Hamburg: "Hullo.

Is this Fritz Zywietz? Yes? This is Jutta Umbach." Pause. "I'm your daughter." *No good.*

"Herr Zywietz, I'm the daughter of Gertrud Umbach. I believe you knew her during World War II in Thüringen? I understand you are my father." *Forget it.*

How about, "Papa, I'm Jutta, your daughter?" *No, way!*

What shall I call my two "fathers" anyway, I wonder? I decide to continue calling my stepfather "Pappi" or "father" and my birth father "FZ" because it was my stepfather who raised me.

Throughout these imaginary phone conversations, I can't help but visualize my mother standing in the open doorway between kitchen and hallway, her slippered feet firmly planted on the ground. I picture her, holding a three-foot ear trumpet with both hands, trying to capture every syllable of my conversation. Contacting my birth father would be too awkward, I decide. Besides, do I even want to become involved with this man? Apparently he hasn't been very interested in me.

I turn my thoughts to a much more enjoyable activity and spend countless hours drawing caricatures. The square little book I am working on is clad in red jute and, except for its size, identical in appearance to the photo album Günter gave me for Christmas the year before. I am creating two stick-figure characters that tell Günter's and my story. Simple scenes recount how we met, how I was imprisoned, and what life was like after that. The last page shows me flying off to the United States, waving good-bye. "See you soon," says the caption. The book will be my farewell present to Günter. I hope he will be pleased.

The days pass by as quickly as the Middle Ages. Sometimes, I think time is standing still. At last, it is Friday, January 27, one day prior to departure. I shipped the cardboard box a few days ago and pack my suitcase in full view now. Günter and I have been in touch only sporadically, and then only for short periods by phone. We agreed that he will pick me up at nine o'clock the next morning, and we expect to arrive in Munich the same afternoon. I cross my fingers and pray that everything will turn out as planned. The fear that another bombshell might explode during the next twenty-four hours keeps an iron grip on me. I want this ordeal to end.

Although I sleep fitfully in fifteen-minute intervals, I also feel a strange sense of peace. Why don't I fret about leaving my hometown, my friends, or even Günter, I wonder? Why don't I agonize what it will be like when I can't see his familiar face anymore, hear his melodic voice, feel his arms around me or his lips on mine? The only intense feeling I am aware of is my overwhelming desire to escape. Throughout the night, I watch the hands of the alarm clock creep toward morning. Tapsi turns onto her back and lets me rub her belly. I will miss my little wiener dog.

Even before daybreak, I rise, make my bed, and tidy up. Then I sit down and wait. My packed suitcase and red cosmetic case beckon from the door. Freedom is almost within reach. Finally, the day breaks gray and pink. From the kitchen I hear the clatter of silverware and dishes. I briefly leave my room to wash up and return to slip into my short-sleeved wool dress, nylons, and high heels. I drape my winter coat and hat over the suitcase. Then I sit down again. How many hours have I spent here dreaming of Günter and of our life together? I peer through the small window into the bare treetops and the tiny patch of sky. How often has this view been my only connection to the outside world? For the last time, I look at a photo of Günter, caress it, and tuck it into my purse.

At 8:30 a.m. the three of us sit down to a continental breakfast. I can't eat. Even the coffee fails to wash down the rolls. They stick to my throat like glue. Promptly, at 8:50, I say, "It's time!"

I get up from the table, wash my hands, and brush my teeth. Then I haul my suitcase and cosmetic case to the front door. Tapsi has been agitated all morning. She runs back and forth. No doubt, she knows something is about to happen. I pick up my little buddy—she is only four years old—cradle her in my arms, and whisper, "I'm sorry, Taps, I'll be back. I promise. Until then, be Mommy's good little girl."

My mother and father remain seated at the living room table where we had breakfast. The apartment is cloaked in an eerie silence. No radio, no television, no human voice to break the quiet. I return to the living room and lean uneasily against the door frame.

"I have to leave now."

My father does not move. My mother rises, reaches for her keys and says, "I'll go downstairs with you."

I take a few hesitant steps into the room. "Good-bye then," I say and look at my father. A tear runs down his cheek. He does not get up. He does not look at me. "*Ich vergebe Dir*—I forgive you," is all he says.

Too much has happened for me to be able to respond. I stand there, the wheels of my mind are spinning, but nothing comes of it. "Bye," I say again. We do not hug, kiss, or shake hands. I turn, walk into the hallway, and proceed to the front door. My eyes are open, but my mind has shut down.

My mother and I step into the tiny lift, luggage and all. It is a tight fit. We descend in silence. On the ground floor, I push open the elevator door with my back. My mother steps into the vestibule and holds open the door. I grab my luggage, and we exit into the cool morning air. As soon as I have negotiated the eight steps to the courtyard and have a clear view of the street, I glance in all directions. *Dear God, let Günter be there. I'm at the end of my wits.*

My heart jumps when I see his red Opel Kadett parked around the corner. *He's there!* A huge weight falls off my chest. *Thank you, Günter.*

Out of the corner of my eye I see the car door swing open on the driver's side. Günter gets out and slowly walks toward us. The air sizzles with tension. *It's almost over.* I put down my suitcase, turn to my mother, and give her a stilted hug. "Good-bye then."

"Good-bye," my mother says. "If things don't work out, you can always come home," she says.

"I know," I say. But I also know that I can't ever live this way again. I have to figure out something else. Anything.

There are no tears. My mother barely acknowledges Günter's presence. He picks up my suitcase, and I follow him to the car. As he places my luggage in the trunk, he asks under his breath, "Everything okay?"

I nod.

He opens the passenger door. I say "Hi," to Dieter, his roommate, who is seated in the back and climb in. Günter takes his seat behind the wheel, starts the engine, and we pull away from the curb. As his car makes its way down the Kuno-Fischer-Straße, turns left into the Kantstraße and heads for the AVUS, Berlin's raceway and feeder road, and finally to the autobahn, I look straight ahead. My eyes are dry. Even as the familiar sights get smaller and smaller behind me, I continue to look straight ahead. I don't ever again want to go through what I experienced these past two weeks.

Going, Going—Gone

GREY SKIES HANG BEFORE US. Everything looks drab. The low hum of worry continues to run through me like a current, even as we enter the AVUS a few minutes later. I still feel my mother's presence and am haunted by her corklike ability to pop up in unlikely places. I half expect her hand to tap me on the shoulder, ordering me to turn back. By the time the AVUS merges into the autobahn ring, I start to settle down. At last. My heart begins to beat normally and I breathe freely as if casting off a constricting skin. *I've done it. I have scaled my parents' confining walls.*

Since we started the journey, no one has spoken. "You have no idea what it was like those past two weeks," I say to Günter, breaking the silence. Turning to Dieter I add, "If you can imagine three planets orbiting the same sun without crossing paths, that's about what it was like. Time moved so slowly, I wondered whether today would ever come. My parents never accepted our decision to spend these last two days together," I say turning back to Günter. "They considered it my duty to save my last hours in Germany for them."

He nods, looking straight ahead, mindful of traffic. "It's over now," he says with that calmness I so admire.

"I know. I'm glad we managed to have at least this time together. I'm glad you thought of it. I only wished it could have been more. Anyway, thanks for whisking me away."

Günter says something, but his words get lost in the passing fog that clouds my thoughts. In its murky mist, I feel like I am standing in the middle of a hairpin turn. The road ahead of me looks entirely different from the one behind me. Until today, my ability to lead a "normal" life has depended on keeping my head down and my mouth shut. My parents punished any small sign of independence with house arrest. I think they tried to strip me of everything that makes me unique. *But now, I am free. I won't have to tiptoe through life anymore. From now on, I'll get to decide when to get up, when to go to bed, what to eat, what to wear, and whom to date. I'll be able to talk on the phone without being cryptic and to sip a cup of cocoa at a café without having to produce the subway ticket that got me there. From now on, I'll be in control of my life.*

"By late afternoon, we should be at my folks' home," I hear Günter say and my frown melts into a broad smile. *Today and tomorrow belong to us.*

At his family's home, we make every minute count. His parents leave us to each other. We walk and talk, and the disparate shards of the past eighteen months since we first met seem to knit themselves together into one coherent picture: every past secret, every past disappointment, and every past victory. Everything seems to make a little more sense now. But we also carefully avoid speaking of the future, afraid of unearthing unexpected complications.

Monday arrives all too quickly, and Günter drives me to the bus depot. On the way, we make idle conversation. We skirt the pertinent issues and speak only of peripheral things. Neither of us knows what to say. We feel close, and yet, we feel uncomfortable. So much is left unsaid.

When the boarding announcement cuts through the din, we jump as if electrified and don't quite know what to do. *This is it.* I fumble through my purse and produce a gold Parker pen. It is engraved with Günter's name on the clip.

"So that you'll write often," I say as I hand him the pen, my eyes fixed on his.

"But I don't have anything for you," Günter says dismayed.

"Doesn't matter. It's my turn. Remember the sexy Parisian umbrella you gave me for Christmas? Black on top with a cloud of burgundy lace underneath? I could never reciprocate with anything half as gorgeous. I shipped it to San Diego, you know, even though they say it never rains there."

We chuckle and hold each other. My tears want to well up, but I swallow hard and extricate myself from his embrace to rummage through my purse a second time.

"This is for you, too." I pull out the small, red book I put together during my last two weeks in Berlin. Creating it seemed to give purpose to my hated confinement. As I hand him the result of my artistic endeavors, my chest is bursting with pride.

He looks as pleased as a stroked cat. Tears roll down his cheek. I have never seen him cry before. Our throats are parched as we drop our voices to whispers. Our hands meet. We embrace.

"Last call for the bus to Luxembourg." The announcement cuts through the joy and sadness that engulf us. Trembling, I place both hands on Günter's shoulders and study his face for the last time. I photograph it with my eyes. I want to memorize it.

"I've got to go," I murmur and stoop to pick up my purse and cosmetic case. One more kiss. Then another. We hang on to each other and refuse to let go.

"I'll come to visit you in the summer, halfway through your stay," Günter says.

"I can't wait. I'm looking forward to it already. Can you imagine how much fun we'll have? My parents nowhere in sight?"

"*Bis bald dann*—see you soon."

One more teary hug and we say good-bye for the last time.

I pivot and join the stream of passengers. "See you this summer," I whisper under my breath. When I turn back, I see him wave. I wave back. Again. And again.

I love Günter with all my heart and can't wait until we are ready to build our life together. As so many times before, my emotions succeed only in choking me. *Why didn't I tell him of my love just now? Why was my tongue tied again? Has my battle with my parents made me incapable of showing emotion?* They have inserted themselves like a boulder between us, forcing us to grow oddly, like two trees twisting around the same rock. We survived the ordeal, but not without harm. It will require hard work on both our parts to normalize things. Our love for each other will have to be our guide.

I store my coat in the overhead bin and place my purse and case underneath the seat in front of me. Then I sit down by the window. As the bus pulls away, we wave and wave. Günter's head gets smaller until it is no bigger than a black dot. Then he is gone. An uncontrollable wave of longing sweeps over me. *What if I never see Günter again?* I crumple up in my corner and begin to sob. Pressing my forehead against the window, I mouth, "Günter, please come soon." My insides feel like they have fallen through the floor.

A few minutes later, I straighten up and try to pull myself together. *What am I doing? I am about to embark on the greatest adventure of my life. I fought for this trip for two full years. I have to become myself before I can be with Günter. I need time to discover and develop my own identity.* I have told myself all this a million times before.

The middle-aged man in the seat next to me says in an American accent, "Hi, I'm Jeff Walker. Will you be staying in Luxembourg or continuing on?"

"On to New York and then on to San Diego in California. My girlfriend lives there," I nod.

"San Diego," he says. "I've lived there for a couple of years. Nice town. Great weather."

"You have? What's it like? Tell me. I'll be there for a whole year."

As the bus zooms down the autobahn, Jeff paints vivid pictures of San Diego's sunny skies and seventy miles of pristine beaches. *Seventy miles?* I am impressed.

When we cross the border to Luxembourg, he tells me about the Hotel Del Coronado where *Some Like it Hot* was filmed. Günter and I have seen that movie. *I'll be able to see for myself where it was filmed?*

"San Diego simply has it all," Jeff continues his narrative. "Within an hour or two, you can be at the ocean, in the mountains, or in the desert."

"In the desert? A few years ago, I saw the movie *Die Wüste lebt*—the Living Desert. It was so hot there that they fried an egg on the rocks. Is that true? Could you fry an egg in San Diego's desert?"

"I haven't tried it, but I bet you could," Jeff says. Then he goes on to talk about a historic gold-mining town in San Diego's backcountry, called Julian. "It's now mainly a mountain getaway where people go to hike and harvest apples in the fall." He follows up with a description of San Diego's picturesque harbor and its old lighthouse on the cliff high above. Next, he recounts his sojourns into the fashionable community of La Jolla.

"I was told San Diego was nothing more than a small Navy town," I am hesitant to interject. I don't want to offend him.

"It is a small town, and yes, the Navy has a huge presence there, but it's also quite charming," Jeff says. He goes on to talk about Balboa Park. "All of the buildings were constructed for the Panama-California

Exhibition, and the zoo is right next door. The San Diego Zoo is world famous, you know. You've picked a beautiful place, believe me."

My imagination is on fire now. My subdued spirits warm up and my melancholy lifts. San Diego has always been the vaguest part of my escape plan. I begin to insert myself into the picture, just as I have done when Sonja first wrote to me. In my imagination, I stand in front of my alpine mountain chalet, my new, temporary home. Holstein cattle graze in the tall, juicy grass that surrounds my abode. From the rolling green hills, I overlook the Pacific and watch the gentle waves caress the miles and miles of white beaches. I stretch my arms toward the sky and bask in the warm sunshine.

My thoughts turn to the Berlin Wall. Ulbricht's regime kept "improving" the monstrosity every year. In 1963, two years into its existence, they replaced much of the stone with concrete. The following year, they added dog runs. On long, retractable leashes, the animals guarded the area behind the *bordermarker,* along with human sentries. By the fifth year, the Wall was fortified with enough barbed wire to circle the earth. Still, the Wall became a normal setting to most Berliners. We came to accept it; many of us even became oblivious to it.

The barriers my parents erected followed a similar pattern. They also started as makeshift impediments. Slowly, their restrictions turned into formidable obstacles, complete with their own guard towers. During our eighteen months together, Günter and I saw my parents' barriers grow higher and higher until they became as difficult to scale as the Berlin Wall. People say that a frog dropped into hot water will immediately hop out. But a frog put in cold water, which is slowly heated, will just sit there until he dies.

I don't want to die like that frog. Today is the first day of my free life. "Keep the fork—the best is yet to come," Tante Michen always said when she cleared the dinner table. She knew that dessert would be even better than the meal. I need to find out how the world works. I need to find out what is inside of me. You're lucky, I tell myself. America will be that equalizer. A year from now, I'll be the person that already lives inside of me but has not had a chance to come out yet. In anticipation, I lean back in my seat, close my eyes, and relax. Everything will work out.

San Diego—here I come!

Afterword

I spent 1967 in San Diego and, for the first time, experienced true independence. Eager to learn and discover, I leapt with zeal into each new day and each new encounter. Soon after arrival I changed employers, rented a furnished apartment, and worked out my own daily priorities. Some nights I stayed up until the wee hours of the morning; some weekends I slept until noon. Although I washed the dishes most of the time, now and then, I let them pile up. At last I was in charge of my life, and I loved it.

That summer, halfway through my planned stay, Günter arrived for a month-long holiday. Prior to his visit I purchased a fifteen-year-old, baby-blue Studebaker to explore the many sights in and around San Diego and Tijuana, the Sequoia National Park, and San Francisco. Freed from my mother's interference, we relaxed and thoroughly enjoyed each other's company. Life seemed as good as life was meant to be.

After Günter left, my girlfriend Sonja moved in with me. We not only shared pesky household duties but, wearing the same size, we also doubled our wardrobes. On my twenty-second birthday that fall I invited everyone I had met during my stay to help celebrate, and I delighted in the knowledge that my mother was unable to dictate who could join the festivities and what time the party should end. I did not even mind being away from home during the Christmas holidays. Soon enough I would return to Berlin, and the year abroad would be nothing more than a beautiful memory.

In early January 1968 the time had come to give notice at the office, terminate my apartment lease, and sell the car. For no apparent reason I dragged my feet. Questions from home grew louder: "When are you coming back?" Two months later I finally purchased an airline ticket. It was for a six-week round trip.

In Berlin I happily reunited with Günter, my parents, my friends, and my little buddy, Tapsi. I explained that I had decided to extend my San Diego stay by six months, primarily because of the new job I had landed a couple of months earlier. In the hiring process I had concealed the immediacy of my departure and now felt like a fraud. Günter was disappointed but graciously accepted the delay. We saw each other every day and spoke of our impending nuptials. Yet a faint uneasiness kept gnawing at me. Was it the fact that everything in Berlin seemed smaller than I remembered? Was it the Wall that still surrounded the city? Did I fear reconstruction of the parental walls? Had I not matured enough during the preceding year to be ready for matrimony?

Slowly I began to grasp that my discomfort was rooted in a growing awareness that, despite my optimism to the contrary, my parents had not appreciably changed during my absence. Most likely I would face continual power struggles once resettled in Berlin. In the past I had tried to brush under the carpet, evade, or outwit my mother's attempts at directing my life. How would Günter cope with my family's quirks? Would he accept them or take issue? Would I be able to stand up to my mother and escape her power field? Was I ready to successfully balance being a wife, a daughter, a mother, and an individual?

When Günter casually mentioned that he regarded cooking to be women's work, this one offhand comment sufficed to trigger one of my worst fears: Did he want a full partner, or did he prefer a girl who liked to limit her involvement to the home? Would I face another series of unilaterally established rules? Would my life always resemble a paint-by-the-numbers picture which is mapped out by others?

Confused, I returned to San Diego. During the extension of my stay I hoped to figure out whether I should stifle my burning desire to test my limits and to put to work everything I had to offer, or whether I should settle for limiting my life's role to that of being a devoted wife, mother, and daughter. Every day I searched my soul. Every day the answer changed. In the end, I penned a heartbreaking letter to Günter, suggesting that we separate.

I chose freedom. I chose to remain in America, first tentatively, then permanently. As I found out, freedom wasn't free, however. The price demanded that I give up everything familiar until then: Günter, family, friends, and my little dog. It demanded that I relinquish many of the customs, the culture, social values, and language that formed my very foundation.

But freedom also gave me something I had craved since adolescence: It allowed me to grow into the person that already lived inside of me. Freedom allowed me to pursue higher education and to marry a man who would encourage and help me become my true self.

The transformation took time and involved many baby steps. When my given name, Jutta, proved too difficult for American tongues, I switched to my middle name, Elke—the first of many changes toward a new identity. Each of my experiences in adolescence had shaped the course of my life: Being an only child, having an overprotective and domineering mother, befriending the Kelly family, meeting Günter, and spending a year in a foreign country. Some people think me courageous for immigrating to the United States by myself. I wonder if it would not have taken more courage to return to Berlin.

In 1989, when I followed the fall of the Berlin Wall on television, I cheered with all my heart for the victims who had been trapped behind that monstrosity for twenty-eight years. As the Wall collapsed, it felt as if the last vestiges of my restricted childhood crumbled as well.

About the Author

J. Elke Ertle was born and raised in West Berlin during the aftermath of World War II when the city had become the focus of an escalating Cold War between East and West. As an only child of a photographer and his wife, she enjoyed a strict and stable childhood. Befriending an American service family awaked her interest in America. While the Berlin Wall restricted her physical liberties, her parental walls curtailed her emotional freedom. Finding the latter as impenetrable as the concrete wall that divided her city, she immigrated to the United States.

In *Walled-In*, Elke describes the first twenty-one years of her life in West Berlin and shares her recollections of the Berlin Airlift, the construction of the Berlin Wall, and the impact of John F. Kennedy's visit when he proclaimed, "*Ich bin ein Berliner.*"

Retired from employment in the public sector, she now lives in San Diego with Burch, her husband of four decades. She holds a masters degree in Industrial-Organizational Psychology from San Diego State University and a Certificate in Fitness Exercise Science from the University of California, San Diego, and currently teaches group exercise classes on a part-time basis.

Discussion Questions

1. Is *Walled-In* a universal story despite its unique setting? Which aspects of the story could you relate to easily?

2. The author hopes to spend one year in the United States in order to grow and mature. Do you believe that time abroad is beneficial to the development of the adolescent mind and spirit?

3. "Obedience, discipline, and loyalty were imparted at birth with the first slap on the buttocks," the author writes. Is her outlook on life shaped by her upbringing? How?

4. During her first trip abroad in the family Volkswagen, the author develops a deep fondness for black Americans. Can this fondness be considered a form of prejudice?

5. As the Berlin Wall goes up, Conrad Schumann, a young East German soldier, leaps across the fence to freedom at great risk to himself and his family. Do you think it is a courageous or an impulsive decision?

6. "All—all free men wherever they may live, are citizens of Berlin. And therefore, as a free man, I take pride in the words 'Ich bin ein Berliner.'" What did John F. Kennedy's words mean to the people of Berlin and why?

7. How does the Berlin Wall influence the author's identity? How about her parental walls? Which is more powerful and why?

8. Despite being deeply in love with Günter, the author leaves for America instead of remaining in Berlin? Why?

9. In *Walled-In*, the author shares with the reader twenty-one years of her life. Did she change during that time? What trigger points can you identify?

10. The author learns on her twenty-first birthday that she is an illegitimate child. Were there earlier occasions which might have lent themselves to disclosure?

11. Does this memoir challenge you to reconsider or strengthen any stereotypes or preconceptions you may have about Germans?

12. What is the most important theme throughout the book? How does it influence the author's journey to freedom?